Urban Operating Systems

Infrastructures Series

Edited by Geoffrey C. Bowker and Paul N. Edwards

Urban Operating Systems

Producing the Computational City

Andrés Luque-Ayala and Simon Marvin

The MIT Press
Cambridge, Massachusetts
London, England

The open access edition of this book was made possible by generous funding from Arcadia—a charitable fund of Lisbet Rausing and Peter Baldwin.

This book was set in ITC Stone Serif Std and ITC Stone Sans Std by New Best-set Typesetters Ltd. Printed and bound in the United States of America.

Library of Congress Cataloging-in-Publication Data

Names: Luque-Ayala, Andrés, author. | Marvin, Simon, 1963– author.
Title: Urban operating systems : producing the computational city / Andrés Luque-Ayala and Simon Marvin.
Description: Cambridge, Massachusetts : The MIT Press, [2020] | Series: Infrastructures | Includes bibliographical references and index.
Identifiers: LCCN 2020002955 | ISBN 9780262539814 (paperback)
Subjects: LCSH: Smart cities.
Classification: LCC TD159.4 .L87 2020 | DDC 307.760285—dc23
LC record available at https://lccn.loc.gov/2020002955

10   9   8   7   6   5   4   3   2   1

Contents

Acknowledgments

Producing this book has been challenging, exciting, and sometimes a lot of fun. There are several people and institutions to whom we owe a debt of thanks for making time to speak to us and for their encouraging feedback, constructive and critical comments, and material and moral support.

We would like to acknowledge the support of colleagues at both Durham University's Department of Geography and the University of Sheffield's Urban Institute, who read draft chapters and listened to our story while providing productive and constructive opportunities for discussion. In particular, we would like to thank the following: At Durham, Colin McFarlane, Harriet Bulkeley, Louise Amoore, Ben Anderson, Oliver Belcher, Mike Crang, and Helen Wilson. At Sheffield, in the Urban Automation and Robotics team: Desiree Fields, Aidan While, Andy Lockhart, Rachel Macrorie, and Mateja Kovacic. At Durham, at different times during the project, we worked with research support from Ruth Machen, Miklós Dürr, and Yu-Shan Tseng. We would like to offer a very special thank you to Ruth Machen, who endured five years of thinking through the book's material, reading draft chapters, and providing insightful comments.

We also had many opportunities to present earlier chapter drafts, either at workshops and conferences both in the United Kingdom and internationally or to colleagues who kindly agreed to read them in advance. We were often struck by the constructive and positive feedback we received on our initial ideas and arguments. For this, we would like to thank Ola Söderström, Stephen Graham, Nancy Odendaal, Ayona Datta, Adrian Smith, Rob Kitchin, Maria Kaika, Erik Swyngedouw, Rob Raven, Shannon Mattern, Philip M. Macnaghten, Rodrigo Firmino, Fábio Duarte, Jeremy Crampton, and James Cornford. We have tried to remember everyone, but apologies to anyone we have missed. Across the world, a number of academic colleagues provided invaluable support, particularly when visiting their cities and countries for fieldwork purposes. Maria Francesch-Huidobro and Yvonne Chiu were especially helpful over the fieldwork in Hong Kong, while Rodrigo Firmino and Bruno de Vasconcelos Cardoso were always there for us during fieldwork in Rio de Janeiro and subsequent periods of reflection on the Brazilian context. In Brazil, we also counted on the support of Alexandre Hojda.

Material support from a number of different funders enabled us to undertake a program of fieldwork over a three-year period. We would like to acknowledge four sources in particular. First, the ESRC/CONFAP awarded us funds for the project "Augmented Urbanity and Smart Technologies: How 'Smart' Are Our Cities Becoming?" (ES/N000013/1). This facilitated meetings between Brazilian and UK researchers, resulting in a collaboration that led to chapter 5, as well as a number of site visits in the UK and Brazil that informed the overall project. Second, a grant was obtained from ORA/ESRC for the proposal "The Knowledge Politics of Experimenting with Smart Urbanism" (ES/N018907/1). This allowed us to make a number of site visits and to attend conferences and workshops. Third, Carillion, a company that is now defunct, funded research time on the program of case studies. Fourth, Durham University's Department of Geography and Institute of Hazard, Risk, and Resilience and the University of Sheffield's Urban Institute funded fieldwork and attendance at conferences.

Special thanks go to those we interviewed in many different cities over a three-year period. In total, they number over 125 people. They were very candid and open in their responses to our questions; they generously gave us their valuable time, and we deeply appreciated the effort they made to show us around study sites, to provide us with access to meetings and research laboratories, and to invite us to civic hacking and other civic tech events, which added greatly to our understanding of the urban context and the politics of digital technologies.

The MIT Press has provided assistance with every step of the publishing process. In particular, the quality and constructiveness of the feedback from both the initial reviewers of the proposal and the final reviewers of the manuscript made this a much better book, even though we have not been able to address every single suggestion. Many thanks go to Katie Helke and Justin Kehoe for their time and effort in putting the book together. The editors of the Infrastructures Series at the MIT Press, Geoffrey C. Bowker and Paul N. Edwards, gave really important, strategic, and focused feedback, which helped us to think about the central contribution of the book. In addition, Kiera Chapman, our own copy editor, helped us with the final production of the text and provided multiple valuable recommendations. To them, we are grateful.

Finally, our families. We owe the greatest debt to Ruth, Anna, Nicky, and Lewis for supporting us through absences from home while we were undertaking fieldwork, as well as through long days and nights of writing.

Flávia Neves Maia, our coauthor for chapter 5, would like to acknowledge Rachel Coutinho Marques da Silva, as well as the support of the Coordenação de Aperfeiçoamento de Pessoal de Nível Superior (CAPES) in Brazil and the Ministry of Science and Technology, Conselho Nacional de Desenvolvimento Científico e Tecnológico (CNPq).

—Andrés and Simon

Chapter Credits

In chapter 1, "Computing the City: A Brief Genealogy" was originally published as Andrés Luque-Ayala, "Urban," in *Digital Geographies*, ed. James Ash, Rob Kitchin, and Agnieszka Leszczynski (London: Sage, 2018), 24–35.

Chapter 2 is a shortened and edited version of Simon Marvin and Andrés Luque-Ayala, "Urban Operating Systems: Diagramming the City," *International Journal of Urban and Regional Research* 41, no. 1 (2017): 84–103.

Chapter 5 is a shortened and edited version of Andrés Luque-Ayala and Flávia Neves Maia, "Digital Territories: Google Maps as a Political Technique in the Re-making of Urban Informality," *Environment and Planning D: Society and Space* 37, no. 3 (2019): 449–467.

Chapter 7 is a shortened and edited version of Andrés Luque-Ayala and Simon Marvin, "The Maintenance of Urban Circulation: An Operational Logic of Infrastructural Control," *Environment and Planning D: Society and Space* 34, no. 2 (2016): 191–208.

Small parts of chapters 3, 4, and 9 appeared earlier in Andrés Luque-Ayala, "Rethinking the Material Politics of the City through 'Interoperable Streams of Data,'" *Dialogues in Human Geography* 9, no. 1 (2019): 117–120.

1 Introduction: Producing the Computational City

The PlanIT Urban Operating System™ is the smartest, most flexible way to converge infrastructure with a world of sensors, devices and people across developments of scale and entire cities. A single intelligent system to manage it all. The PlanIT UOS enables systems such as energy, water, waste management, transportation, telecommunication, healthcare, security and potentially everything around you to communicate intelligently with each other—and with a world of ever-proliferating sensors and devices. And because we do this in ways that make obvious bottom-line sense, almost everything is about to change.

—Living PlanIT (n.d.)

Cities could soon be looking after their citizens all by themselves thanks to an operating system designed for the metropolis. The Urban OS works just like a PC operating system but keeps buildings, traffic and services running smoothly. The software takes in data from sensors dotted around the city to keep an eye on what is happening. In the event of a fire the Urban OS might manage traffic lights so fire engines can reach the blaze swiftly. The OS completely bypasses humans to manage communication between sensors and devices such as traffic lights, air conditioning or water pumps that influence the quality of city life.

—*BBC News* (Moskvitch 2011)

Technology companies are targeting a new market, producing hardware and software to run cities. Using preexisting technologies developed in a corporate context, international players like IBM, Hitachi, and Cisco have gained a foothold in a new sector that is attractively framed by aspirational narratives centered on smart cities, transparency, and open data. IBM has developed Smarter City, Urbiotica has the City Operating System, and Microsoft has produced CityNext, all software-hardware packages that claim to transform the city. They promise to improve the quality of urban services, to make the city more efficient and sustainable, and to automate the operation of urban infrastructures. Alongside these commercial innovations, municipal authorities are mobilizing resources toward the development and operationalization of a variety of digital platforms aimed at transforming both service delivery and infrastructures. Meanwhile, a loose network of IT aficionados is creating a vast informal ecology of digital projects aimed at the systemic operationalization of the urban world (Marvin, Luque-Ayala, and McFarlane 2016). The vision of those working in this area is that these computational interventions will eventually control the essential hardware, software, and data components of the city. The aim is that they will sit quietly in the background, directing urban informational flows, and will interface with one another via shared languages that ensure interoperability across multiple infrastructures. Within the IT and built environment industries as much as in the media (Living PlanIT, n.d.; Moskvitch 2011), these products, platforms and ecosystems integrating the digital and material domains of the city are often referred to as *urban operating systems*—the Urban OS.

Urban Operating Systems: Producing the Computational City explores the rationalities and techniques that constitute these emerging computational forms of urbanization, including work on smart cities, digital urbanism, and, more recently, platform urbanism. A wave of enthusiasm for smart cities, urban data, and the Internet of Things has produced the impression that the mobilization of computation in the city can resolve almost any urban problem. Far from being new, these claims have a long lineage, stretching back over six decades. At their base is the assumption that rational calculation and transactional decision-making can account for every part of the urban world. This book examines the cultural, historical, and contemporary contexts in which urban computational logics have emerged, with the intention of subjecting the claims of the current wave of digital urbanism to critical scrutiny. Taking our cue from David Golumbia (2009), we argue that computation is a metaphor, method, and organizing frame that occupies a privileged but underanalyzed role in urban studies. Drawing on this, our book investigates the ways that digital products, services, and ecosystems (and a very specific set of conceptual logics embedded within them) are reshaping the ways in which the city is imagined, known, and governed. In so doing, we explore the reconstitution of the contemporary city through digital technologies, practices, and techniques, including data-driven governance, urban sensing, digital mapping, predictive analytics, digitally enabled control rooms, civic hacking, and open data narratives. Focusing in particular on how power in the city operates and urban control is achieved, we interrogate the way that code, software, hardware, and platforms—and their underlying logics—entrench the status quo while also underpinning radical changes in contemporary urbanization.

For over three decades, urban scholars have pointed to the critical role of urban infrastructures in structuring and delineating the experience of modern urban life. Urban infrastructures, in "subtle and powerful ways . . . define, shape and structure the very nature of cities" (Graham and Marvin 2001, 30). Electricity grids, water and transport networks, and sanitation, waste collection and telecommunication systems, among others, have long been considered key physical and technological assets of cities. They "provide the technological links that make the very notion of a modern city possible," enabling exchanges and dynamic relationships between different actors, and embodying capital and knowledge investments in the city (Graham and Marvin 2001, 13). However, they are neither limited to material technological devices nor free from political, cultural, and symbolic representations and implications. Alongside their function as a collection of material components and flows (pipes, cables, switches, buildings, resources), they operate as political and symbolic devices supporting a visionary ideal of the city's future (Nye 1999). Both a means and object of governing, infrastructures are sociotechnical assemblages that include practices, regulations, and standards, as well as a range of state and nonstate actors and human and nonhuman agencies (Hughes 1983; McFarlane and Rutherford 2008; see also Bennett 2010). In this book, we will examine the tensions, contradictions, and limits of the coming together of computational logics and these assemblages. We argue that computation dramatically transforms the very nature and meaning of urban infrastructures, engendering not merely new infrastructural capacities within the city, but also new infrastructural forms altogether.

Our central argument is that, in constituting the urban as a calculative entity and advancing functional simplification and heterogeneous reintegration at a city scale, the Urban OS puts in place a new technology of governing—a calculative diagrammatic of control focused on the *operationalization* of the urban. This is, in Deleuzian terms, a new diagram of power, an abstract machine generating "a new kind of reality, a new model of truth" (Deleuze 2006, 30; Knoespel 2001). As an abstract diagram, paraphrasing the French philosopher Michel Foucault (1995), the Urban OS transmutes a mechanism of power into a function and vice versa. This effectively makes the Urban OS into a political technology, but one that is particularly concerned with depoliticizing urban processes while prioritizing operational efficiency, optimization, and management. Such a theoretical position sees the Urban OS as an overarching urban infrastructure operating as a non-neutral matrix through which meaning in the city is generated and negotiated. Paired with the traditional infrastructures of the city, the Urban OS engenders a new generation of infrastructures, both digital and corporeal, co-constituted through the affordances of each other—an intelligence incarnate of the urban (cf. Dillon 2003) that, now inescapable and endlessly mutable, operates through *infrastructural trans-actionability*. Through a range of computational logics, from datafication to sensing, among others, the urban operating system becomes a form of knowing that takes bodily form. This is an urban infrastructure that is always already co-constituted with digital technologies.

One of our core aims is to understand how the city has emerged as a key site for the systemic commercial and societal application of digital systems, through what initially appeared to be computational products that were designed for the urban market. The Urban OS puts in place a form of control in which the city is governed through computational logics—ways of thinking and ways of knowing—that assume that the urban can be treated as a calculable entity. Giving primacy to computational processes, it is claimed, leads to an audited, rationally managed, efficient, controlled, and integrated city: the urban realm as a commodified logistical enterprise. *Urban Operating Systems* traces the transmutation of these processes and approaches from military, corporate, and logistical domains to the city and interrogates the politics and ways of operating of this emerging wave of digital urbanism.

Examining Urban Computational Logics

This book aims to produce a multifaceted account of the formal and informal constitution of the Urban OS across diverse urban contexts. Our wide-ranging analysis focuses on the politics of municipal open data platforms and the work of civic hacking communities, municipal and citizen sensing platforms, digital mapping, predictive analytics platforms, digitally enabled control rooms, and the mobilization of an ecology of digital technologies in support of prodemocracy protests. We have identified seven urban computational logics, each of which is the subject of a chapter of the book. They are operationalization, datafication, sensing, mapping, prediction, circulation, and (digital) resistance.

In chapter 2, we examine *operationalization* and analyze the "diagrammatic abstractions" present in the marketing material written by corporate providers of urban operating systems. Our aim is to uncover a logic that underpins all aspects of the computational city. This chapter therefore provides the initial building blocks for a critical analysis of the rationalities at play in the practical rollout of digital urbanism. It traces the historical roots of the Urban OS within the military and corporate domains, focusing on the means by which computational logics transmute from defense and business contexts to the urban environment. By reconstituting the city as a set of ordered relationships, the Urban OS sets the foundations for the ways in which all things urban are to be measured and calculated. As such, this technology digitally operationalizes the city in a way that establishes future rationalities for governing it.

An important argument mobilized in this chapter is that the Urban OS tends to collapse corporate and urban problematics so that the city is increasingly viewed and managed as a corporation. In transmuting the logistical and corporate rationality of software packages, such as enterprise resource planning (ERP) systems, to the city, the urban becomes amenable to digital interventions aimed at developing interoperability, interconnection, and integration. However, these make a series of assumptions about how the city is envisioned, known, and acted upon. While in the Western world the city has always been seen as a site for business and exchange, where the boundary between urban and commercial worlds is never clear-cut, its ideal condition as polis both results from and depends upon citizen debate, contradiction, contestation, contingency, and a multiplicity of viewpoints and ways of being. Yet the latter are anathema to the singularity, functional simplification, and overall consistency required by a computational structuring of the world. The collapse of the division between city and corporation can therefore be seen as the first step of the Urban OS toward the removal, or hollowing, of the political from the city on account of operationalization and flow.

In chapter 3, we examine the computational logic of *datafication*, through an analysis of the making of New York City as a data-driven city. With the constitution of data as a key urban flow that underpins a new type of urban utility (data-as-infrastructure), the Urban OS arguably creates a common language for all urban processes. Like operationalization, datafication underpins all aspects of the Urban OS; through interventions such as municipal open data platforms and the work of civic hackers, among others, it enables the possibility of recombination and *trans-actionability*— the generative power of recombining urban processes and the city's traditional ecological flows (of water, transport, waste, air, and so on) into new flows, processes, and bodies. Critically, *the interplay between datafication and urban infrastructures embodies urban data*; as data lines flow in the city, their binary (im)materiality is reconstituted as a powerful urban flow. The resulting city-in-formation embodies data toward a form of *intelligence incarnate of the urban*: the materialization of data through urban flows on account of flexibility, mutability, and adaptability, a process that affords power and effects control.

Chapter 4 looks at the computational logic of *sensing*, drawing on a case study of sensors and sensor platforms in Barcelona. Sensing, like datafication, is a strategy to render calculative intelligibility across urban processes. It also *embodies* the informational diagrammatic characteristic of the Urban OS: the urban sensor is the body that translates and mediates between the digital and material domains of the city; in doing this, it creates new bodies and urban forms. Sensing effectively fragments urban flows into discrete and small spatiotemporal units of data and thus plays a key role in the ability of the Urban OS to dis- and re-assemble urban circulations. In so doing, sensors afford the technomaterial substrate of the city a new urban economy based on the way in which data flows create new circuits of commodification and profit. Sensors therefore constitute a new technology for both governing and monetizing the urban. They remake the sites of value creation of the city and generate new forms of value via digital assets. We describe this as a form of *urban commodification through digital hyperfragmentation*, and we argue that it is likely to lead to a relocation of value through flows.

In chapter 5, we examine the computational logic of *mapping* via its digital incarnation in Google Maps. Through an analysis of efforts to map Rio de Janeiro's favelas, we uncover the ways in which the process of digital mapping simplifies and homogenizes the city, integrating all urban territories into global circuits of economic flows. Within Google Maps, in the coming together of space and the database characteristic of this urban computational logic, the database of business is prioritized. This process recasts what is considered a "point of interest" in the city, emphasizing entrepreneurial sites and narratives and excluding urban knowledges and practices that are not amenable to digitalization. Furthermore, techniques of enumeration and spatial calculation are used to exert power and relocate sovereignty: new forms of territorial control emerge as the computational logic redefines which groups have the ability to gather and control information and therefore to shape market configurations and capital flows. We argue that this amounts to *the computational production of territory*.

Chapter 6 homes in on the urban computational logic of *prediction*, based on an analysis of the use of predictive analytics platforms in Chicago. Prediction reworks time and space via mathematical calculations, producing an understanding of the city as a calculative machine. It is a process that translates space into standardized units of data, enabling interoperability across seemingly disconnected urban domains while also allowing for calculating the urban across time. In practice, prediction is about targeting and spatial fragmentation: a conceptualization of the city via microgeographies or the use of a microgrid. Despite numerous claims about the transformative potential of predictive analytics in the city, we argue that it is a process that reinforces and reproduces the status quo.

Interventions like digitally enabled control rooms and digital dashboards underpin the computational logic of *circulation*, whereby the city is reconfigured as a logistical enterprise. We examine this in chapter 7, focusing on Rio de Janeiro's Operations Center (in Portuguese, the *Centro de Operações Rio* or COR), designed and implemented by IBM. We argue that the control room represents a new mode of urban infrastructure, based on the partial and selective rebundling of urban space in order to achieve real-time, efficient, and effective circulatory flow under conditions of disruption. This form of Urban OS is increasingly mobilized in response to growing conditions of economic, political, and ecological turbulence across the world. Here, through the close coupling of crises and the everyday, the city's political debates take a backseat to an operational rebundling aimed at guaranteeing flow maintenance. Constant information flow becomes the new nature of the city, the milieu that needs to be created. The emphasis on circulation, achieved via the rationalities and technologies immanent to the Urban OS, is so strong that it risks becoming the end as well as the means of governing the city. Forcing this emerging digital city to remake itself in the image of its own narrow epistemology, the Urban OS gives precedence to circulatory management over agonistic politics and thus contributes to the digital hollowing of the polis mentioned earlier.

Chapter 8 asks questions about the possibility of thinking about *resistance* as an urban computational logic. Through an analysis of the 2014 prodemocracy movements in Taipei and Hong Kong and the role of a mashup of digital urban systems within them, the chapter explores the extent to which civic hacking and a range of digital interventions can configure an operating system for occupation. From the Arab Spring to New York's Occupy Wall Street, contemporary political protest within cities operates through logics of occupation—immobilizing the very flows that enable urban life. In this chapter, we look into the possibility and significance of the mobilization of a loosely connected ecosystem of urban digital platforms, social media, digital communication tools, and other IT interventions, in support of contemporary political protest. Computation plays a role in enabling the disruption needed for protest, by raising local, national, and international awareness and enabling the agglomeration of diverse groups of people who might have an interest in participating. Yet sustained occupation also relies on traditional urban flows (e.g., energy, potable water, waste collection) and a temporary infrastructure for the occupation itself (e.g., sanitation and logistics). The material obduracy of urban occupation therefore resists and challenges the power of the Urban OS: such protests rely on the sustained presence of human bodies on the street and on a range of infrastructural forms that provide basic forms of life support. In this context, the power of computation is relatively limited; the mobilization of digital systems for political protests in cities highlights the limits of digital systems and the preeminence of traditional material infrastructures and urban flows. Ironically, the attempted contribution of the Urban OS to contemporary forms of occupation is, to a large extent, about operationalization, and therefore it is a move that does not offer unorthodox perspectives by failing to question the epistemologies embedded within the digital.

The remaining sections of this introduction place the Urban OS in a historical context, looking at both professional practice and academic inquiry within digital urbanism. They also provide a guide to the Urban OS and an outline of the conceptual approach of the book, explaining how we under-took our research and offering a preliminary summary of our argument. Our hope is that our work illustrates how the seemingly banal and hidden ways of thinking embedded within computation are being refocused on the city in ways that have far-reaching implications for almost every aspect of contemporary urban life. We hope it shows the ways in which calculative technologies, techniques, and rationalities are transforming urban flows and modulating urban infrastructures, reshaping the politics of the contem-porary city through a new set of relationships with networked technologies.

Computing the City: A Brief Genealogy

The ideas that we present in this book build on an extensive body of critical work within the humanities and social sciences on the role of digital tech-nologies within the city. For over two decades, human geography, urban studies, STS (science, technology and society) studies, sociology, computer science, architecture, urban studies, media studies, and other disciplines have examined the interface between computing, information communica-tion technologies, and the city. We draw significantly on these works, but we argue that there is also a need for studies that unearth the history of com-putational logics in the city, in order to develop a deeper critical analysis of the relationship between urbanism and computational technologies. Such an approach is important because it complicates popular ahistorical, norma-tive, and technodeterministic narratives of the digital urban. Uncovering the role of military, corporate, logistical rationalities in this history can provide an insight into the ways in which digital technologies can be used not only to govern and control the contemporary city, but to enclose new parts of its infrastructure for privatization and surplus value creation. Furthermore, such an approach calls into question the notion that technical forms of urban knowledge, control, and calculation are ideologically neutral, instead foregrounding the profound political, epistemological, and ontological con-sequences attached to the adoption of urban operating systems.

Cybernetic Cities: 1960s–1990s

Since Norbert Wiener outlined the principles of cybernetics in the 1950s, urban researchers and practitioners have increasingly viewed the city as a communication system (Light 2003; Meier 1962; Webber 1964). Drawing on a set of information technologies developed by scientists working within the American defense industry, they reconceptualized the urban as both a machine and a living organism. From the 1960s onward, urban planners sought to apply advances from mathematics, systems analysis, and computing technologies to the urban, transforming it into a domain for high-tech intervention and decision-making. American cities such as Pittsburgh, New York City, and Los Angeles started experimenting with their urban renewal programs, using a combination of computing, cybernetics, and military expertise to take a more problem-oriented approach to local administration. Urban planners and administrators began to frame the city from a militaristic/defense perspective, looking for solutions to urban problems in the informational management of urban processes. The city thus became a "battleground" on which experts fought "a war on poverty"; urban problems were a matter of processes going awry, arguably to be solved via the implementation of better feedback loops and continual self-adjustment (Halpern 2014; Light 2003). The *Journal of the American Institute of Planners* hailed computers as the drivers of a revolution in urban planning (Harris 1966): with their databases and simulations, they were not only capable of enhancing existing planning tools, such as maps and 3-D models, but also of handling large datasets and visualizing problems in novel ways. Most importantly of all, computers were seen as having the ability to turn planning into a scientific endeavor (Light 2003). As examined in more depth in chapter 2, information systems became a form of urban response that was notionally capable of producing scientifically verifiable outcomes from a value-free, neutral perspective, thus depoliticizing the planning process.

Beyond the domain of urban planning, from the 1960s onward (and perhaps all the way to the early 1990s), the growth in computer use led to a belief in the dematerialization of society—one that would arguably undermine processes of urbanization, threatening the very existence of the city. The "theology" of cyberspace—a belief in the ability of computers, digital systems, and new media to create an immaterial world of information that we can inhabit (Bolter and Grusin 2000)—underpinned a futuristic and euphoric technological utopianism in which reality was to be replaced, bit by bit, by information. Insightfully captured by Steve Graham in his pioneering *Cybercities Reader* (2004), this was a period when scholars and technologists (from Marshal McLuhan [1964] and Alvin Toffler [1980] to Nicholas Negroponte [1995] and Bill Gates [1995]) regularly commented on the extent to which digital communications would overcome the need for spatial proximity, causing cities to collapse. Of course, such predictions never came to fruition, in part because this posturban fantasy had failed to grasp the complex relationship and multiple interdependencies between computer technology and the city.

The Networked City: 1990s–2000s

Rather than causing cities to collapse, the world of information technology and computers has facilitated global urbanization (Graham 2004). Throughout the second part of the twentieth century, global telecommunications developed in parallel with the urban transformations characteristic of advanced industrial societies; to an extent, the configuration of the postindustrial city became a matter of the relationship between the two (Graham and Marvin 1996). No longer were cities simply dense physical nodes of buildings, transport networks, economic activity, and cultural life; they also became electronic hubs, the centers of demand for telecommunications, and the powerhouses of global digital communications. The ubiquitous nature of computing established an urban world governed more by interconnectivity than by boundaries. In the emerging *networked city*, the urban was no longer defined by physical enclosure (i.e., the city walls), but by digital connectivity (Mitchell 2004). Here, "control of territory means little unless you also control the channel capacity and access points that service it" (10). The production of the internet itself provided a form of urban geography, with selected cities playing an important role in its genesis through the clustering of IT activities (Townsend 2001; Zook 2008). From the physical networks that allow digital connectivity—fiber optics, copper cables, communication towers, antennas—to the patterns of employment and political-economic landscapes associated with the digital economy, information technologies materially co-constituted the city. Three dimensions of this networked city attracted significant critical attention within the social sciences: hybrid spaces, surveillance, and social sorting.

In 1992, Christine Boyer developed one of the first critical analyses of the popular dematerialized account of cyberspace, challenging the way in which the technologically oriented city was envisaged as a huge megalopolis without a center (Boyer 1992, 115). Advancing the idea of the *cybercity*, Boyer instead highlighted the hybrid material and sociotechnical nature of the informational network that was developing in the contemporary urban realm. In response, social scientists who engaged with the cybercity, particularly within human geography, began to foreground the roles of space and materiality in the digital world. In contrast to earlier discussions, academics no longer saw technology as a substitute for the city or embodied experience, but rather as a force mediating social, physical, economic, and cultural relations (Graham 2004). Digital technology, they argued, effectively transforms the cultural geography of the city and everyday life in a myriad of ways (Crang 2010). Wakeford, for example, draws on feminist approaches to examine the hybridity of internet cafés and the ways in which digital mediation affects the gender identities of their users. She argues that the city forms part of a wider technological and computational landscape, consisting of a multiplicity of hybrid spaces and forming a set of "material and imaginary geographies which include, but are not restricted to, online experiences" (Wakeford 1999, 180). Following a similar approach, Forlano (2009) examines the ways in which Wi-Fi technologies produce sociocultural and economic reconfigurations of the city, thus generating a set of new *codescapes*.

Perhaps some of the most discussed hybrid spaces in the interweaving of digital technology with the city are the *spaces of surveillance*. Digital technologies facilitate and enable urban surveillance not simply through data collection and recombination but also through techniques of visualization and simulation (Graham 1998). Taking Foucault's notion of panopticism to new heights, and drawing on the ability of computers to store and recombine large quantities of information in near real-time, Graham and Wood (2003) suggest the imminent emergence of a super-panopticon: "a system of surveillance without walls, windows, towers or guards"(Poster 1990, 93; cited in Graham and Wood 2003, 230). In this way they point to a quantitative change in the state's ability to govern via direct surveillance. The implications of this process, they suggest, go significantly beyond issues of privacy and/or disciplinary control. From CCTV and smart utility metering to social targeting and marketing facilitated by data collection, surveillance fuels the growing information economy of the city while supporting a particular political-economic configuration. This continuous and real-time tracking of bodies and behaviors supports a segmentation of service provision (differentiating users between levels of ability to pay, risk, or eligibility) and fosters a neoliberal logic that prioritizes the privatization of public services, the commodification of the city, and the development of urban markets (Graham and Wood 2003, 229).

As both academics and the wider public became more aware of the potential inequalities embedded in the urban operations of code, interest in *software-sorted geographies* rose. Studies began to explore the digitally mediated sorting techniques applied "in efforts to try to separate privileged and marginalized groups and places across a wide range of sectors and domains" (Graham 2005, 562). Software-sorting, exemplified by face-recognition, CCTV, and electronic mobility systems, illustrates the role that code and programming can play as mediators of urban practices, shaping both the city and its politics (Kitchin and Dodge 2011; Thrift and French 2002). Such a digitally mediated city is a *sentient city*, a ubiquitous computing environment that is "not a passive backdrop but an active agent in organizing daily lives. . . . It is a world where we not only think of cities but cities think of us" (Crang and Graham 2007, 789). This ubiquitous computing characteristic of the contemporary urban condition, described by Greenfield (2006) as *everyware*, "seeks to embed computers into our everyday lives in such ways as to render them invisible and allow them to be taken for granted" (Galloway 2004, 384).

Smart Urbanism: 2010s–Present

The idea of the *smart city* has grown in popularity recently, as an extension and actualization of digital utopianism. Promoted by the corporate sector, international organizations, and national and local governments alike, the dominant vision of the smart city is one of a digitally enhanced urbanity that combines intelligent infrastructure, high-tech urban development, the digital economy, and electronically enabled forms of citizenship. Narratives around smart cities are deeply rooted in seductive and normative visions of the future, in which technology stands as the primary driver for change (Luque-Ayala, McFarlane, and Marvin 2016), an idea that has gained global recognition through the publicity associated with the IBM-owned product Smarter Cities. However, the smart city concept also inherits elements from academic ideas developed in the 2000s around *intelligent cities*, which emphasized a problem-solving approach to the urban—advocating partnerships among academia, business, and government in which ICT (information and communications technology) operates as a key input for regional innovation, competitiveness, and economic development (Caragliu, Del Bo, and Nijkamp 2011; Komninos 2002).

Since its inception, the smart city has been a vague and nebulous concept. It comes charged with aspirations for a better future, alongside expectations that it can help achieve environmentally sustainable growth, infrastructure flexibility, new urban services, transparency, demand responsiveness, and social inclusion. Smart city interventions take a broad range of forms, and in most (but not all) cases these foreground the role of urban computing and digital technologies. Emblematic examples include Chicago's SmartData Platform, an experimental predictive analytics platform; Barcelona's Sentilo, a municipally owned open-source platform aimed at operating and collecting data from urban sensors; and Rio de Janeiro's Operations Center, all of which will be analyzed later in this book. Smart city initiatives are often an amalgam of loosely connected projects of various sizes, under the leadership of both public and private stakeholders. For example, the Amsterdam Smart City initiative involves a collection of around two hundred projects involving a broad range of stakeholders and digital technologies.

Over the past decade, scholars within geography and urban studies have started to ask critical questions of the smart city (Hollands 2008; Luque-Ayala and Marvin 2015). How are these new forms of digital technology transforming urban flows and reshaping urban politics and governance? What are the dominant logics and pathways in play, and to what extent can the smart city embrace a progressive agenda? How do different forms of urbanity and various citizen imaginaries take shape through the smart city, and to what extent does the smart city allow their contestation (Luque-Ayala and Marvin 2015)? Analyzing this literature, Kitchin, Lauriault, and McArdle (2016, 17–22) have identified a set of common critiques of the smart city. First, there is the argument that advocates of the smart city advance a reductionist form of technocratic governance, one that presumes that all aspects of a city can be measured or monitored. In this view, smart cities treat urban problems as technical problems, and accordingly prioritize technological solutions. Second, critics argue that the smart city is buggy, brittle, and hackable: it is "prone to viruses, glitches and crashes" and "vulnerable to being maliciously hacked" (Kitchin, Lauriault, and McArdle 2016, 17–22). Third, in line with the critique of digital surveillance identified in the previous paragraphs, academics have argued that the smart city's mobilization of big data leads to dubious forms of panoptic surveillance, predictive profiling, and social sorting. Finally, many writers have contended that smart city interventions and their mobilization of data create the illusion of neutrality, overlooking both urban politics and the politics of big data. Data collection and code development, they argue, are not value-neutral and as such constitute a political intervention in the city. One strand of criticism that is discussed more fully in subsequent chapters argues that the smart city plays a major role in the corporatization of urban governance (Barns 2016; Greenfield 2013; Söderström, Paasche, and Klauser 2014; Townsend 2013; Vanolo 2014). Both smart urbanism and urban big data can be seen as agendas mobilized by ICT corporations to enclose government functions and develop them into new market opportunities. The smart city, in other words, can be a commercial endeavor advancing entrepreneurial goals.

During the late 2010s, these critiques have been refined and nuanced, as academics have opened a new set of theoretical questions, many of them in dialogue with feminist critiques of science and postcolonial urban theory (cf. Elwood and Leszczynski 2018). This work problematizes common understandings of smart urban spaces as straightforwardly "mediated" through digital technologies. Authors are careful to avoid granting excessive agency to digital technologies, and they also challenge the emphasis within conventional critical social theory on resisting digital intervention. Here the human is brought back into the picture; this is an inventive and creative posthuman agency, "both mediated through techniques and diverse" (Rose 2017, 779). Agents, in this view, actively work toward progressive new modes of urban activism through a productive and proactive engagement with digital urban technologies (Cardullo, Di Feliciantonio, and Kitchin 2019; Lynch 2019).

A broader engagement with critical social theory has "provincialized" the smart city in myriad ways, as writers have rethought its narratives from the perspective of the Global South—for example, unpacking the "smart citizen" as a postcolonial subject and exploring the gendering of the smart city (Datta 2019; Datta and Murray 2018; Datta and Odendaal 2019; Gurumurthy, Chami, and Thomas 2016; Strengers 2014). These perspectives follow long-standing traditions within STS and geography that unpack the symbolic and material power of technology, recognizing the extent to which "smart and digital technologies are now the key policy and political tools of postcolonial states to embrace and imagine new urban futures" (Datta 2018, 417).

All of the critiques cited in previous pages unpack the power/knowledge dimensions of digital urbanism. At times, critics have focused on the ways in which digital and smart cities, as techno-utopian discourses, promote neoliberal rationalities and specific private interests; at others, they have adopted a cautiously optimistic approach to explore the epistemological implications of encountering the city through digital narratives and technologies. Our work is inspired by this body of analytical literature, but focuses more clearly on the relationship between the Urban OS and traditional infrastructures of the city in order to shed light on the political and economic consequences of using these technologies to come to know (epistemology) and generate new urban spaces and flows, altering their ways of being and becoming (ontology). It is to this subject that we now turn.

Urban Operating Systems as the Urban OS

In this book, we point to the need to question the ontological and epistemological implications of what is now a pervasive computational urbanism. We argue that in order to understand how digital technologies transform and shape the city, it is necessary to analyze underlying computational logics themselves. Research on digital urbanism, in other words, cannot simply be limited to a disconnected analysis of individual technologies or to an examination of where and on whose behalf they are used. Drawing on philosophy and media studies, we see computation as a "metaphor, method, and organizing frame" (Golumbia 2009, 1) for the city; an abstract machine that "constructs a real that is yet to come, a new type of reality" (Deleuze and Guattari 2004, 157). As such, urban operating systems are not simply a "top-down attempt to discipline citizens"; neither can they be "challenged by a simple inversion of this relation, via a bottom-up liberation of technologies in the name of people" (Krivý 2018, 21). In other words, the implications of the corporate takeover of urban functions via digital technologies cannot simply be counterbalanced by embedding into the latter the "liberal humanist values of inclusion, empowerment, sustainability and digital privacy" (Krivý 2018, 21). Seeking to transcend simplistic top-down versus bottom-up analyses of the smart city, we argue that the emerging wave of digital urbanism, regardless of who it is enacted by and for, puts in place a distinctive regime of urban governance. This is a regime that, in instilling a new way of mapping and shaping relationships between forces, inscribes particular ways of seeing the city, representing relationships and anticipating a changed material future through the making of new connections, disconnections, and flows.

The entry point for our analysis of urban computational logics is the Urban OS, as an abstraction made of pluralities. Scholars have not themselves critically evaluated urban operating systems previously, but they have discussed the idea of the city as an operating system in a number of contexts. First, urban studies scholars have drawn metaphorical comparisons between the complexity and processes of the city and those of a computer. Such comparisons often draw on an early understanding of an operating system (OS) within the IT sector, developed to control multiple and different processors within a computer and to provide a language of interoperability for handling inputs and outputs (cf. Cloot 1965). In computers, the OS acts both as a technology for controlling and coordinating separate processes and as the medium for handling and interconnecting complexity. Used metaphorically to describe a city, this understanding of the OS becomes a way of emphasizing complexity and control within the city: the urban becomes a complex information processing system based on exchange of goods, information, and cultural practices—an operating system in its own right (de Waal 2011).

Second, developing this idea further, Pieterse (2014, 208) suggests that a participatory and "democratic, horizontal, network-based, 'Wiki' model of urban development" could provide an alternative "operating system" for cities, an urban equivalent to a nonproprietary response to the dominance of the "ubiquitous Windows computer platform." A nonexclusionary form of urbanism that is not based on ability to pay is thus imagined in the language of the OS. The comparison between a computational OS and the city starts to move beyond metaphor here. Other scholars have taken a still more literal approach to the ways in which digital technologies are giving rise to a new city-scale operating system, exploring the new ways in which they are coupling information and infrastructure. Written in software code and capable of sensing individual actions in real time, this type of OS aggregates data to effect action at a distance. The resulting real-time city operates through sensor networks that aggregate data streams into new services and products for consumers or citizens (Townsend 2000, 2015).

Third, academics have focused on the links between infrastructural development and wider questions of urban control in relation to a city-scale OS. Easterling has examined how a new combination of infrastructure space, sensors, and software uses the medium of information to envisage the city as a collection of "invisible, powerful activities that determine how objects and content are organized and circulated"—calling this "an operating system for shaping the city" (Easterling 2014, 5). Here, the concept of an OS is that of a platform that is both updated over time and unfolding in time to handle new circumstances and situations, using software "protocols, routines, schedules and choices" to encode relationships between buildings or to manage infrastructural logistics (Easterling 2014, 6). This moves significantly beyond earlier formulations of the OS as a relatively straightforward coordination mechanism between different urban processes (discussed earlier), instead seeing it as a set of integrated informational products, platforms, and interventions loosely interconnected into a broader digital ecosystem *that imposes a form of order on the urban context.* This is the meaning of the Urban OS that informs our work: we wish to emphasize chaotic bundles of hybrid techniques, tools, products, and systems, rather than a standardized unified product. Urban operating systems of this type are being trialed and tested in multiple configurations and urban contexts, with potentially transformative implications for how the city is imagined, planned, and governed (see, e.g., Gabrys 2016 and Halpern et al. 2013 on ubiquitous sensing and data recording infrastructures; Kitchin, Lauriault, and McArdle 2015 and Mattern 2015 on digital urban dashboards; and Barns 2016 and Perng and Kitchin 2018 on municipal open data platforms and civic hacking practices). Viewed in this way, the Urban OS attempts to develop informational/computational ecosystems for urban applications, generating the capacity to integrate the functional and informational dimensions of the city and to coordinate between the previously separate (or, at best, loosely coupled) spheres of infrastructure networks, public services, and everyday life.

In our definition of the Urban OS, we emphasize the ways of thinking, knowing, acting, and being that are embedded in these calculative technologies, and the ways that urban planners, civic technologists, consultants, and business entrepreneurs are using digital and IT systems to establish particular ideas of urban order. The Urban OS is a way of both knowing the city and making it actionable. As such, we are interested in the mechanisms at play in the ongoing transformation of the city via digital technologies. Our concern thus is not so much the technological arrangement itself (e.g., hardware, software, sensors, platforms, clouds, etc.); rather, we are concerned with *how* that technological arrangement is re-assembling the city. The Urban OS, therefore, could equally be *singular* (and often commercial) packages of information systems put together by large and small IT and software companies, or *collective and loose* ecosystems of technologies and associated practices operating in tandem (yet with varying degrees of integration). They seek to coordinate and integrate services across fragmented urban functions, and comprise software (databases, predictive systems, analytics, modeling and simulation) and associated hardware (computers, sensors, control rooms) assembled into a purpose-built urban system aimed at functional and spatial integration. What makes both of these configurations of urban digital assemblages into a form of Urban OS is not the fact that they are digital technologies applied to an urban setting but that they both operationalize, homogenize, reintegrate, and simplify the urban.

As singular commercial packages, urban operating systems are largely based on preexisting, large-scale integrated computational products that were initially produced for the corporate market. ERP systems, initially developed in the 1980s and central to the ascendancy of the corporate business model, are a clear antecedent of the contemporary Urban OS. They consist of software management systems aimed at integrating business processes (e.g., payroll, procurement, quality management, customer acquisition, and product/service delivery) through common databases and information flows across corporate departments (sales, accounting, human resources, etc.). These are complex products, and their implementation in the corporate sector is an expensive and demanding process that has been criticized. The problem is that the assumptions built into the software tend to reshape the organization of the corporate entity implementing it in significant and material ways (Kallinikos 2011). As a result, ERP systems often generate a range of inflexibilities and obduracies described within the business world as *electronic concrete*. This configuration of the Urban OS is perhaps better illustrated in the book by Rio de Janeiro's Operations Center, designed by IBM based on an integration of some of its preexisting software packages (see chapter 7). The grounding of the Urban OS within ERP systems is important because it underpins the idea that the corporation and the city are alike, and that they suffer similar problems of functional integration that require separate and disconnected processes to be fragmented, reaggregated, and digitally integrated.

Currently, however, the Urban OS is being constituted in a multiplicity of ways that move far beyond the simple repurposing of ERP systems toward urban functions. As such, it transcends code/software/hardware, as well as corporate configurations, to include the work, views, and politics of a multiplicity of stakeholders who, by using digital technologies, interact with, complement, build upon, reinterpret, and transform city systems in ways that can be considered to have broader systemic qualities. Here the Urban OS is not the result of a single product or package, but a loosely connected assemblage of IT practices and technologies—an ecosystem made of digital platforms, social media, mobile phone apps, clouds, software packages, and sensing devices, but also coding practices, civic hackathons, data activism, and so on. While this provisional, territorially dispersed, and distributed assemblage (cf. Anderson and McFarlane 2011; Li 2007) of urban digital interventions is characteristic of all urban operating systems, in the book this configuration comes across more explicitly when analyzing the work of civic hackers in support of Hong Kong's prodemocracy movement (chapter 8). As such, using the language of Easterling (2014), the protocols, routines, schedules, and choices embedded in digital urban technologies transcend a single software package, to shape the politics of emerging and dispersed forms of digital or smart urbanization. We therefore argue that it is critically important to understand the systemic qualities of the computational logics that underpin the Urban OS and the ways in which this, as an emerging computational urbanism, is transmuted and reapplied toward governing a much wider set of urban processes.

Conceptual Lenses: An Emerging Urban Computational Apparatus

Drawing on governmentality literature, Chris Otter (2007) and Patrick Joyce (2003) have explored the historical relationship of infrastructure, technology, and power in the city. Both authors are concerned with the consolidation of urban infrastructures in the nineteenth century and the ramifications of this for governing the city. Otter criticizes traditional perspectives on governmentality (e.g., Dean 2010; Miller and Rose 2008) for focusing on bureaucratic and discursive governmental techniques, silencing "the brute materiality of technology" (Otter 2007, 578). He suggests that technological systems are endowed with an agency of their own and play a key role in the creation of the self-disciplining liberal subject. Their materiality carries a political charge, enabling "government *through* and *by* technology" (Otter 2007, 580; original emphasis). Here, multiple machines and sociotechnical networks, from roads and sewers to electricity grids and gas networks, secure in a dispersed way while materializing an indirect mode of rule. In the city, these infrastructures operate as technosocial solutions of a political nature. As with later digital technologies, like the Urban OS, their politics is enhanced by the fact that the solution that they offer is apparently "technical" and therefore seemingly neutral and external to the agonistic world of politics (Joyce 2003). As explored in more depth in chapter 2, urban infrastructures and the practices associated to their use and establishment imposed a new diagram of power, with implications that mapped and shaped wider societal relationships. As historians and sociologists of the nineteenth- and twentieth-century city have argued (Joyce 2003; Osborne and Rose 1999; Otter 2007), the materiality of urban infrastructures plays a critical role in territorializing government—signaling the urban as a domain for the exertion of government and authority, as much as a laboratory for generating new truths about the social world.

The Urban OS continues this historic imbrication of technology in the establishment of modes of governing and the generation of truths about the city (cf. Osborne and Rose 1999). Yet the contemporary moment intensifies the relationship between power and infrastructure present in earlier configurations of the city by bringing together material and digital flows—an *intelligence incarnate of the urban*. A calculative logic is thus mobilized as the supreme rationale for imagining the city and for effecting actions to change it. Drawing on a Foucauldian interpretation of power as creative, enabling, and productive of subjects, meanings, and interventions (Miller and Rose 2008; Patton 1998), our analytical framework seeks to understand the emerging urban computational apparatus as a governing device, with an embedded politics that, in transmuting the city into a calculative and logistical enterprise, does not question established orders. Instead, it seeks to ensure their maintenance without changing organization, ownership, or orientation. This mobilization of technical domains in the making of the city represents an *eclipse of politics* (cf. Agamben 2009), an operationalization of the urban that speaks of management as "a pure activity of government that aims at nothing other than its own replication" (Agamben 2009,

22; see also Braun 2014, 61). As mentioned previously, we describe this as a *digital hollowing of the polis*. The diagrammatic logics of the Urban OS signal toward new ways of imagining the city, establishing urban meaning and opening or closing modes of inclusion; this is a regime that embodies important presumptions about what constitutes appropriate knowledge and forms of decision-making.

Researching the Urban OS

Far from being passive backdrops to technology, cities complicate, enable, disrupt, resist, and translate the Urban OS. However, there is a lack of comparative analysis and a dearth of knowledge about the range of urban contexts within which the Urban OS is emerging. To analyze the social and political implications of the Urban OS and examine how specific urban conditions enable and constrain digital urban technologies, we needed to generate new knowledge about the forms, dynamics, and consequences of the Urban OS in an internationally comparative context. We sought to address three key challenges in particular. First, we wanted to examine the Urban OS from the inside, rather than relying solely on promotional and publicity material from product developers or on secondary literature. This meant we needed to engage with the participants who were involved in shaping urban operating systems across the world, undertaking fieldwork across a range of sites in which it is being applied. Second, we wanted empirical research to inform the priorities of the fieldwork in an iterative manner that would allow us to trace pathways emerging from interviewee feedback. This led to a reconceptualization of the Urban OS halfway through the project as both a singular and formal commercial package and an informal, multiple, and unbounded ecosystem of urban digital technologies operating in loosely connected ways. Third, in the absence of a single source of funding for the project, we adopted creative, flexible, and improvisatory approaches that were able to make use of financial and practical opportunities as they arose.

As mentioned previously, we have identified seven computational logics that are driving the political transformation of the city and its infrastructures: operationalization, datafication, prediction, sensing, mapping, circulation, and resistance. This list is not meant to be exhaustive, nor is each logic exclusive to the specific empirical case study that illustrates it. However, we do believe that these computational logics are emblematic of the types of processes at play in the digital re-assembly of the city. We examine each from three distinct perspectives. First, we analyze the *production* of computational logics, uncovering the domains in which these calculative ways of thinking were initially developed. Here, looking into the histories of the specific digital products and computational techniques at play gives us an insight into the origins and lineage of the logic before its adoption within urban contexts. Second, we trace the circulation of computational logics in different contexts and the specific mechanisms for their *transmutation* into the urban. This illustrates the context of emergence of the logics. It also shows the extent to which, underpinned by broader ecosystems and ways of thinking (such as the military, logistics, or the corporate world), they go beyond specific digital technologies or software products and both engulf and transcend computation. Third, we investigate the *urban politics* that result from the implementation of computational logics in the city, examining the forms of support and resistance that they provoke, with a view to identifying their implications and how they reshape the governance of urban infrastructure.

We began by researching single computational packages developed by the IT sector and aimed at municipalities. We were able to inquire into these products via visits to IBM labs in Dublin and Delhi, conducted as part of a wider university relationship. We also carried out pilot work by visiting smart city projects and facilities in Glasgow, Bristol, and London and by interviewing IT professionals working in these cities. During this initial period, we discussed our intentions with (and at times interviewed) software engineers working in both the academic and the private sectors, including colleagues and friends. We also conducted a desktop analysis of the marketing material prepared by large companies to promote their developing range of smart city products. The critical issue that our early analysis raised was the extent to which forms of knowledge and rationalities embedded within broader computational products and processes also provide the foundational underpinnings for the wider set of technologies and products aimed at the urban segment, in this way giving shape to a new form of computational urbanism.

We then traced the development of particular systems, platforms, and digital ecosystems, through a bricolage of approaches and taking advantage of a range of funding opportunities. The role played by municipal open data platforms and a process of datafication quickly emerged as a central component of the Urban OS, providing the primary data flows for other urban applications. To explore this, we used small-scale project funding to carry out a series of interviews in New York City. We also briefly participated in the local civic hacking scene, which was particularly lively partly thanks to the Bloomberg administration and its conceptualization of New York as a data-driven city. We advanced our analysis of sensing platforms through a case study of Barcelona, where the city council was at the time working with private sector partners to develop specialist skills in the construction and testing of sensor-based technologies. As in other cities, our research involved site visits and interviews with government officials and businesses, particularly start-ups involved in deploying sensors in the city.

We examined the implications of digitally mapping the city by looking in depth at an initiative by Google Maps to map favelas in Rio de Janeiro. We were able to do this thanks to UK and Brazilian research funding available for the development of international research networks, and most importantly via a collaboration with Dr. Flávia Neves Maia, a Brazilian academic and practitioner looking at the role of digital technologies in Brazilian cities. Thanks to this collaboration, our analysis of Google Maps in favelas involves not only interviews but also participatory observation, as well as an extensive review of documents and marketing material associated with the initiative.

Meanwhile, our analysis of predictive analytics platforms focused on Chicago, given the high profile achieved by the city on this front. Here we also took part in events within city's civic hacking scene, alongside interviewing a number of active and former senior government officials who were playing pivotal roles in developing the use of predictive analytics to police and manage the city. In 2014 and 2015, we visited the Rio Operations Center (COR), a control room in Rio de Janeiro designed with extensive input from IBM. Combining site visits with interviews and media analysis, this led us to identify circulation as one of the main logics advanced by the Urban OS.

Finally, we initially focused on the Sunflower Movement in Taipei for our examination of the role of digital technologies in forms of political resistance and urban protest. While visiting Taiwan, we established relationships with civic hackers through a number of interviews and participation in civic hackers' conferences. These interactions, occurring toward the end of 2014, revealed links between Taipei's Sunflower Movement and the then-evolving Umbrella Movement in Hong Kong. As a result, the focus of our examination shifted, and we did fieldwork in Hong Kong by visiting the protest sites and conducting interviews there while the occupation of the Umbrella Movement was still active.

In total, our fieldwork activities extended across eleven cities, where we conducted over one hundred interviews involving more than 125 IT professionals, government officials, civic hackers, activists, and IT aficionados. Where these interviews are used in the book, they are either indicated by double quotation marks or set off, and preceded by a brief explanation of the working context of the interviewee. With very limited exceptions, all of the interviews were audio recorded. In all cases, we complemented these methods with site visits, document reviews, and desktop research targeting relevant web-based sources. In some cases, we also analyzed a range of forms of digital media (e.g., Facebook pages, smartphone apps, "collective interviews" conducted via the Hackpad real-time collaborative text editor, platforms created by civic hackers) and video sources (available through online media channels). We were able to make two visits over a period of two years to four of the five case-study sites that are discussed in chapters 3 to 8 (Chicago, Rio de Janeiro, Barcelona, and Hong Kong/Taiwan; the exception was New York City, which we visited only once). This allowed us to conduct follow-on interviews with key respondents.

Andrés conducted the bulk of the fieldwork, while Simon was able to participate in most of the follow-on fieldwork visits. When we analyzed the case of Google Maps in Rio de Janeiro's favelas, the interviews, participatory observation, and site visits were conducted by Dr. Flávia Neves Maia, who focused on four of the twenty-five favelas where Google has had a presence: Cantagalo, Pavão-Pavãozinho, Santa Marta, and Vidigal. Flávia and Andrés jointly conducted additional documentary analysis. We enriched the research with additional visits to "model" smart city initiatives and IT labs in Glasgow, Bristol, Delhi, and London. Overall, through attending political demonstrations (Hong Kong), carrying out participant observation in civic hacking events (Taipei, Chicago, and New York), spending social time with corporate developers of urban operating systems, seeing how communities in favelas engage with digital technology, and sitting in the staff coffee room of Rio de Janeiro's COR, we were able to build rich and in-depth understandings of the key dimensions of the applications of computational logic in exemplar cities.

In the practical world of city-making, the Urban OS is not a single informational product but rather a varied set of computational ecosystems, from digitally enabled operation centers to municipal data platforms, mapping initiatives, infrastructural sensing systems, and predictive analytic models, among others. Differentiating among these has enabled us to identify the specific techniques through which digital urbanism operates and the way that these stake a claim to a new form of authority that is transforming the ways in which the city is governed. Chapter 2 provides a more detailed analytical understanding of the Urban OS as an informational product, exploring the ways in which it conditions understandings of the city. Chapters 3–8 then analyze specific computational ecosystems through empirical detail. These are understood both as ways of thinking and acting (means, mechanisms, procedures, instruments, tactics, vocabularies) and the very material and digital technologies involved (cf. Dean 2010). We argue that it is through these techniques that the political rationalities embedded within the Urban OS effect change, bringing about new forms of urban control and reconfiguring the nature and meaning of urban entities. Chapter 9 reviews the main argument that an evolving range of digital logics are advancing new ways of imagining, knowing, and governing the city. This conclusion is careful to show how contested, multiple, and often contradictory logics are being developed in this experimental phase of digital urbanism, drawing on these tensions to develop a future research agenda.

2 Operationalization: Diagramming the City through the Urban OS

This morning we heard a discussion of the near-term potential of information systems to support a variety of urban functions. . . . The tone of the session was certainly optimistic, and this attitude, I believe, is appropriate. Important progress has been made in the last decade in the general field of information systems—both in developing new hardware and with regard to systems design and development so that the new information hardware can be exploited in an urban planning context. . . . This development has major implications; a powerful tool is available to make it possible for you to do a better job.
—Charles J. Zwick, RAND Corporation[1] (Zwick 1963, 1)

Computational systems, and the logics that they embed, have become ubiquitous, pervading every aspect of contemporary life. They are used in every institution and are involved in the production and sale of almost every product and service. However, their presence is far from neutral. As we discussed in chapter 1, computational systems (like other forms of infrastructure) play an active role in governing society. They provide a means through which particular rationalities of governing operate and the ways by which political positions find tangible and material expressions. Computation (the method used by computers) and its rhetoric (a belief that computerization can produce a superior form of social and political organization) play a role in legitimating emerging and established institutional powers (Golumbia 2009)—by consolidating specific rationalities as important ways of conceiving the world, and producing knowledge about it (Cowen 2014; Rossiter 2016). We argue that there is a pressing need to examine these rationalities from a critical viewpoint, exploring how they resonate with (and inhibit) established structures of urban control.

This chapter lays the background for an examination of the computational logics embedded within the Urban OS, and for the subsequent analysis of how these logics (chapters 3–8) shape the city itself as much as they shape how governing and power operates within it. We begin by tracing the historical roots of the Urban OS within military and corporate domains, examining the transmutation of computational logics from defense and business to urban contexts. We explore the dis- and re-assembly of the city by the Urban OS following a rationale of greater flexibility, and the ways in which this frequently achieves the opposite result: a loss of flexibility, the impossibility of customization, and the imposition of ways of being. We subsequently inquire into the production of computational logics and the underlying rationalities of these systems, particularly the claims for the superiority of computation as a form of organizing society. Our aim is to break down the ways of thinking that are embedded within these urban computational ecosystems and to subject them to critical questioning.

Our conceptualization is guided by the idea that the Urban OS reconfigures the city as computational space by implementing a range of diagrammatic abstractions. We draw on Deleuze and Guattari's notion of the diagram as a creative device that, beyond representing the world, "produces a new kind of reality, a new model of truth" (Deleuze 2006, 30; Deleuze and Guattari 2004; Knoespel 2001). Diagrams offer particular ways of looking at how a given reality is both shaped and rendered comprehensible. As representational devices, they illustrate an attempt to simplify complexity, a process of translation in which some elements are left out while others make it in. Yet Deleuzian diagrams are not meant to be conceived within the realm of the visual. As simplified rationalities, in visual, narrative, or cognitive form, they map and shape the relationships between forces, imposing a form of conduct through spatiotemporal composition and serialization.

We discuss the diagrammatic abstractions embedded within the Urban OS through an analysis of graphics and illustrations associated with five of its paradigmatic framings, produced by Hitachi, Microsoft, and IBM.

The five paradigmatic framings of the Urban OS that we identify understand the city as a cybernetic entity or a system of systems; a set of disconnected strata or overlapping IT layers; a type of computer processor or urban CPU; a set of closed informational flows, in a closed loop of data collection, analysis, insights, and action; and a space of possibilities for the digital dis- and re-assembly of urban circulations. Relaying the urban as an efficient logistical enterprise and operating as a piloting device (cf. Deleuze and Guattari 2004), the Urban OS appears as an emerging urban diagram introducing an informational diagrammatic of control. Through the Urban OS, a new corporate rationality of control, based on functional simplification and heterogeneous reintegration, takes hold in the city, supported by a logic of optimization, productivity, reengineering, agility, modularity, flexibility, and configurability.

Our aim is to move beyond the formalized and commercial side associated with the production of urban operating systems (exemplified by, e.g., Barcelona's City OS [chapter 4] and Rio de Janeiro's Operations Center [chapter 7]). Instead, we use diagrammatic abstractions to discuss more broadly the ways in which computational logics are reshaping the framing of urban problems. These logics are a common element across many urban applications from many producers, both formal and informal, as well as commercial and noncommercial, constituting a novel bricolage of hybrid informational ecologies for the city. This looser and more expansive way of understanding the Urban OS is perhaps best illustrated by the collection of loosely connected digital practices and technologies that protesters are using in Hong Kong's prodemocracy movement (chapter 8).

Placing the Urban OS: From Defense to Urban Applications

As an information system put together by large and small IT and software companies working alongside local authorities and social actors, the Urban OS seeks to coordinate and integrate services across fragmented urban functions. It is comprised of software (e.g., databases, predictive systems, analytics, modeling, and simulation) and associated hardware (e.g., computers, sensors, control rooms) assembled into a purpose-built urban system that aims to produce functional and spatial integration between infrastructure networks and public services. In practice, this system operates as a chaotic bundle of hybrid techniques, tools, products, and operating systems (rather than as a standardized and unified product). Consequently, cities across the world are trialing urban operating systems in multiple configurations. Through interventions such as open data platforms (chapter 3), sensing platforms (chapter 4), digital mapping (chapter 5), predictive analytics systems (chapter 6), digitally enabled operation centers for the integration of municipal functions (chapter 7), and even a hotchpotch of systems and applications used in support of urban protest (chapter 8), the Urban OS attempts to develop informational and computational ecosystems for the city and its operations.

While the twenty-first century has seen a significant increase in computational applications for the city, the idea that the urban could be conceived as a complex digital system to be managed through data flows originated in the mid-twentieth century. In 1968, Arnold E. Amstutz, writing from his desk at the Massachusetts Institute of Technology (MIT), made the case for a new style of city management. Amstutz, then and now a relatively unknown professor of management, believed that systems analysis offered the key to commanding complexity in the modern city. We do not intend to suggest that Amstutz was a pivotal figure in this process; rather, the opposite. He was one of many people (academics, managers, computer scientists, urban planners) who imagined that computer technology could achieve a rationally ordered city. In his view, the city could be rendered responsive to human needs via a threefold strategy: structuring the spatial environment into categories and subcategories, developing clear objectives and criteria for their evaluation, and using computers to "synthesize and maintain a representation of the total environment" (Amstutz 1968, 21). His claims illustrate a wider trend toward using cybernetic thinking and systems modeling to solve what John Collins, the mayor of Boston between 1960 and 1967, described as "the crisis of the cities, the greatest domestic crisis to challenge America in a century" (cited in Forrester 1969, vii). Amstutz's approach rested on the delegation of authority to computer systems, and expressed confidence in the idea that the availability of more data and better modeling would provide the correct answers: thanks to the preprogramming of urban functions, city executives would "finally" be able to approach urban problems with "increased effectiveness due to the availability of more meaningful data and an increased (model based) understanding of [the] environment" (Amstutz 1968, 21).

In the late 1950s, and drawing on the principles of cybernetics developed by Norbert Wiener (see chapter 1), the city increasingly came to be seen as a communication system (Meier 1962; Webber 1964; see also Light 2003). Social science and policy analysts alike increasingly relied on flowcharts and data visualizations to compensate for the unknown, while data recombination and a search for patterns reorganized knowledge about the city and developed new forms of urban cognition (Halpern 2014). This understanding of the urban as a space of data flows and environmental modeling draws on the digital computation work of Jay W. Forrester (1961, 1969), the father of system dynamics and a pioneer in the application of modeling techniques to social systems. Forrester, also one of the forefathers of the "science of cities" (Batty 2013; see Townsend 2015 for a critique), saw the urban as a complex yet linear system of interacting parts, each of which was experiencing growth, equilibrium, or stagnation. Those parts could be modeled by calculating urban flows and providing an account of conditions in their surrounding environment. Technology was not to target the symptoms of urban decay; rather, it would provide unique access to "the dynamics of urban structure," allowing city administrators and planners to develop "a set of revival policies that can reverse a city from economic stagnation" (Forrester 1975, 247, 249). Such belief in computer applications, system dynamics, and digital modeling as mechanisms to solve urban problems was quickly espoused by a generation of American planners and technologists. By 1966, the *Journal of the American Institute of Planners* was reporting on a practical and theoretical revolution within the discipline as a result of computerization (Harris 1966; Meier and Duke 1966). By the early 1970s models that emphasized change over equilibrium as well as the spatial dimensions of urban modeling had emerged (Batty 1971), consolidating the relationship among mathematical modeling, urban planning and computation, and its potential use in urban theory and planning practice.

Yet computer science, modeling, and simulation were not the sole sources of inspiration for this urban revolution. It was underpinned by the vast amount of knowledge around systems analysis developed by scientists working within the American defense and aerospace industry. This early history of the cybercity, traced in detail by historian of science and technology Jennifer Light (2002, 2003), reveals how the military-industrial complex of the mid-twentieth century provided important sets of tools to city planners (see also Farish 2010). Organizations such as NASA, the Lockheed Corporation, the RAND Corporation, and other defense contractors operated as consultants to municipal governments, transferring techniques and technologies from military research programs into urban management. This act of translation was promoted by the de-escalation of the Cold War, as companies in the IT-defense sector recognized the need to transfer their innovations and technologies to new markets, something that intensified after they were hit by reductions in government spending resulting from the missile test ban (combined with increasing limitations on the budget associated with the Apollo program). City planning and management quickly emerged as "targets of opportunity" (Light 2003, 46). The postwar association of urban planning with military research, cybernetics, communication sciences, and computation had long-term epistemological consequences, as new ways of observing and knowing the city were developed. This coincides with a broader period of transformation in urban cognition. Data visualizations and "the interface" became central concerns, while the urban came to be produced via "new techniques of calculation, measurement and administration" (Halpern 2014, 17). For historian of technology Orit Halpern, cities became "systems with an endless capacity for change, interaction and intervention, and problems of urban blight, decay, and structural readjustment [came to] have no clear definitive endpoint" (2014, 121). In this new model of the urban, structural categories like race, gender, and class were replaced by "the environment," and urban politics negotiated through design, aesthetics, and personalization. Urban planners began to argue that enormous amounts of quantitative data constituted a new form of objective truth, which pointed in a straightforward way to the best course of action. Ethics and politics thus became matters of calculation (Halpern 2014).

The confluence of urbanism and the military-industrial complex in the postwar period changed the way in which urban academics and practitioners saw the city, embedding it with new meaning. The urban became a "battleground," with city officials "fighting a war on poverty," "battling against urban chaos," and combatting "blight" and "unrest" (Farish 2010; Graham 2004b; Light 2003; Vanderbilt 2002). As the city and its problems were framed in this militaristic/defensive language, urban planners came to view solutions as a matter of processual management. As Jennifer Light explains, urban planners initially saw computer simulations as an extension of existing planning tools such as maps and 3-D models, as a kind of additional instrument that they could use to perform monotonous tasks, to handle large numbers of variables, and to visualize problems in new ways. Gradually, the city became redefined in cybernetic terms, as systems analysis and computing offered an opportunity for unifying different planning traditions that saw cities as either organic systems or as machines. Key to this was the incorporation of action and feedback in tools such as databases and computer simulations, in which real-time information could properly represent cities and urban processes in ways that maps and models could not. Together, these developments meant that planners increasingly saw their profession as a scientific endeavor.

After the failure of the American Housing Acts of 1949 and 1954 to achieve the objective of urban renewal, planning professionals sought to enhance their prestige and to access federal funding by remaking their field through data and computer models. The information systems approach offered them a form of urban response that seemed capable of depoliticizing the planning process while achieving scientific and verifiable outcomes. This led to a major expansion in government initiatives on urban dynamics and urban cybernetics, under the leadership of the United States Department of Housing and Urban Development. It involved incentives to create closer relationships between military and urban experts through funded programs of urban experimentation, leading to urban observatories, urban data centers, and urban information systems (Light 2003). Planning was to be redefined in cybernetic terms, described by a data contractor for the city of Los Angeles quoted by Light as "a 'control mechanism' to improve decision-making [and] . . . 'solve complex urban problems'" (2003, 48). An amalgamation of diagrammatic abstractions—both ways of seeing and doing—led city planning to adopt a language of feedback, homeostasis, and control. Over time, however, the computing rationalities, techniques, and technologies imported from military operations into urban planning proved to be practically ineffective. By the mid-1970s, the Vietnam War had undermined confidence in military techniques, and several high-tech initiatives around urban systems had closed after they were shown to be unsuccessful in solving urban problems (Light 2003). Yet the knowledge that these programs had created about computer systems and the faith that they had expressed in modes of "IT-thinking" did not vanish, but instead became firmly established in a different market.

Coding Organizational Behavior: Modes of IT-Thinking

The urban context was not the only domain where experimentation with computing technologies beyond military applications was occurring. Corporations, in particular, were interested in the potential of computer systems to streamline corporate production processes. In 1957, IBM supported the foundation of the American Production and Inventory Control Society (APICS), a nonprofit dedicated to knowledge generation within supply chain and operations management. Soon afterward, a computerized, time-based planning and inventory control system quickly became a flagship for operations management within APICS. It gained popularity in the wider corporate context throughout the 1970s (Jacobs 2007; Mabert 2007), though it was only in the late 1980s that software engineers developed computer packages capable of integrating "all" aspects of corporate operations (Jacobs 2007). The global market for these enterprise resource planning (ERP) systems was over US$38 billion by the turn of the century (Rashid, Hossain, and Patrick 2002), consolidating IT as the largest area of capital expenditure in US business.

The influence of ERP systems on city-making is not the direct result of their use within municipal government.[2] Rather, their deployment by business organizations, and the resulting refinement of corporate rationalities through technological systems, saw ERP packages emerge as the antecedents to the Urban OS, promoting a computational solution to urban problems. As the business sector adopted ERP systems, a particular regulatory regime was inculcated within organizations. ERP packages function by linking all business operations to a single database, to "promise the seamless integration of all the information flowing through the company—financial, accounting, human resources, supply chain and customer information" (Davenport 1998, 121). One result of this is that ERP systems force businesses to reengineer systems in order to accommodate their software logic (Rashid, Hossain, and Patrick 2002). When a business implements an ERP system, therefore, it has to not only integrate operations across functions and production sites, but also alter how the corporation is shaped and governed (Kallinikos 2011). The ERP system inculcates a systemic logic and a series of data-based relations that establish a standardized way of receiving inputs and prescribe ways of instrumenting and conducting operations. As a result, organizations are drastically simplified, operating through normative workflows that stipulate transactions and processes. ERP systems therefore limit capacity for contextual and local adaptation in a variety of ways: the presumptions of the software package cannot be overridden, evaluation is restricted to a limited number of criteria, and cognition processes rely on the identification and deployment of common elements across experiences. The black boxed nature of the technology (the software) protects it from deliberate manipulation or transformation, further increasing rigidity within the resulting configuration.

ERP systems advance a rationality that superimposes logistical think-ing onto the practices of organizations, thereby achieving "a technology of governance and control" (Rossiter 2016, 9). Critical information systems scholar Jannis Kallinikos has analyzed the ways in which corporations come to be governed by the very technological systems that enabled their rise. His work points to the ways in which specific forms of software programming embed ways of thinking about the world, constructing forms of agency and establishing a micro-order within the everyday. In an effort to render inter-nal relations predictable and controllable, off-the-shelf information pack-ages such as ERP systems come to transcribe the organization's complex reality "into the language of the package" (Kallinikos 2007, 61). Coding language embodies routines and procedures that generate particular forms of perception and cognition, shaping and governing behavior "thanks to the variety of strategies of *functional simplification* and *reification* by which it lays out its prescriptive order" (Kallinikos 2011, 7; original emphasis).

Kallinikos looks in detail at different techniques of coding, focusing par-ticularly on object-oriented programming. An intensely structured form of software coding that is highly governed by structures and procedures, object-oriented programming divides reality into objects, which are then subdivided into other objects, each one possessing a series of attributes. By recombining these attributes, the software allows the relationships between objects to be reconfigured. This computational logic by which reality is rendered as information is sustained by an elaborate vertical integration. Through an emphasis on modularity, predetermined structural features, and intrinsic qualities, IT packages and knowledge are constituted as both specialized and transferable from company to company or organization to organization (Voutsina, Kallinikos, and Sorensen 2007). The use of ERP sys-tems implies a functional understanding of the organization, where the fragmentation of operations into functions and subfunctions is crucial for the appropriate functioning of the whole. Organizational operations are reconstructed after a detailed breakdown of components into sites, agents, functions, and relationships. This logic of interoperability reconfigures the everyday business of organizations using ERP systems into a collection of standardized procedural steps, patterns, functional categories, modules, and cross-modular transactions. The resulting outcome loses sight of strat-egy, with processes being replaced by procedures—a linear sequence of transactional steps (Kallinikos 2007).

The implications of an informational diagrammatic of control for corporations have been profound. Underpinned by modularity, transferability,
and a superficial flexibility, this diagrammatic of control is based on functional simplification and selective integration. It implies the establishment
of narrow channels for knowledge circulation alongside specific forms of
decision-making. Despite claims for multiplicity and widespread interconnectivity, technique and procedure become obligatory passage points, and
data flows become a tangible route to a new cartography of power. Rather
than increasing the flexibility and adaptability of organizations in dealing
with important changes in the external environment, these systems have
instead increased obduracy and rendered internal relations predictable and
controllable as they become reduced to transactional steps embodied in
software. Yet these ERP-type systems have been rebadged and lightly reconfigured into a new set of corporate IT technologies targeting the urban environment. The fact that they are the forerunners of the Urban OS raises
questions about the transfer of these IT-based rationalities of control to the
urban context. The next section will therefore explore the implications of
these diagrammatic abstractions within an urban context.

Diagramming the City

The application of computation to the city is likely to have long-term effects,
impacting the ways in which cities are known and governed. In this section, we will argue that computational logics do not merely simplify existing complexity via a series of communication and information techniques
for rearranging flows. They account for a novel diagram of power; a new
way of mapping and shaping the relationships between urban forces; a new
series of techniques for imposing a form of conduct through spatiotemporal
composition and serialization. We argue that this logic operates as a Deleuzian diagram—an abstract machine or a transitory relay producing "a new
kind of reality, a new model of truth" (Deleuze 2006, 30; Knoespel 2001).
    Over thirty years ago, Peter Taylor uncovered the way in which scien-
tific diagrams hold the power to create their very object of study. In his
analysis of ecosystem diagrams within mid-twentieth-century ecology,
Taylor examined how ecologists rendered the complexity of ecosystems
comprehensible, manageable, controllable, and predictable (Taylor 1988).
Technologically based analogies between energy circuits and ecosystems

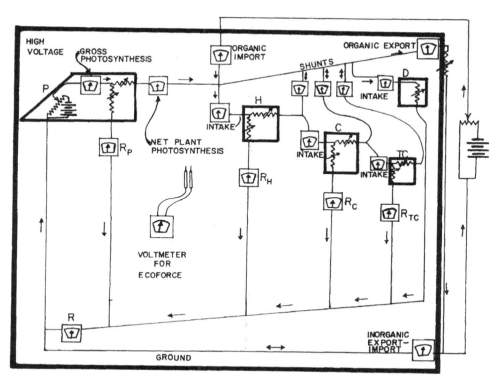

Figure 2.1

H. T. Odum's conceptualization of an ecosystem through electrical analogies, examined by Taylor 1988. *Source:* Odum 1960, 4.

(e.g., Clarke 1954; Odum 1960; see also figure 2.1), where ecosystems were understood as energy flows, constructed the idea of the ecosystem in particular ways. These diagrams—as forms of representation—determined, among other things, which organisms and relations were included and excluded in the ecosystem, what flows through it, what are its limits and its contents, and how it is accounted for. Taylor argued that ecosystem diagrams, based on physical analogies with energy and engineering, framed and translated ecological processes while allowing ecologists "to act as if ecological relations were decomposable into systems and could be managed by analysis external to the system" (Taylor and Blum 1991, 275). This is not far from the way in which computational logics shape how we understand the contemporary city.

Somewhat echoing the work of Taylor, Deleuze and Guattari's understanding of the diagram offers a useful analytical device to understand the power of computational logics in shaping space. However, their perspective transcends representational approaches in which the diagram is an abstract visual simplification that, in representing the world, creates its object of study and intervention (e.g., Taylor 1988; Taylor and Blum 1991). The diagram for Deleuze and Guattari *"does not function to represent*, even something real, but *rather constructs a real that is yet to come*, a new type of reality" (Deleuze and Guattari 2004, 157; our emphasis). It functions as a non-neutral matrix through which meaning is negotiated and generated (Knoespel 2001). It has a future-focused capacity to operate "as a means of seeing something never seen before," embodying momentum toward further definition and elaboration (Knoespel 2001, 147). The meaning of the diagram is framed by its setting and enforced by the narrative within which it is placed. The diagram can be seen as having a dual role, both stabilizing and society in the making (Callon 1987). Knoespel (2001, 147) points to Deleuze's understanding of a diagram as a "piloting device" that "embodies a practice of figuring, defiguring, refiguring and prefiguring." As an abstraction, its effect is not bounded by an attempt to reproduce or imitate, but by a productive, pragmatic, and creative essence (Deleuze 2006).

Critically, the diagram transmutes a mechanism of power into a function, and vice versa. Foucault's understanding of the diagram is linked to his analysis of panopticism. The panoptic as a diagram is not only a carceral optical arrangement (affecting visible matter and allowing prison guards to "see without being seen"), but a "polyvalent" abstract technology that can operate in multiple sites (Foucault 1995, 205). Deleuze explains this further, seeing the panoptic as an abstract machine that seeks to "impose a particular conduct on a particular human multiplicity" (Deleuze 2006, 29; original emphasis removed). The diagram thus acts as an immanent cause, penetrating, permeating, and overlapping the whole social field and, in doing so, executing the relationships between forces so that these take place "'not above' but within the very tissue of the assemblages they produce" (Deleuze 2006, 32). Originating and evolving within an entity, such diagrams enclose together intentionality and technique for acting. As explored in the following section, the Urban OS as an emerging technological diagram of the city collapses governing intent, technique of action, and material technology.

Osborne and Rose (1999) examine historic diagrammatic conceptions of the city as a space of government and authority, or the territorialization of government through a diagram of power. Their overarching aim is to understand how contemporary modes of power operate, this time with the city as "a governed and ethically saturated space . . . a way of diagramming human existence" (737). They write: "These diagrams are neither models nor Weberian ideal-types but operative rationales. Each diagram depicts and projects a certain 'truth' of the city which underpins an array of attempts to make urban existence both more like and less like a city" (738). Using a governmentality perspective (Foucault 2009), where governing is not limited to the thoughts, policies, and strategies of those in formal positions of power but occurs through silent and informal styles of self-governing, they examine how urban diagrams have transformed modes of governing throughout history. The Greek polis, as the emblematic diagram linking urbanity with political forms around citizenship and participation, embeds the immanence of an authority that results from political sociability. It is linked to a form of "natural government" in which, rather than calculated intervention, what predominates is an antagonism that gives rise to self-government. In the nineteenth century, the urban diagram changed to reflect an alteration in the forces of power, as governing the city became *"inseparable from the continuous activity of generating truths about the city"* (Osborne and Rose 1999, 739; original emphasis). Truth and government became entangled through spatiality—a truth that, just like with the Urban OS today, was technical rather than philosophical or political. This practical urban thought operated through the management (the gathering, organizing, classifying, and publishing) of information (Osborne and Rose 1999), albeit in combination with its own material form by way of urban infrastructures (Joyce 2003; Otter 2007).

In this process, authority was linked to specific knowledges and forms of technical expertise, something that has continued in the laudatory contemporary attitude toward urban digital technologies and the Urban OS. The exercise of power was no longer concerned with the imposition of overt forms of discipline and subordination, but instead with a "regulated and civilized freedom." In this view, liberal thinking did not create the liberal city; rather, a technologically driven change at the diagrammatic level altered the way in which the city was conceived as a milieu for realizing and modulating freedom, positioning the city as a laboratory of conduct (Osborne and Rose 1999, 740). The emerging urban diagram of the nineteenth century, for instance, rather than focusing on domination, sought to balance an autonomous public sphere, markets, individual liberty, and the rule of law. The sanitary city, in particular, positioned Victorian public health and sanitary systems as a privileged technology for governing the urban (Rabinow 1995). In the context of urban slums, the collective body of the citizen (a population) became a privileged governing site. Within the diagram imposed by the sanitary city, a eugenic logic pointing to what was seen as the city's immanent tendency to produce degeneration, corruption, and illness is juxtaposed with a social logic that sees the virtuous social forces of the city and its machines of morality channeled toward the establishment of remedies (e.g., renewal through water infrastructures and progressive social housing schemes; Osborne and Rose 1999). Over the course of the following 150 years, a variety of other urban diagrams made their mark in the history of conducting human conduct, subjectivity, and life, including the garden city, the colonial city, and the zoned city (Osborne and Rose 1999).

In this book, we argue that a new diagrammatic of urban power is emerging through an ecosystem of technologies loosely grouped within what we refer to as the Urban OS. This twenty-first-century diagram is based on new ways of managing information and flows, and is the contemporary outworking of the interface between information communication technologies and the very material infrastructures identified by Joyce (2003) and Otter (2007) as the force behind the full—yet subtle—expression of liberal politics of the nineteenth century. As anticipated by Osborne and Rose, this emerging computational diagram based on "telematics and informatics [and] computerized models of flows of power, water, traffic" allows life in the city "to be governed in a new way" (1999, 750). Here, entangled with metaphors around "configuring and reconfiguring, flexibility, multiplicity, speed, virtuality [and] simulation . . . [the city] marks out a concrete field of localization and concentration where the exercise of government appears potentially possible" (749). A practical and material manifestation of the digital, smart, or computational city, the Urban OS embeds new ways of thinking about the city and new rationalities for governing it.

The Urban OS as an Emerging Urban Diagram

In the context of contemporary smart city narratives, the definition of an urban market for IT applications rests on narratives establishing analogies between corporate and urban contexts. With an estimated market value for smart city technologies of US$463.9 billion by 2027, and a compound annual growth rate (CAGR) of 24.7 percent (Grand View Research 2020), the urban market has emerged as a strategic priority for IT corporates (Paroutis, Bennett, and Heracleous 2014). The Urban OS, distinct from the use of software and ERP systems in municipalities given its outward-facing aim, provides of a set of techniques and capacities for bringing together urban infrastructures, urban services, and everyday life—techniques and capacities that often sit outside direct municipal control. City functions that are usually kept separate and loosely coupled (e.g., waste collection, transport provision, energy services, security, and emergency response) are reconfigured into a more integrated and tightly coupled relationship.

In transmuting the logistical and corporate rationality of the ERP system into an urban product, a collapse between corporate and urban problematics is required. The *IBM Intelligent Operations Center for Smarter Cities Administration Guide*, for example, identifies key problems of the city as fragmentation and dispersal of control, lack of real-time updates, system isolation, and inability to generate insights from existing data. In this context, the Urban OS "addresses these and many other challenging issues by providing insight, management, and oversight capabilities for any city or enterprise *(as they both face many of the same issues)*" (IBM 2012, 3; our emphasis). By imagining the problems of a city in this way, IBM makes them amenable to the type of intervention that software/hardware packages make possible: the solution becomes one of interoperability, interconnection, and integration, which are conveniently also the things provided by preexisting software packages designed for the corporate environment. As we are told by an IBM engineer involved in preparing the guide, the objective is to develop solutions for urban problems based on a range of "IBM-linked software components that already exist in the market, that have been working for some time and that are trustworthy . . . integrating all these components into a solution, [the software puts in place] a platform that can be applied to a diversity of domains or market segments of a city or of industry." IBM's local teams limit their contribution to that of coding the integration, "because you use the packages you already have."

Technology companies, then, are applying knowledge practices from the information communications sector to urban environments in ways that treat the city and the corporation as similar. A solution architect for Smarter

Cities working for IBM informed us that years of experience in developing products for the public sector had taught her that the key contribution made by IBM to any client, beyond software or programming, lay in the operationalization of processes via protocols. She drew a comparison between the development of products for cities and customer relationship management (CRM). Her argument was that the two are not so different: "You need to have processes to answer a client, to address the problems they have, and then to redirect them to the correct area that fixes their claim." The process itself in all its richness (e.g., dealing with a disgruntled customer) is better understood by the company or organization purchasing the software or ICT service than by IBM (in this case, a city administration). However, as she pointed out, through the development of standard protocols and replicable communication flows "there is an optimization of work and resources . . . we call that the operational model, because that includes the procedure itself, but also the governance of who responds to whom . . . who is the owner, who is the leader . . . and which agencies must have a representation." Inevitably, such forms of standardization from the world of systems engineering give rise to new structures of power. But what vision of the city, and what diagram of power, is created through the deployment of these digital standards and protocols?

We argue that the Urban OS establishes a diagrammatic form of relationship with the city. Just as the ERP system reshapes the corporation, the Urban OS attempts to generate particular urban futures by imitating a horizon of thought. It functions as a vectoring tool, suggesting and testing new connections while extending the possibilities of thought (cf. Deleuze and Guattari 2004). This section examines how the city is being diagrammed, as we investigate the system manuals and promotional materials of the Urban OS. We focus on the illustrations associated with five paradigmatic framings found within this literature, taken from *Hitachi's Vision for Smart Cities* (Hitachi 2013, 14, 21), the *Microsoft CityNext Technical Reference Model Overview* (Microsoft 2013, 3, 7), and the *IBM Intelligent Operations Center for Smarter Cities Administration Guide* (IBM 2012, 15). These five paradigmatic forms combine to illustrate the Urban OS as an emerging urban diagram, transmuting a corporate informational diagrammatic of control to the city.[3]

The Cybernetic City: A System of Systems

Marketing material for the Urban OS shows the city as a *system of systems* (figure 2.2), a total bounded entity that renders the city as a set of ordered

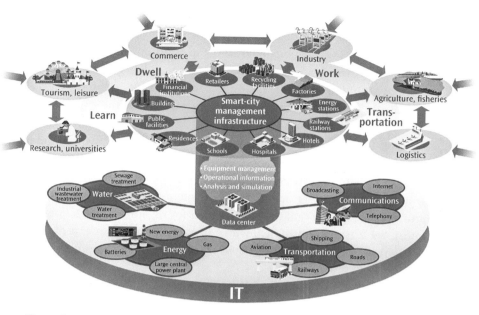

Figure 2.2
The cybernetic city, illustrated by a figure included in *Hitachi's Vision for Smart Cities* with the original caption "Relationships between smart cities and IT." *Source:* Hitachi 2013, 14.

relationships. It speaks of interconnected complexity, yet simplified and rendered manageable. Using metaphors from technology, biology, and cybernetics to describe a combination of human and technological systems (Light 2002, 2003), this paradigmatic framing calls upon imaginaries of interconnection, integration, and intelligence. The city is constituted through a multiplicity of separate systems (e.g., water, energy, schools, and buildings) feeding into different urban domains (e.g., agriculture, commerce, industry, tourism, and energy). The Urban OS is conceived as a platform able to make connections between what is currently separate. Both the software and hardware components of the Urban OS sit at the center, making connectivity possible while also echoing analyses of smart city narratives as obligatory passage points for the technological urban (Söderström, Paasche, and Klauser 2014; see also Callon 1986). Most importantly, data collection, storage, and flow—also occupying a central stage—is positioned as the primary mode and language for interoperability.

The city as a system of systems operates through techniques of classification, resulting in the provision of a system for organization and, in this way, a framing for an objective reality. This involves the development of typologies, the establishment of hierarchies, and a broad mapping of connections between these components. It seeks to connect formerly segmented functions, motivated by the desire to render the entire system of internal relations within the city predictable and controllable. Its emphasis on classification also has an ontological function, determining the city's components and establishing sets of relationships between them, thus creating entities and boundaries. Beyond a proposal for integration, the framing of the city as a system of systems is concerned with dissecting the complex nature of the city into steps and then foregrounding the manageability of the city/organization. It is less about the adaptability of the city to external contingencies than to build a detailed map for organizational action and control. Yet it is difficult to distinguish between the form of organization proposed and the city itself, two aspects that collapse into each other.

The City as (Disconnected) Strata
The Urban OS conceptualizes the city as a series of homogenous and sorted layers, typically structured around a set of domains of urban life such as the social and/or economic, technological/infrastructural, governmental, and environmental (figure 2.3). Categorization and taxonomy are important here, as the resulting model aspires to functional simplification. Each layer is composed of relatively homogenous, sorted, and ordered components that are the product of earlier phases of sorting and cataloging. A further presumption is that these layers are functionally self-contained, discrete, and poorly coordinated. Such a layering process becomes critical in providing the real or material city for digital systems or "smart" processes—rationalities, techniques, and technologies—to work with, as new Urban OS infrastructures are coupled above and below urban domains.

This horizontal understanding of the city as a collection of overlapping layers is akin to what Deleuze refers to as *strata*: an assembly of consistent homogeneous elements. Strata, as a diagrammatic formation playing a role in the genesis of form and thus creating reality, stands in direct opposition to the *rhizome*, a nonhierarchical form more amenable to hybridization (Deleuze and Guattari 2004). Layering the world in hierarchical manners, strata depends on sorting machines, devices that take a multiplicity of objects and their heterogeneous qualities and distribute them into uniform layers (De Landa 2000). Thus the Urban OS—in effect a sorting

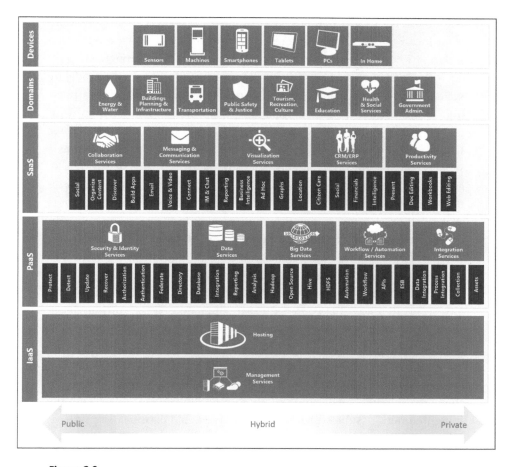

Figure 2.3

The city as (disconnected) strata, illustrated by a figure included in the *Microsoft CityNext Technical Reference Model Overview* with the original caption "CityNext capabilities across devices, domains and service layers." *Source*: Microsoft 2013, 3.

machine—constitute the city as a set of disconnected, separate, closed, loosely coupled layers. Each layer is configured and sorted according to particular techniques and history. It enables a link back to earlier regimes of control, suggesting that a form of integration across layers is needed.

Just like the cybernetic city, the city as (disconnected) strata operates through classification and taxonomy, not only providing an order but, beyond that, establishing an ontology. It generates categories, attributes, and subcategories and, in doing so, creates their very object of intervention. Here, local specificity is lost as a result of the primacy of binary models that assign attributes to objects and establish differentiation through the presence or absence of such attributes. A homogenizing drive (via modeling systems) takes over. The city as disconnected strata, operating as a piloting device, introduces new players and establishes new hierarchies, with the very materiality of IT systems and/or devices as foundational layers. In figure 2.3, these are represented by the notions of infrastructure as a service (IaaS); security, data, and workflow platforms as a service (PaaS); and software as a service (SaaS). The city is, in essence, subject to a form of modularization and cataloging according to a set of predefined criteria that are then reflected in the nature of the software system. In a way, in order to apply these systems in an urban context, you have to work upon the city through these forms of standardization, modularization, and classification. This is a process of breaking down the city into a multiplicity of objects and components. In a hierarchical manner, this unbundling of the city occurs in a way that is predefined by the nature of the software itself: through the data fields, datasets, and types of services that are involved in digital systems. Yet within the IT industry, there is concern that there are no common standards for classifying the components of different urban layers. As companies such as Cisco have pointed out—in a way that compares their city-building task to the configuration of biological knowledge of the Enlightenment—"subjects such as botany have had classification systems for more than 100 years. . . . However, there is no equivalent agreed-upon taxonomy for city information" (Cisco 2012, 7).

One of our interviewees, a computer scientist, linked this diagrammatic abstraction with the analytical fragmentation characteristic of object-oriented programming discussed earlier: "There are a number of objects. For example, hospitals, [which have] doctors; doctors, which have certain capabilities or skills . . . basically everything can be broken down into its most fundamental components . . . you can actually break everything down until eventually you get to the lowest possible element in the system." The emphasis is on the reduction of the complex and particular to general and universal objects so that these can be integrated into wider systems. In this way, in a highly vertical and hierarchical fashion, different urban systems are modeled and understood in the same way: "it all links; it is hierarchical . . . each of the [components], as transport and energy, might be modeled in the same way." Thinking of reality as a hierarchically organized "stack"—also a popular way of conceptualizing protocols, data formats, and software among computer engineers—ensures that each layer handles "the same base information simultaneously, but at different levels of abstraction" (Straube 2016, 5).

This act of configuring a city as disconnected strata echoes Bratton's analysis of global computing as a stack, where a software-based, modular, and interdependent vertical order gives rise to a planetary-scale political geography based on communication platforms. This layered and inescapable political machine, linking earth to users and everything in between, is made from both computational forms and "social, human and concrete forces" (Bratton 2015, 11). Extrapolating stack thinking to the city means that different urban systems (such as health, transport, energy, or waste) are modeled and understood in the same way and then hierarchically organized into an overall system. But critically, "the stack is not simply an enumeration of different elements that constitute a whole. Instead, each of its layers is an articulation of a specific logic and already encompasses the entire system" (Straube 2016, 6). In other words, both Bratton's stack model and the Urban OS claim to produce a coherent totality. In practice, as we will see in the chapters that follow, this totality is nothing more than an illusion—an ideal vision that, in claiming totality and consistency, seeks to legitimize its political scope and mode of intervention. Instead, an entropic tendency inherent to computation and data precludes the possibility of totality and foregrounds the role of contingency and randomness (Parisi 2013). This is one of the many points of breakdown of the Urban OS, as well as a contradiction internal to control systems.

The Urban CPU

Digital urbanism is re-assembling local connections between the different layers of the city and is therefore playing a critical role in the formation of new urban ecosystems. The Urban OS is a way of organizing these interconnections through the development and positioning of new centers, this time in a markedly "arborescent" manner (cf. Deleuze and Guattari 2004; figure 2.4). In this reconfiguration, a special class of "operators, or intercalculatory elements, is needed to effect this interlock" (De Landa 2000, 39). As figure 2.4 suggests, these emerging technosocial ecosystems are organized around an obligatory passage point: the core, center, or platform around which the

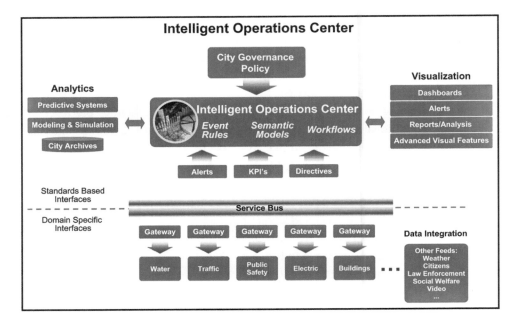

Figure 2.4
The urban CPU, illustrated by a figure included in the *IBM Intelligent Operations Center for Smarter Cities Administration Guide* with the original caption "IBM Intelligent Operations Center architecture." *Source:* IBM 2012, 15.

wider ecosystem is organized. This archetypical framing not only shows the critical role of the Urban OS in assembling connections between software and hardware within an overall system architecture, but also establishes a form of relation between the internal governance of the city and the virtual and physical networks outside. It suggests interlayered networks, interfaces, and data integration, assembled together in a new control system that sits across/above/within the layers of the city. Disconnected and separate layers are now potentially linked by new analytic and control functions.

The example presented in figure 2.4 positions city governance as a form of input into an Urban OS or operations center. It breaks the city down into a series of event rules, a set of semantic models and workflows that are supported by key performance indicators, directives, and alerts. Providing a tangible link to urban big data debates (Kitchin 2014b; Klauser and Albrechtslund 2014; Townsend 2015), this characterization of the Urban OS brings together forms of analytics (data analytics, predictive systems, modeling, and simulation; see chapter 6) and a standardized set of city archives (e.g., a municipal open data platform; see chapter 3). The analytics generated by such urban big data are then fed to a set of visualizations, such as dashboards and alerts (see Kitchin, Lauriault, and McArdle 2015). Such schemes, through a *service bus* (a term used in software design to refer to communication interfaces between mutually interacting software applications) and digital gateways aimed at data integration, act upon the city, on buildings, electric networks, public safety, traffic, water, and so on. It both represents and brings into existence a model for the Urban OS to connect the core operating system to a set of other urban capacities, through specialist software and smaller companies or communities of knowledge with particular expertise in infrastructure.

A computer scientist we interviewed highlighted the similarities between this illustration of a city's intelligent operations center (figure 2.4; see also chapter 7) and a computer processing unit (CPU). Pointing to the hardware-centric nature of the terminology used, he identified analogies between this way of representing urban operations and ways of representing computers themselves. The urban is reframed by a language that emphasizes control nodes, data flows, memories, gateways, and interfaces. The Urban OS, as an operations center in the center of the diagram, "would be like the arithmetic logic unit of the CPU, which does the adding and subtracting and multiplying." Like a personal computer, this understanding of the urban is based on the idea of an internal processor (the intelligent operations center) working with external memory (analytics) to produce a visible outcome on a display (visualization on a screen or monitor or, in the case of a hypothetical smart city, dashboards and alerts). The illustration emphasizes the interfaces between components, which act as permeable boundaries that define the form of interaction with the outside world. This urban CPU "would be connected to your registers, which are local stores of information, and also your control unit, which tells you what to do . . . so there you are: the 'city governance policy unit' is the control unit!" he explained.

Urban Data Flows: Circular Autarky

Central to Urban OS operations are circular and closed processes of data acquisition, analysis, and action (figure 2.5). The key premise is the establishment of a single data set that feeds the operating system—sometimes referred to within the industry as the "golden record" or the "single version of the truth" (IBM 2009, 1). Through the modularization of layers,

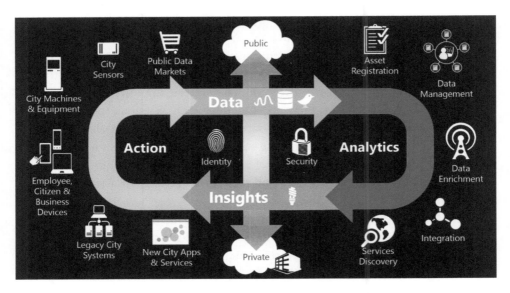

Figure 2.5
Urban data flows and circular autarky, illustrated by a figure included in the *Microsoft CityNext Technical Reference Model Overview* with the original caption "A wealth of city data fuels a continuous cycle of insight and action." *Source:* Microsoft 2013, 7.

examined in previous pages, the Urban OS is able to predefine and standardize inputs and outputs for any urban context and process. The aspiration here, referred to in figure 2.5 as "science in action," is the creation of a closed loop of data collection, analytics, insights, and action. The flow connects public and private clouds, through city sensors, mobile and desk-based computer devices, data management, and public data markets. However, such a tight understanding of data flows and knowledge acquisition squeezes various forms of knowledge and expertise out of the picture.

The Urban OS presumes a mode of information flows that is inward looking, exclusionary in terms of the social interests involved, and largely depoliticized. The assumptions and presumptions of the Urban OS focus data within the system itself and tend to ignore other forms of knowledge and expertise that lie outside the system—particularly outside of the formal lexicons of planners and modelers—advancing a city with limited learning capacities (cf. McFarlane 2011). It thus foregrounds an urban epistemology that excludes a wide range of voices, priorities, stakeholders, and viewpoints, a process often embedded in techniques of automation. Characterized by

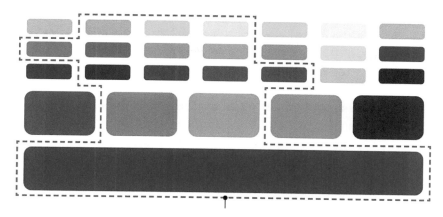

Figure 2.6
Dis- and re-assembling urban circulations, illustrated by a figure included in *Hitachi's Vision for Smart Cities* with the original caption "Design Framework—Example combination for a particular urban development project." *Source:* Hitachi 2013, 21.

the primacy of data over other priorities, the Urban OS becomes an internalized and technocratic system that is not open to challenge, innovation, or creativity, unless this is done through the language and logics of the system itself. This is a closed world, characterized by forms of closure and self-referential behavior that are shaped by software configurations. Urban processes, agents or stakeholders, in order to be part of *analytics, insight,* and *action,* have to be inside the presumptions of the software system itself.

Dis- and Re-assembling Urban Circulations

The city, already dis-assembled in layers and data, is then selectively re-assembled in an arborescent fashion through an attempt to construct a coherent aggregate. These are highly selective processes that dis- and re-assemble on the basis of the categories and presuppositions of the Urban OS. It involves a suggestion that flows and other aspects of urban life can be un- and rebundled to achieve flexibility, efficiency, and optimization. Figure 2.6 provides a simple but powerful illustration of this process of re-assembly in the Urban OS. It is powerful precisely due to its simplicity, where colored blocks with no particular reference to either the city or the computing world are reaggregated by a dashed line, which notionally integrates them toward a new urban function. Or, as Hitachi puts it, "daily-life services infrastructure can be broken down (dis-assembled) into the various different services provided by the city," pointing to *"the disassembly and reassembly* of the daily-life services infrastructure *as one way to create new value* for smart cities" (2013, 23, our emphasis).

The need for modularity, interoperability, and transferability across systems—and cities—revokes local specificity. The same process incorporates diversity and the ability to develop relationships beyond the local, albeit in its own terms. By fragmenting and re-assembling the city, the Urban OS produces a flow of information that is theoretically transferable across geographically and culturally divergent places. Explicitly referring to processes of unbundling and rebundling, it relies on techniques of modularization and categorization to claim a unique capacity to reimagine and reconfigure the urban. It is claimed that these "customized packages of service delivery" can serve the unique circumstances of individual cities, yet local particularities can enter the system only in the form of standardized data, and it is solely by combining datasets that the city can be reconfigured. The Urban OS works upon the comprehensive design of items, relations, and transactions that can be molded into a management model that could be brought to bear on any organization. This process of disaggregation is made possible by reconfiguring the components of the city into data blocks that can later be worked with, recombined, or reprocessed. The city is laid bare—dis-assembled into its constituent parts, defined by the categories created and used by the Urban OS—and then re-assembled into new, more desirable configurations and flows. Urban processes, now distilled into immaterial data packages, can be reconfigured in a variety of ways. From this perspective, the Urban OS operates through techniques of digitalization and datafication (chapter 3), converting the life of the city into standardized and decontextualized units of data that function as a kind of common language.

Conclusions: Governing through the Urban OS?

In this chapter, we have foregrounded the critical need to place the Urban OS within a longer-term historical framework. The idea of applying information technologies and computational logics to urban problems developed in the United States during the 1960s, when new techniques and technologies of computing and communications were explicitly reoriented from the military and defense sectors and applied to urban contexts. This cybernetic turn that viewed the city as a system of systems made comparisons between cities and both technological/communication systems and ecological concepts to achieve balance and homeostasis. Although these initial efforts toward the computational city were relatively short-lived, they are an important historical antecedent of the contemporary applications of computing technologies to urban issues. Critical information, organization, and management studies have provided us with important insights into the ways in which information communication packages such as ERP systems (clear antecedents to the Urban OS) have simplified decision-making into functional steps and integration through standardized operating procedures that fit the premises and assumptions of the software packages—a process that works to the detriment of flexibility and local sensitivity. It is important to place the contemporary shifts toward digital, platform, and smart urbanism in this wider context in order to understand some of the limits, tensions, and dangers that may be inherent in this new approach to managing the city.

We have also outlined five paradigmatic framings, which illustrate how the Urban OS imposes order on the city, reshaping it as a problem and an object for intervention and suggesting a series of defined solutions in the shape of reconfigured flow relationships. The Urban OS, the inheritor of earlier waves of urban computing and a product of the interface between corporate, logistics, and IT thinking, represents an attempt to construct new rationalities for a regime of control. This emerging regime is based on functional simplification and heterogeneous reintegration, mediated through computational ecosystems that embody important presumptions about what constitutes appropriate knowledge and forms of decision-making. The diagrammatic abstractions of the Urban OS, which are examined in more detail in the chapters that follow, signal toward new ways of imagining the city, establishing urban meaning, and opening or closing modes of inclusion and participation. The collapse between city and corporation has significant implications: it is a first step in the digital hollowing of the polis, advancing the removal of agonism, difference, and multiplicity in favor of operationalization and efficiency. The singular logic of the business enterprise, just like that of a computational structuring of the world, requires operational drive, functional simplification, and overall consistency. It is incompatible with the *polis*—the idealized form of democratic urbanity and citizenship that results from and depends upon participation and debate, forms of inclusion, the recognition of multiple forms of being, contestation, and contradiction.

Our analysis sees an emerging computational urban diagram operating beyond simple representation, playing a role in creating a new type of reality. The Urban OS frames (effectively mediating and recreating) urban circulations, imposing computing technology as an obligatory passage point. In it, both urban flows and the city itself are increasingly viewed as a logistical enterprise in search of efficiency and optimization. In this sense, the Urban OS as an urban diagram is both a design for the city and a template for its operations, exercised through a range of urban computational logics—six of which will be examined in the following chapters: datafication, sensing, mapping, prediction, circulation, and resistance.

3   Datafication: The Making of Data-as-Infrastructure

Socrata believes firmly that the public sector must treat data today as more than an afterthought. . . . In order to improve quality of life and services to their citizens, governments must treat data as a resource, just like they would water or electricity. They must provide an infrastructure around it and make it accessible to the public. In short, today is the era of data-as-a-utility.
—Socrata (2015, 1)

This chapter examines how data is being constituted as an urban infrastructure. We want to move beyond understandings of this infrastructure in terms of the physical platforms that support and enable data flows, such as servers, data centers, networking devices, routers, fiber networks, and the like. Instead, when examining the making of data-as-infrastructure, we want to draw attention to the data itself as a flow that underpins a new type of utility and creates new infrastructural capacities. Rather than simply being transmitted and processed, data in the city *flows*, just like water, energy, or transport. In the emerging digital city, data operates as an underlying and systemic infrastructure, helping to manage other networked infrastructures, transforming urban services, and creating new opportunities for the enclosure of urban infrastructure by capital.

In the coming together of data and traditional infrastructures, data-as-infrastructure co-constitutes a new generation of urban infrastructures that are simultaneously digital and corporeal. Data in the city is generative, allowing for recombination while giving birth to a new nature of place and flow. Through an entanglement of digital and material forms, data-as-infrastructure does not simply advance an epistemology of the urban but rather advances an ontogenesis of infrastructural operations, a digital operationalization of infrastructural flows as productive and inherently relational. The main ontological implications of data in the city are examined in the following chapter, while this chapter discusses the idea of data-as-infrastructure in more depth.

Our understanding of data-as-infrastructure draws heavily on the work of Susan Leigh Star (Star 1999), who argues that infrastructure is made at the point of resolution of tensions between the local and the global. Rather than a preexisting form of substrate, infrastructure is emergent; it "emerges for people in practice, connected to activities and structures" (Star and Ruhleder 1996, 112). In doing so, it puts in place a new set of relationships and acquires meaning according to the cultural context in which it is mobilized. In this process, as "substrate becomes substance" (Star and Ruhleder 1996, 113), the balance of power shifts. Data, the primary flow that underpins the computational logics discussed in each of the following chapters, endows the Urban OS with the power to recombine urban processes into new flows, processes, forms, and bodies. We capture this idea through the computational logic of *datafication.*

Datafication relates directly to two of the diagrammatic abstractions that we examined in chapter 2: circular autarky, or the generation of inward-looking, depoliticized data loops (figure 2.5); and the dis- and re-assembly of urban circulations by means of computation (figure 2.6). Datafication, we argue, gains its fundamentally recombinant force through three distinct processes. First, *decoupling* disconnects data from questions of origin and ownership, separating notions of source from notions of flow. Second, *content distribution* reframes data as an asset that can be commodified and distributed across a range of different channels. Finally, *embodiment* captures the ways in which data combines with traditional infrastructural flows to form new urban materialities, and through this the generation of a new form of "intelligence incarnate." Combined, these processes amount to a new urban ecological flow and a new infrastructural form—modular, socially embedded, transcendent, built on an installed base, and developed from within a community (cf. Star 1999).

Following Dalton and Thatcher's agenda for critical data studies, instead of examining urban data from an instrumental perspective (i.e., asking how close it would bring us to a mythical objective truth), we ask questions about what it means for something to be quantified in particular manners and "what possible experiences have been opened and which have been closed off" (Dalton and Thatcher 2014). In this chapter, we examine the pervasive and constantly reproducing narratives that surround data in the city (e.g., sharing, accountability, innovation, open access, open government, transparency, economic value, evidence-based decision-making, social entrepreneurship, citizen innovation, etc.). These, in the view of critical data scholars, both provide a practical rationale for its use and legitimate it (Kitchin 2014a).[1]

Within industry and professional circles, discussions around the role of data in the city are full of optimistic narratives that foreground the benefits associated with an unrestrained flow of data (open data), advancing ideals of transparency and accountability in local government. While we do not fundamentally disagree with the value of qualities such as transparency and accountability, our analysis takes a different stance. Beyond prioritizing transparency and accountability, data-as-infrastructure installs a form of governing through calculative recombination, where interoperability underpins political ideals as much as the material possibility of transforming the city via a new nature of urban flows. Datafication accounts for a new logic of urban management, which sets the foundations for a transformation of the role of local government in the delivery of urban services, establishing a new type of relationship between the public sector and technology professionals by expanding data usage in the urban context.

Datafication involves a combination of governing logics: a collapse between the formalized and corporate responses embedded within the municipal open data platform and the informal, decentralized, and "alternative" responses of the civic hacker. This occurs in the context of, first, the urban adoption of open data principles, with civic hacking (or civic tech) communities and open government movements actively demanding data, contributing to the development of platforms, and experimenting with the use of urban data; second, an urban service reorganization, in which national states push local governments to use data to better organize interoperable and more efficient and transparent local government services; and third, a push for urban regeneration and economic development through an engagement with ICTs, in which, as noted in the previous chapter, the city is seen as being similar to a large company in need of technology. The city provides vast quantities of data that need to be managed as an opportunity to be exploited as an asset by the private sector, resulting in the need for data flows and platforms as infrastructural capacities for the generation of new circuits of economic exploitation.

This chapter briefly reviews the broader development of municipal open data platforms, but we primarily focus on New York City, reimagined by the Bloomberg administration (2002–2013) as a data-driven city (New York City 2013). We discuss the establishment of the NYC Open Data portal and the role of the civic hacking community in its development, alongside the various narratives that transform data-as-infrastructure into a way of thinking about, and remaking, the city. We show how a cadre of municipal leaders (often with private sector backgrounds) have been working alongside the private sector, sponsoring programs and experiments with urban data in order to advance a newly intensified understanding of local government as an enterprise. In this context, the coming together of interventions and discourses around free and open data flows, transparency, and accountability feed into an attempt to create a standardized data infrastructure through which the urban can be recombined in specific and commercial ways.

The Data Revolution Encounters the City

Data and calculation are not new to the city. For around two hundred years, data collection and statistical analyses have played a key role in configuring the urban, making data into an instrumental tool for running cities. As discussed in chapter 2, since the 1960s, information systems and urban computing have influenced how we know and imagine the city. Long before that, in the nineteenth century, the development of modern statistics led local authorities to a form of "government by numbers," replacing an older "political arithmetic" whereby data collection was in the hands of the centralized state (Joyce 2003). Outside of the bureaucratic apparatus of the state, an "enlightened" and technically skilled cadre of professionals and opinion makers, such as doctors and clergymen, began to generate knowledge about the social conditions of the city. From the collection of "facts" carried out in the early nineteenth century by the Manchester Statistical Society to John Snow's mapping of cholera incidence in London in the 1850s, people began to recognize the power of numbers to influence local governance and to shape urban interventions (Joyce 2003; Rose 1991). Becoming what Bruno Latour identified as an *immutable mobile*,[2] numbers in the city have, for over two centuries, acted as the "trace that can be made both visible and stable, and hence knowable and therefore manageable for the ends of power" (Joyce 2003, 25; see also Latour 1987).

Data-Driven Urbanism

With the dawn of digital computing, the pressures to collect and process ever-higher volumes of urban data grew. *Big data* now constitutes a new type of economic and knowledge asset in the shape of large, complex, and unstructured datasets that require computational processing to reveal patterns, trends, and associations. Over the last decade, scholars and commentators alike have argued that the arrival of big data heralds "a new era of data-driven urbanism" (Kitchin, Lauriault, and McArdle 2018). This era is characterized by the ubiquity of ICT and the creation of markets through digital technologies, or, as we see in chapter 5, the territorialization of global flows (see also Barns 2016; McCann and Ward 2011). The promise of urban data (both big and small) is that it can create efficiency savings and find solutions to problems across diverse urban areas, acting to optimize a new range of public services and making the city more effective, accountable, transparent, responsive, and flexible.

Data advocates argue that the use of data in the city enables real-time analysis, new and more effective modes of urban governance, and the possibility of more sustainable, competitive, and productive cities. Some add that the free and open flow of urban data is a force for democratization, encouraging accountability and a constructive public discourse while also "providing a transparent measure of progress" toward societal goals (Mahoney 2013, 10). These advocates for urban data praise it as providing "the raw materials to drive more effective decision-making and efficient service delivery, spur economic activity, and empower citizens to take an active role in improving their own communities" (B. Goldstein 2013, ix). In Barcelona, for example, experiments with data collection via wireless sensors in waste bins claim efficiency improvements in municipal waste collection (Thomson 2014). In Boston, Kansas City, Washington DC, and Sydney, a smart phone application similar to Uber called BRIDJ has used data from multiple public and social media sources to optimize public transport routes, resulting in a model of on-demand transport that claims a "40–60% more efficient trip (on average) than traditional transit" (BRIDJ, n.d.).[3] In Moscow, wireless sensors collect data on parking usage and notify drivers of available spaces via a mobile phone app. Worldsensing, the company behind Moscow's Fastprk system, claims a measured reduction in congestion, pollution, and driver's stress (Worldsensing, n.d.). In Chicago, datasets in the hands of civic hackers have been used to support parents in identifying the sites and times of free flu vaccinations, and in finding school routes for their children that avoid areas with high levels of criminality (Whitaker 2012). Examples like these abound, and we have no doubt that our readers will be familiar with other similar stories in their own cities and regions.

However, alongside this optimistic reading of urban data, there are other, more skeptical views. Critics of the data-driven city have long argued that it facilitates surveillance and systemic profiling, leading to a degradation of key citizen rights and a loss of privacy. Graham and Wood (2003, 228) contend that it has facilitated "a step change in the power, intensity and scope of surveillance" through a ubiquitous form of computing that collects and recombines data and displays the results through new methods of visualization. This surveillant city links data from CCTV, smart metering systems, electronic transport ticketing, credit and financial institutions, social media, and many other data-based technologies to "monitor, control, and guide social processes with unprecedented precision and power" in ways that are "virtually invisible and formally unregulated" (Graham 1998, 496). This leads not simply to a generalized condition of "surveillant anxiety" (Crawford 2014), but an "anxiety of control" generated by a tension between our desire to limit the disclosure of personal data and a growing awareness that any attempt at exerting such control is futile (Leszczynski 2015a, 965).

The New Urban Science
Within academic circles that embrace the idea of urban analytics, data underpins a new science of cities, in which an understanding of the urban is largely achieved through various forms of computer modeling. In this view, following an understanding of cities as "more like organisms than machines" (Batty 2013, 1), data enables the abstraction and analytical simplification of complex urban processes in order to uncover the properties of the city's flows and networks. Urban knowledge is constructed as a calculative exercise, wherein an understanding of the city is to be achieved not simply by observing flows and networks but rather by numerically predicting them (Batty 2013; Bettencourt et al. 2007). Despite the fact that urban big data can potentially impact both long- and short-term planning,

practically speaking, it is decisively shifting the emphasis "from longer term strategic planning to short-term thinking about how cities function and can be managed" (Batty 2013, 274; see also Batty 2017).

The ways in which data is conceived within such forms of urban analytics, as well as the science of cities itself, have been criticized for being reductionist, mechanistic, essentialist, and deterministic (cf. Mattern 2013; Morozov 2014). Highlighting the epistemological implications of a science of cities, Rob Kitchin sums up the risks associated with thinking the city through data:

> These approaches adopt a realist epistemology that supposes the existence of an external reality which operates independently of an observer and which can be objectively and accurately measured, tracked, statistically analyzed, modelled and visualized to reveal the world as it actually is. In other words, urban data can be unproblematically abstracted from the world in neutral, value-free and objective ways and are understood to be essential in nature; that is, fully representative of that which is being measured (they faithfully capture its essence and are independent of the measuring process) . . . they promote an instrumental rationality that underpins the notion that cities can be steered and managed through a set of data levers and analytics and that urban issues can be solved through a range of technical solutions . . . [and] fail to recognize that cities are complex, multifaceted, contingent, relational systems, full of contestation and wicked problems that are not easily captured or steered, and that urban issues are often best solved through political/social solutions and citizen-centred deliberative democracy, rather than technocratic forms of governance. (Kitchin 2016, 4)

Governing the City through Data

Critics of the science of cities approach remind us that data, big or small, is never neutral and raw, but always shaped by the cultural landscape where it is created. It is the result of specific contexts with distinctive social practices and therefore imbued with the beliefs and biases inherent to such practices (Dalton and Thatcher 2014). By foregrounding the ways in which contemporary data usage has both political and epistemological implications (Cheney-Lippold 2011; Crawford, Gray, and Miltner 2014),[4] they offer a contrasting account to that of urban data practitioners, drawing attention to the influence of power (social privilege and social values) on the production of urban knowledge via data (Kitchin 2014a). As Stephen Graham puts it, "code-based technologized environments continuously and invisibly classify, standardize, and demarcate rights, privileges, inclusions, exclusions, and mobilities and normative social judgments across vast . . . domains" (Graham 2005, 563). The databases and data models that enable the operations of the computational city thus encode "fundamentally political questions about who—what bodies—are considered normal on the urban street and whose bodies are deemed 'deficits' to the collective urban imagination" (Wilson 2011, 868).

If traditional infrastructures, such as public lighting, water, and sanitation, have previously played an important role in establishing modes of governing (Joyce 2003; Otter 2008), the same could be said of the evolving data infrastructures of the contemporary city. Klauser, Paasche, and Söderström have examined an emergent form of governing through code and the use of data to order and regulate everyday life, coding "social life into software" (2014, 870). New urban technologies, such as the urban dashboard, establish new and narrow ways of knowing the city based on instrumental rationalities. Here, "the city as visualized facts" is "open to manipulation by vested interests" (Kitchin, Lauriault, and McArdle 2015, 6). As a new urban utility, data gradually becomes "a part of how we see the world," changing notions of causality and our understanding of space (Thrift 2014, 1264). If the smart city is seen as a vehicle moving toward the corporatization of the urban (Barns 2016; Söderström, Paasche, and Klauser 2014; Vanolo 2014), data is the flow that enables digital infrastructures to reconfigure the city as a business-led, entrepreneurial, highly attractive, and competitive corporate entity.

Remaking Data as Urban Infrastructure

Increasingly, thinking about the future of urban infrastructure demands a reading of infrastructure through data and of data as infrastructure—a future that, in the view of many, is enabled first and foremost by forms of data collection, data release, and data analytics. Cities all over the world are engaging in a broad range of data initiatives, as exemplified by the proliferation of urban dashboards, open data platforms, and dedicated analytics teams within city governments. Speaking of data as a utility—"flowing through the city's 'pipes'" (Mayor of London 2014, 21)—city authorities increasingly see data as playing a decisively "material" role in the city, rebundling it and integrating its pieces—or, as the consultation document of the London Infrastructure Plan 2050 puts it, acting as "the 'glue' that integrates transport, energy, health, waste and housing" (Mayor of London 2014, 21). Information flows are positioned both as a way of configuring essential public services and as a public good in their own right.[5] As data flows through the city, this data-as-infrastructure is transforming how the city operates, adding a new infrastructural layer operating over, through, and in between layers of waste, water, energy, transport, and other utilities and services.

The current embrace of data at the urban level emerges in the context of national level pressures and opportunities related to efforts to advance open government. Driven by the desire to embrace a digital economy and to reduce costs via efficiency gains, states are promoting the adoption of open data at national, regional, and local levels. In the United States, for example, the White House has been critical in promoting standards and mechanisms for increasing data use in local government. In the United Kingdom, the Government Digital Service is advancing the Government as a Platform policy, with a set of data-based products and templates that can be used in any local authority.[6] At stake is the application of a set of techniques for local service reorganization, a push from the central state for municipal governments to use data to better organize interoperability and efficiency in local service delivery.

Consequently, it is not surprising that the most popular way in which cities are mobilizing data initiatives is through open data platforms (aka open data portals). In recent years, they have become common in a broad range of organizations, including businesses, multilateral agencies, scientific institutions, nonprofits, and government agencies at all levels. In 2017, the software company Opendatasoft published a list of over 2,600 open data portals across the world, hundreds of which have been developed by city governments. The list includes the usual suspects (large cities with well-developed IT clusters such as Chicago, Rio de Janeiro, Amsterdam, and London), alongside a cadre of smaller and perhaps less well-known cities (such as Fortaleza in Brazil, Rosario in Argentina, Basildon in the UK, Bandung in Indonesia, and Umeå in Sweden).[7] These municipal open data platforms aim to standardize forms of data collection in the city and to make the collected data available to the general public. They provide users with data on a range of topics of local interest, such as transport, education, crime and public safety, sanitation, local budgets, and the environment. The emphasis is not so much on the visualization of data (as it would be on the urban dashboard) as it is on the provision of raw data *in machine-readable formats* that are licensed for public and private use (covering both commercial and noncommercial uses).

A strong force behind the establishment of open data platforms across the world has been the *open movement*. Strongly rooted within the worlds of IT and internet development, this is an eclectic call for openness, transparency, collaboration, and free access across a variety of domains, from software development and science to government. The open movement calls for collaborative solutions to "many of the world's most pressing problems" via open data, open science, and open-source software (Open Knowledge Foundation, n.d., "Glossary"; see also OECD, n.d., "Open Government"; OECD, n.d., "Open Government Data"). In doing so, it plays an important role in promoting contemporary narratives of open government, which emphasize openness as "part of the conditions of possibility of all politics" (Tkacz 2015, 3).

Interoperability: Governing through Calculative Recombination

Beyond simply a technological fix for society's problems, what becomes apparent here is the mobilization of a model of governance (Barns 2016; Tkacz 2015)[8] in which ideals of democracy, transparency, public scrutiny, and accountability are seen as achievable through interoperability and the free flow of data and information facilitated by ICT technologies. This emerging form of local governance is underpinned by open data, with the latter defined by the World Bank–supported Open Knowledge Foundation as "data that can be freely used, re-used and redistributed by anyone— subject only, at most, to the requirement to attribute and sharealike" (Open Knowledge Foundation, n.d., "What Is Open Data?").[9] At the heart of this definition sits a desire to maximize interoperability: "If you're wondering why it is so important to be clear about what open means and why this definition is used, there's a simple answer: interoperability. Interoperability denotes the ability of diverse systems and organizations to work together (inter-operate). In this case, it is the ability to interoperate—or intermix— different datasets" (Open Knowledge Foundation, n.d., "What Is Open Data?").

Open data platforms mobilize a way of governing through calculative recombination, imagining a type of city that mimics the ways in which digital information systems operate. The attention given to the requirement of machine-readable formats is relevant (e.g., XLS or CSV files, as opposed to PDF files), as this is precisely what allows other computers to access and use data for the purpose of calculation or visualization—allowing for interoperability in practice and, through this, data recombination. The emerging form of urban governance advanced by the open platform is based on the possibility of rebundling the fragmented city and continuously reassembling urban processes through digital recombination.

Municipal open data platforms reconstitute the role of government as data or platform provider, a move that illustrates the influence of data-driven narratives and practices in framing responses to urban challenges. In this *government-as-platform*, local authorities are narrowly framed as the providers of "a marketplace for the delivery of third-party software services to citizens" (Barns 2016, 556). The open nature of the model relocates the possibility of calculation outside the public sector, underpinning a desire for economic development via a data-based innovation that, in theory, is to emerge through the integration of the city's economic sectors and urban processes. This particularly favors the IT sector, as well as local authorities and businesses with the skills to act at the interface between information communication and data processing, as the following case study of New York City illustrates.

New York City: The Data-Driven City

NYC Open Data

In February 2012, the New York City Council approved the Open Data Law, requiring all city agencies to open their data by 2018. New York followed San Francisco, California; Portland, Oregon; and a handful of other US cities and counties in enacting legislation to make a wide range of government data freely available to the public via online platforms.[10] The law set ambitious objectives, calling for an accessible repository of machine-readable data that "will make the operation of city government more transparent, effective and accountable to the public." Its purpose was not simply to streamline intra- and intergovernmental communication and interoperability, but also to open up possibilities for "the public to assist in identifying efficient solutions for government," to "promote innovative strategies for social progress," and to "create economic opportunities" (New York City Council 2012). The Open Data Law was one of the landmark interventions of Michael Bloomberg, a mayor who had come from the private sector and was convinced of the potential for data to transform the city.

The Bloomberg story illustrates the transmutation of corporate rationalities into the urban world. This is a story underpinned by narratives around data-driven efficiency and information as a tool for empowerment, and substantiated by the possibility of decision-making informed by real-time data streams (Bloomberg 2001).[11] Bloomberg's involvement in the making of New York as a data-driven city is salient not because he is a businessman, but because his business is founded on data flows. Twenty years before becoming mayor of New York, he developed the Bloomberg Terminal, a purpose-built computer terminal that enabled real-time access to financial market data on an electronic trading platform. An important antecedent to the urban dashboard (Mattern 2015), the Bloomberg Terminal uses multiple panels to provide simultaneous (rather than sequential) streams of information in real time (figure 3.1). Involved in hundreds of thousands of financial decisions every day, the terminal embodies a faith in the power and profitability of data.[12] Bloomberg wanted to transform New York City into a *data-driven city*, meaning "a city that intelligently uses data to better deliver critical services, while increasing accountability through transparency" (New York City 2013, 7). In his foreword to *The Responsive City*, a book that argues the merits of digital technologies as an opportunity to "revolutionize local government" (Goldsmith and Crawford 2014, 1), he speaks of the importance of data for improving municipal service delivery, empowering public servants, increasing quality of life, and saving taxpayers' money. He credits himself with bringing to the public sector a private sector approach that relies on ICTs, data mining, and real-time quantitative measuring to prioritize efficiency, effectiveness, and cost savings. In his words: "I have a rule of thumb: if you can't measure it, you can't manage it. And I brought that approach with me from the private sector to New York's city hall. . . . Harnessing and understanding data helped us decide how to allocate resources more efficiently and effectively, which allowed us to improve the delivery of services" (Bloomberg 2014, v, vi).

Bloomberg's Open Data Law committed New York to a single web portal via which all agencies would share their information with the public. This became NYC Open Data (https://opendata.cityofnewyork.us/), advertised as "a powerful tool that ensures transparency and fosters civic innovation within our City to help improve the quality of life for all New Yorkers"

Figure 3.1
The Bloomberg Terminal. Photo by Giulia Forsythe. Creative Commons CC0 1.0
Universal Public Domain Dedication.

(NYC Open Data 2017; figure 3.2). As of July 2014, the city had made nearly
1,300 datasets available to the public through the portal. By 2018, the portal housed over two thousand open datasets and had twenty thousand
users every week. A range of events raised public awareness of its existence,
including an annual Open Data Week. In 2018, this included thirty sched-
uled events and featured over fifty government, industry, and community
partners. One of these was Socrata, a software company specializing in data
as a service (DaaS) and responsible for storing and maintaining NYC Open
Data.[13] Socrata has pioneered the market for data management within the
public sector, making it a primary illustration of the manifold ways in
which corporate systems and expertise are now entangled in the generation
of data as a public infrastructure. Focusing on public sector clients, Socrata
supports governments in making data searchable and discoverable. To use

Figure 3.2
Screen capture of NYC Open Data as of March 2019. *Source:* https://opendata
.cityofnewyork.us/.

their own terminology, they *surface* data from a variety of platforms into
the cloud and make it open to the public.

In addition to Bloomberg's Open Data Law, arguments about value generation and public engagement played a pivotal role in the introduction
of NYC Open Data—in particular, the justification that this type of public
engagement would strengthen the regional economy by encouraging private entrepreneurial involvement. As a staff member of New York City's
Department of Information Technology & Telecommunications (DoITT)
put it, "We are interested in how open data can boost the city's economy
and help create new businesses and drive entrepreneurship . . . [we want
to] create business around data." The Open Data Law explicitly stated that
the desire was for the public to assist in identifying solutions for government, encouraging a form of cooperation between civic technologists and
the city's government. While this allowed digital economy businesses like

Figure 3.3
Hacknight evening in New York City. Photo courtesy of La Vesha Parker/Progressive HackNight.

Socrata to get involved, it also enabled input from civic hackers, open data activists, and urban technologists (figure 3.3)—described by that same City of New York staff member quoted here as "a group of activists that were really interested in boosting the transparency and accessibility of city information, working closely with City Council . . . an amazing and engaged community of activists and civic technologists who are focused on access to government information." They played a particularly important role in the development of the platform, advising on its initial phases and agitating toward the release of particular datasets. They were drawn together by BetaNYC, the civic organization behind New York's weekly Civic Hacknights—evening meetings that operate as "weekly project night[s] for technologists, designers, developers, data scientists, map makers, and activists who are working on 'civic technology'" (Hidalgo 2015). These events function as data advocacy spaces, but also as a critical site for the civic tech community to reimagine, discuss, and shape the contemporary coming together of technology and local government. Participants, like many others within the civic tech movement, see technology as playing a key role in streamlining government processes, sometimes improving what already exists, while at other times circumventing existing processes and replacing them all together.

Hacking New York, Part 1: Transforming Government through Liberating Data

Recent academic analyses of civic hacking have emphasized its role as a form of data activism and advocacy (Schrock 2016; Schrock and Shaffer 2017; Thakuriah, Tilahun, and Zellner 2017). We expand, complicate, and problematize this perspective, agreeing with scholars for whom civic hacking actually creates a particular type of city that is imbricated in a series of "alternative place-making practices . . . [recreating] urban governance, community engagement, and the meaning and practice of urban everyday life" (Perng and Kitchin 2018, 2; see also Townsend 2013). Politically, the status of civic hacking is controversial. For some, it genuinely empowers citizens to respond to social issues; for others, its trendiness masks dubious libertarian values (de Lange et al. 2015). In terms of political economy, hackers put into practice a desire to transform the status quo through the donation of free labor, suggesting a challenge to conventional forms of production and mechanisms for capital accumulation. Wark describes hacking as a free, cooperative, and self-organized form of labor associated with computing programming, which "presents something of a challenge to the social order" (Wark 2006, 321). Hackers work on their own time, set their own goals, and work "on common property for the good of all" (Wark 2006, 321). In *A Hacker Manifesto* (2004), Wark discusses hackers as a social class with the ability to abstract information, to separate it from capitalist forms of production that operate through the monopoly of property ("intellectual property"), and thereby to liberate it for the common good—opening the potential for information to overthrow class rule. Yet, our experience during fieldwork, in the spaces where the hacker meets the city, suggests that Wark's reading of hackers as a distinct and revolutionary class movement is idealistic. In evening meetups and civic hack nights, civic hackers operate as part of a community of data activists; during the daytime, they are more likely to be consultants or developers working for Google, Facebook, eBay, or other IT businesses advancing the digital economy. Their provision of an idealistic free labor, as discussed in the pages that follow, is quickly subjected to enclosure by capital for the creation of surplus value. Transcending top-down versus bottom-up narratives in the search for an "alternative" digital city (Luque-Ayala and Marvin 2015), civic hackers both represent and challenge dominant powers.

Civic hackers across the world argue that their agenda is largely apolitical.[14] They tend to view themselves as neutral agents who are bringing together transparency and technology for the public good. Rooted within ideas of open source and open government, the narratives they espouse combine a belief in technology and automation with libertarian political perspectives valuing freedom and a skeptical attitude to authority. This is a DIY citizenship that "update[s] the Reaganite philosophy of self-governance for a new, technologically literate generation" (Gregg 2015, 194). As an influential civic hacker in Taipei's Sunflower Movement explained: "There is not really a central agenda, so to speak other than of course being transparent. . . . The agenda is around transparency, the information transparency and the sort of the collaborative culture, of debate and things like that. And the government happens to have most of the data that we need to have intelligent discussions around many issues. . . . You could say it is about governments but it is not necessarily a government."

Civic hacking is not about seizing power, though it is about ways of governing. This helps us to unpack how the coming together of activism, data, and digital technologies informs the configuration of urban politics (a topic further discussed in chapters 4 and 8, in the contexts of Barcelona and Hong Kong). Though hackers sometimes claim that they are apolitical and neutral, they recognize that there are political implications to their activities and that their aim is to put in place a series of commitments to a certain style of governing. The Taiwanese civic hacker quoted earlier continues her explanation by qualifying the role of government, foregrounding the intent to govern, yet lowering the emphasis on the institution itself: "government is just a by-product . . . people notice [that] government is in some places hindering this progress [i.e., transparency and collaboration], and so we have to work with government to get this changed or change their usual [manner] of operation." Her words resonate with those of a prominent civic hacker in New York. Describing his activities to us, he differentiated between the *civic* and the *hacking* parts of the term:

> The hacker part of it is using technology to improve the experience. And that can be anything from making a visualization . . . [to] engaging with the government to pick up new processes that use technology in a better way. . . . . Government

somehow does not understand this for certain processes, so the civic hacker is there to either build it for them, and bypass the government—sometimes . . . [or] maybe build it as a proof of concept, to show the government that it is possible and feasible to do this cheaply. . . .

The civic hacking movement . . . is taking those data feeds and taking that knowledge of internal processes of government, and applying twenty-first-century concepts to it in terms of how we process information, how we surface information. It relates back to the notion that knowledge is power.

The actions of the hacker contribute to efficiency and effectiveness within government, yet bypassing government if needed, thanks to the mobilization of information flows supported by data feeds. As the preceding quote hints at, the unrestricted flow of data is essential for civic hacking. With data as hacking's primary source material, the possibility of civic hacking depends on data flows, making open data platforms into an ideal (albeit not the only) site for resource access. However, data in practice is never a homogeneous nor static category. A remarkable amount of time of a civic hacker goes into working with data. Perng and Kitchin's (2018) ethnography of a civic hacking community in Ireland shows that urban data, to be useful, needs to be qualified, calibrated, acquired, extracted, collected, sourced, crowdsourced, ordered, removed, verified, validated, volunteered, clustered, processed, analyzed, cleaned, anonymized, exchanged, calculated, made intelligible, visualized, and so on.

Our fieldwork revealed that, above all, civic hackers prioritize the need for urban data to be *liberated*. In New York, they spoke about data in particular ways, explicitly and often talking about surfacing data, liberating it, making it searchable and discoverable. In the words of a self-titled data evangelist (one of a growing number of data professionals and activists describing themselves in this way): "*that* is what the open data movement is all about, freeing that information. . . . [It is] how we surface information." In effect, this surfacing of data increases its utility, and through this, its value: "once it is in the platform is more valuable." A significant portion of the efforts of civic hackers in New York goes into ensuring that data is available for anyone who might want to use it. At the time of our fieldwork, the civic hacking community was particularly joyful about the government's release of the city's motor vehicle collision data, which shows the location of any traffic crash reported to the police, as well as how many people were injured and how many fatalities occurred. For years, members of the city's civic hacking community (as well as other community groups) had been

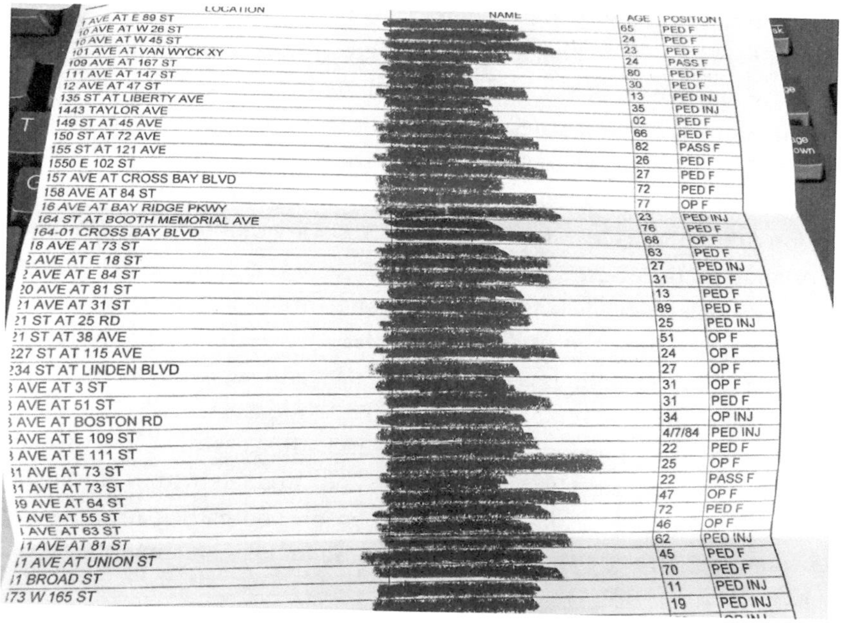

Figure 3.4
Traffic crash data in non-machine-readable format. Photo courtesy of New York Public Radio/WNYC News.

requesting such data, only to obtain it in fragmented ways—for example, via Freedom of Information Act (FOIA) requests. Prior to the formal release of the data, the New York Police Department (NYPD) would only issue the data through monthly PDF reports. These not only were "riddled with errors" (Hinds 2014) but also used a non-machine-readable format (figure 3.4). Civic hackers would *scrape* the data (i.e., find ways to extract it, even if this means manually copying the data) to upload into a database so that others would have access. "People have been clamoring for that [data] for years," explained one interviewee. "One of the members of our community has been doing an ongoing scraping operation, so that every month when they release the new data, he takes it out of the PDF and releases it and makes it downloadable in open formats." When the city finally agreed to publish the data in 2014, it used the city's iconic hackathon, the BigApps competition, to invite the city's civic tech community to use the datasets toward identifying ways for reducing traffic fatalities.

Hacking New York, Part 2: Experimental Entrepreneurialism

Urban hackathons are characteristic of a growing experimentation in governance forms associated with urban computational logics. They are spaces where municipalities partner with the IT sector, students, and technology aficionados to devise ways for using data for city life. Since 2009, NYC has been hosting BigApps, one of the world's most popular city-based hackathons (figure 3.5). Organized by the New York City Economic Development Corporation, the event is supported by a range of IT corporations, including Facebook, eBay, Google, and Microsoft. Software developers, designers, and entrepreneurs are asked to "apply their know-how to improve New York City" and "submit solutions that leverage data and technology to solve . . . major issues for New Yorkers" (BigApps, n.d.).

Scholars have previously associated hackathons with a low-risk and low-cost prototyping space for business and products within the digital economy (Carr and Lassiter 2017). For sponsors and participants, the city, encountered through its data, is a playground for experimentation. In New

Figure 3.5
New York City Mayor Michael Bloomberg at the 2010 BigApps award ceremony. Photo by Steven Rosenbaum. Creative Commons Attribution-NonCommercial-NoDerivs 2.0 Generic (see https://creativecommons.org/licenses/by-nc-nd/2.0/legalcode).

York City, the BigApps competition advocates for government transparency and the involvement of citizens in local government, but also emphasizes the promotion of entrepreneurship. Several winners have secured funding to further develop their products, in some cases becoming start-up companies within the digital economy. Embark NYC, for example, a mass transit app and one of the winners of the third version of the annual competition (2011/2012), subsequently secured investment from BMW to develop a product beyond the prototyping stage. It was later acquired by Apple. Similarly, Roadify, a transport smartphone app and one of several winners in 2010, went on to become an established multimodal transit information distributor and aggregator.[15] In 2017, nearly seven years after winning the BigApps competition, Roadify announced strategic partnerships with leading US digital signage companies such as AVI Systems, Capital Networks, DigiChief, and Four Winds Interactive.

In New York, the convergence of the city's civic hacking community, the Open Data Law, and the NYC Open Data platform illustrates a type of local governance built upon marketplaces for software entrepreneurship (see also Barns 2016). Here, private individuals with ICT skills compete to identify potentially lucrative solutions for public needs and problems. Blurring the boundaries between public and private domains, this form of hacking "appeals to an elite group of individuals who recognise themselves as agents of their moment (Streeter, 2014), whose proficiency equips them to carry the burden of civic duty and deliver services" (Gregg 2015, 194). In this context, datafication, as an urban computational logic, merges three things: the formalized approach of the municipal open data platform, which, underpinned by narratives of openness and transparency, seeks to make the data flow consistent and reliable; the informal responses and applications developed by the voluntary labor pool of civic hackers; and entrepreneurial forms of engagement with the city from those who seek to invest in the solutions suggested not by public servants, but by an emerging cadre of urban technocrats that sit outside government. A key question at stake is to what extent the mobilization of urban data is transformative for local government and, if it is, in what direction.[16] Service provision, as the traditional role of local government, becomes at risk of being superseded by the provision of clean data. In parallel, data provision becomes a public service for the development of further commodities (digital applications) that potentially enclose and privatize parts of the flow.

Datafied Urban Flows: Recombinations through Dis- and Re-assembly

The datafication of the city advances a threefold transformation in urban flows. First, it decouples data flow from its origin, a form of dis-assembly. Second, it selectively re-assembles data as a form of content distribution. Finally, datafication embodies traditional urban flows with new materialities while also embedding data flows with material forms.

Decoupling

In the datafied city, data, in its flows, is increasingly disconnected from both origin and ownership—an inevitable condition of dis-assembling and repurposing data. Liberated urban data, decoupled and free to flow, is recast as an asset in its own right. In an interview with an app developer, a former winner of the BigApps competition, the limited attention placed on data ownership after its opening becomes foregrounded. When we asked about examples of municipally owned data that feed the application he developed, the response we received was puzzled: "I should know the answer to this question and I'm sorry if I don't. I don't spend a lot of time thinking about, you know, who actually owns the data, the data that's there." Of course, this is only a momentary lapse of memory. Within the legal structures of the company, the origin and ownership of each data line is clear. But the fleeting moment illustrates the extent to which the origin of data, once that data "surfaces," becomes inconsequential. What matters are the recombinatory possibilities this liberated data offers. Continuing the interview, we commented: "For the purpose of your applications, whether the data comes from the state level or from the municipal level, it's almost irrelevant as long as the data is there and available." "Exactly!" replied the app developer. "It doesn't matter so much; it's really just about being able to update and use it. . . . I think what we're going to see is more sharing of information at the app level or the platform level that's one degree removed from the primary source."

Content Distribution

The consequence of datafication is the possibility of repackaging urban data as a commodity, turning the city into a megaplatform for "content distribution." Emerging digital platforms relying on urban data operate as distribution channels for urban flows. Like traditional media content (e.g., television shows or news), urban data is surfaced, repackaged, and distributed as content across digital channels such as Google, Google Maps, web pages, smartphone apps, and so on. This process involves the mediatization of urban infrastructure (examined in chapter 7) and is perhaps best illustrated by an app developer working with transport-related open data in New York City: "We are taking that data and we push it out through different types of distribution and exhibition channels, our own model applications, public digital signage, [etc.] . . . and then through third-party applications and websites. . . . Transportation information is content, [just like a] television program is distributed through cable and via satellite and all then broadcasted over the internet . . . [this] is also content."

Critically, this form of data-as-infrastructure is not just about commercial interventions that are enabled by the generation, assembly, and relay of data within and through public domains. It embodies a way of thinking about governing, where local government is reinterpreted as a convener of platforms, the provider of a marketplace for a new urban flow (Barns 2016). Municipalities increasingly provide data; entrepreneurs increasingly take care of the recombination. As the same app developer previously cited puts it, "Municipalities should produce the best clean as possible data, the best data, the cleanest data possible. But I don't think they should be in the business of creating businesses around [it]." In his view, it is more flexible and efficient for public agencies to work with third-party sources and services to enable end user applications for the data. As he emphasized, "[The] city should focus on collecting data, making it clean and then providing it elsewhere."

Embodiment: City-in-Formation

Perhaps the most important characteristic of the datafied city is the embodied nature of urban data. As data lines flow through the city, they are reconstituted as urban flows encapsulating a multiplicity of urban materialities. Urban data, no longer inmaterially digital, gains its power through the ability to materialize itself through a coupling with urban processes and flows. As Wark puts it in *A Hacker Manifesto* (2004, 15), the hack depends on its ability to interact with the material world: "It is at once material and immaterial. It discovers the immaterial virtuality of the material, its qualities of information." It is precisely through such materialization that data-as-infrastructure commands power and effects control.

Here we draw upon the work of Michael Dillon, a critical security studies scholar who has spoken about the condition of corporeality in the digital age and the powers engendered through the materialization of digital information. Drawing on Deleuze's (1992) "Postscript on Societies of Control," Dillon suggests that the power of digital information lies in its ability to find material form. Reflecting on the role of data in transforming contemporary military operations, he explains how engaging with code and data brings about "an intelligence incarnate."[17] The corporeality of information opens possibilities to "command systems of operational combination . . . that bring things to presence, order them in their presence and remove them from presence: the violent comings and goings of power relations" (Dillon 2003, 124). This power finds a tangible expression in the capacity to control reproductions. Paraphrasing his words, but replacing his references to the military with the vocabulary of the city, Dillon provides analytical tools to understand the embodiment of data and code in the urban infrastructural and the endless mutability resulting from this:

> As a function of code, [the city] must be endlessly mutable . . . the way to command this mutability is to develop a strategic virtuosity in the employment of information in order to refashion . . . bodies-in-formation according to any and every eventuality. . . .
>
> Omniscient, omniversal, omnisensorial, omnidirectional, the new strategic discourse embraces a corporeality designed to realize the [urban] intelligence incarnate. (Dillon 2003, 129)

The Urban OS emerges as omniscient, omniversal, omnisensorial, and omnidirectional, providing the city with a new set of infrastructural bodies that navigate and modulate contingency at the point of connection between the local and the global. Critically for us, the growing reliance on data flows in the city puts in place data as a common language and a new configuration of power that operates through code. In the words of Donna Haraway, datafication effects *"the translation of the world into a problem of coding"* (1985, 83; original emphasis). The function of data and code is supposed to make the resulting city-in-formation flexible, mutable, and adaptable in order to refashion infrastructure, territory, and bodies into new configurations according to different eventualities and programs of development. This society of control is driven by information technologies, and it operationalizes open information systems "into modes of self-regulation and self-reproduction" (Dillon 2003, 143). As we will show in the following chapters, data thus finds new materialities, interweaving itself into traditional urban flows and processes such as those associated with water, energy, transport, real estate, and protest.

Conclusions

At the turn of the century, the American sociologist Susan Leigh Star embarked on a project to understand infrastructure through ethnography. Her intellectual program sought to foreground the extent to which infrastructures are sociotechnical, relational, and ecological, and her work debunked previous understandings of infrastructure as a preexisting and static material substrate that simply supports activities and processes. She demonstrated that infrastructures are always emergent, appearing only in practice and as part of a broader ecology, as people use them in connection with a set of structured and localized activities (Star 1999; Star and Ruhleder 1996). Star's conceptualization substantially contributes to our reading of data-as-infrastructure—a notion that far exceeds the physical networks that support and enable data flows (servers, data centers, etc.). Data-as-infrastructure, as a type of utility, is embedded or sunk into a range of social and political structures and arrangements, but it also works to transform them, as the example of civic hackers (and the venture capitalists supporting them) shows. Data-as-infrastructure transcends its own domain of operation by functioning as a tool for horizontal integration and system recombination, supporting other urban flows through automated systems of information collection, command, and visualization. It also engenders a specific community of knowledge, which takes its ordering of reality for granted and the members of which are willing to campaign for data's further liberation on both ideological and commercial grounds.

Urban data, relational and enabling, becomes infrastructure the moment it is asked to resolve (in a rather naturalized fashion) a growing set of tensions between local and global circulations. Datafication, with its logic of calculative recombination, supports the development of new ways of governing the city. It emerges in the context of an urban service reorganization that prioritizes efficiency and entrepreneurialism, both to be achieved via interoperability. Datafication materially aligns an entrepreneurial governance mode with a change in how we conceive the role and means of the public sector, where, as we examine in more depth in chapter 7, governing is not so much about providing services but facilitating circulations. Illustrating the transmutation of corporate rationalities to the public sector, data becomes the means for a lean, efficient, and optimized government, arguably unlocking potential and opportunity. Reframing the city as a business entity, this process materially enrolls the city and its local flows into global circuits of accumulation. Data-driven narratives and practices set the new frame for how to respond to contemporary urban challenges, reconstituting the role of government as data or platform provider. While the narrative states that the ideals of democracy, transparency, public scrutiny, and accountability are to be achieved through interoperability, the free flow of data is mobilized toward business creation.

Datafication is a technique for unbundling and rebundling the city, recombining urban processes and flows into new flows, processes, forms, or bodies. It operates through the city's infrastructural ecosystems, and in doing so becomes one of them, creating new capacities for other computational logics. In chapter 2, we examined how data operates as a critical layer within any computational logic: the Urban OS depends on information flows that can support the ordering, sorting, and calculative capacities of the operating system. Its operation relies on functional simplification and transactional mechanics, establishing a closed world of data-software interaction. Moving on to the material we examined in this chapter, we see how it is through data that computational logics are embedded into the materiality of the city; data's capture and mobilization functions as a translation technique, making the city actionable in new ways. Datafication involves three parallel processes. First, liberating data, which requires decoupling source and flow material. Second, following a logic of commodification, data becomes content; the opportunities engendered are to be realized through its distribution. Finally, the coming together of data and the more traditional infrastructures of the city generates new urban forms—a flow that simultaneously embodies data and transforms the body of infrastructure. Through techniques such municipal open data platforms and the work of civic hacking communities, data is reconstituted to encapsulate multiple (urban) materialities. Here lies the main source of power of the Urban OS: the ability to materialize data through a coupling of information with urban processes and flows—the emergence of an intelligence incarnate of the urban. As Donna Haraway (1985, 83) recognized over three decades ago, this means that "the biggest threat to such power is interruption of communication."

4   Sensing: Commodification through Hyperfragmentation

For me, smart cities are about the digitalization of public space . . . and sensors are what allows you to digitize public space. I say that my business is one of real estate. When I install a sensor . . . all the value that I virtualize is converted into digital and can be exploited, by me or by third parties . . . enabling the creation of an economy underpinned by [electronic] dispositifs. . . . In cities, this generates an infrastructure that virtualizes public space, generating a pool of information in real time for which third parties generate applications.

—Founder of an urban sensors company (Interview, Barcelona, 2015)

Sensors are the physical devices that stand between digital and material flows. They convert the flows of urban space into data signals, bringing together the traditional materiality of the city with the digital world. By transforming urban flows into datasets, sensors play a key role in enabling the Urban OS to *dis- and re-assemble urban circulations* (see chapter 2). Along with metropolitan sensing platforms, they enable novel ways of "actioning" all things urban. Owned by local authorities, the private sector, and/or citizens, both sensors and their platforms are transforming how we interact with the city's environmental conditions, resource flows, and networked infrastructures—from humidity and air pollution to transport, water, waste, energy, and many others. Their use is framed by an assumption that flows and other aspects of urban life can be unbundled and rebundled to increase value and unlock hidden potential. Their mobilization responds to multiple desires, from the city administrator's search for ever-increasing operational efficiency and optimization to the urban activist's idealistic dream of continuous, real-time citizen involvement. However, sensors also have their drawbacks, exemplified by the inevitable loss of local specificity and complexity resulting from a process in which contextual understandings can enter the decision-making system only in the form of data. Sensors are not only a critical connector in the datafication of urban flows (chapter 3); they also *embody* the informational diagrammatic that characterizes the Urban OS, constituting an emerging set of infrastructures that are remaking the sites of value creation in the city.

This chapter focuses on the urban computational logic of sensing, the transformation of potential into action resulting from the digitization of all things urban, and the extent to which this coming together of the material and digital domains of the city renders every dimension of urban life a potential source of value. We see sensing not simply as a process of capturing data in order to know the city and its processes, but as a strategy to render calculative intelligibility across urban processes. We argue that this practice is generative of a particular type of urban environment, providing the technomaterial substrate for a new urban economy based on data flows. Beyond simply providing tools for efficiency and optimization, or for citizen activism, urban digital sensors both embody and enable computational urbanism's desire to create new forms of value via digital assets, further advancing a commodification of urban processes and, at times, public goods. This novel configuration of economic development accelerates the remaking of the commons into commodities. The urban computational logic of sensing, functioning through the Urban OS and following an economic logic of hyperfragmentation, operates as a way of monetizing urban space and flows. Urban sensors thus transform and generate value chains within the city, reconfiguring the urban economy.

Generative Sensing: From Epistemology to Ontology

There are multiple definitions of sensors, each driven by the specific sector of its application. In generic terms, sensors are devices that detect changes in a physical environment and relay this information to another domain. They convert a physical parameter into an electronic signature that can circulate across specific domains for processing. In common with other digital technologies shaping the city, sensing technologies have their antecedents in military and industrial contexts. In the military, from the mid-twentieth century onward, sensor technologies played an important role in the solidification of a command-and-control logic, providing valuable ways of knowing the enemy from afar and enabling the exercise of power at a distance.[1] Acoustic and seismic sensors were used in the Vietnam War as a way of alerting command to the presence or approach of the enemy (Deitchman 2008; Dickson 2012; Edwards 1996; Gregory 2013).[2] Used in tandem with newly emerging computer technology, they enabled centralized and remotely controlled operations that were justified on "rational" and statistical grounds. They helped to generate a technological optimism about the war effort, despite the gloomy assessment of those on the ground. In the politics and culture of the American Cold War, sensors were pivotal to the computational making of an inward and self-referential "closed world": technological packages and practices that Paul Edwards identified as facilitating a "metaphorical understanding of . . . politics as a sort of system subject to technological management" (1996, 7).

Within industrial contexts, the application of advanced sensing technologies has played a critical role in manufacturing, production workflows, and supply chains (National Research Council 1995). In complex, integrated, and automated production systems, sensors are a core tracking and monitoring element, mobilized as a means of maximizing value extraction within material flows. Sensors in advanced industrial applications frequently cover the entire physical spectrum of environmental parameters, including light, radiation, pressure, level, acceleration, and flows of materials. By effectively controlling key processes, they have a decisive influence on quality and safety. As the business world sought to integrate supply chains through a logic of logistical control—linking suppliers and factories to warehouses, distribution networks, and finally customers via last-mile operations—sensing technologies played a critical role in improving efficiency and enabling the logistical flow. Intense use of sensor technologies is now moving outside of the boundaries of manufacturing plants and business parks and into the urban domain. The critical question, then, is in which ways and with what implications a logic of sensing that historically has been primarily focused on tracking, security, and operational efficiency transmutes into wider urban contexts.

Remaking the City

Over the past decade, digital sensors have had a profound impact on the ways in which we come to know and understand the city. The IT sector argues that urban sensors are a critical innovation that can contribute toward enhancing quality of life, increasing efficiency, achieving sustainability, and making cities more responsive (Cisco/Guardian Labs, n.d.). Their widespread deployment, both in actual practice and as part of an imagined techno-utopian future world, stems from three technological shifts that are unrelated to urban planning: the ubiquity of telecommunications; an increase in computing capabilities, enabling the rapid processing of large datasets; and a decrease in the size and increase in the efficiency of battery technology. These technological advancements have not only facilitated the close tracking and monitoring of a range of urban processes; in encountering the urban, they have taken a generative character, remaking the city while hinting at a redefinition of the idea of networked urbanism.

Researchers have produced a stunning proliferation of academic and conference papers on the subject of urban sensors. Within engineering, telecommunications, and computer science, a raft of information frameworks for sensors and sensing platforms promise a new type of city or, as one of these models puts it, "the realization of smart cities through the Internet of Things" (Jin et al. 2014, 112; for a selected but well-cited sample, see Bonomi et al. 2012; Dastjerdi and Buyya 2016; Hernández-Muñoz et al. 2011; Khan et al. 2012; Li, Xu, and Zhao 2015; Petrolo, Loscrì, and Mitton 2017). This prolific literature is full of informational architectures, roadmap specifications, and technical guidelines for networked connectivity. In line with the material discussed in chapter 2, this literature views cities as scaled-up buildings or factories, operating via communication protocols, service interfaces, coding languages, cloud infrastructures, fog computing, modes of system interoperability, and distributed databases (Gaur et al. 2015; Gubbi et al. 2013; Filipponi et al. 2010; Vlacheas et al. 2013). Placing their faith in technological utopianism, such writers share an understanding of the urban Internet of Things as "a communication infrastructure that provides unified, simple, and economical access to a plethora of public services, thus unleashing potential synergies and increasing transparency to the citizens" (Zanella et al. 2014, 22). Introducing sensors within the now-common computing services language of infrastructure as a service (IaaS), software as a service (SaaS), and platform as a service (PaaS; see figure 2.3), these frameworks propose a sensing and actuation as a service (SAaaS) paradigm—where sensing underpins an emerging service model for the city (Longo et al. 2017; Mitton et al. 2012; Perera et al. 2014).

Scholars within critical urban studies and allied disciplines have questioned these technologically driven views, offering an alternative reading of the transformations associated with the "sentient city." Here, sensors underpin an emerging ambient intelligence that does not simply operate in the background, but rather plays an active role in organizing people's lives. They have created an urban condition "where the environment reflexively monitors our behaviour" (Crang and Graham 2007, 789). Writing over a decade ago, Crang and Graham outline three potential different scenarios in which this sentient city may emerge: first, a fully marketized city, with memory and anticipation, where sensors use radio-frequency identification (RFID) technology to track the microcirculation of people and things, constantly reshaping the spaces of the city in ways that target our individual consumption preferences; second, a city driven by the imperatives of securitization, where sensing and surveillance systems (RFID tags, algorithmic video cameras, data mining, and biometrics) reconstitute the city and its infrastructural grids into a digital battleground for the war on terror; and finally, a city where social actors use the potential of augmented spaces for art and activism, and where sensors enable alternative forms of public action.

At the scale of the street, sensors promise a form of ubiquitous computing, in which information processing is able to penetrate almost all domains of everyday life, creating an "everyware." Far from being neutral, this is "an extension of power into public space . . . determining who can be there and what services are available to each one of them" (Greenfield 2006, 65). Sensors have also been instrumental in putting in place a form of metropolitan dashboard governance, where a widespread perception of urban processes coupled with the performance of control come together in redirecting the future of the city (Mattern 2015). Speculating on what happens when digital sensors become one with materials, Nigel Thrift (2014) has spoken of a city where data becomes embedded in surfaces, from walls and windows to cars and trees; where our notion of causality and our sense of place are altered by a newfound ability to perceive urban processes simultaneously near and far, unfolding in front of our eyes in real time. This "sensory skin" of the city has become a new way in which we "make sense" of the urban; a metered and calculative rationality that embodies the multiple limitations of previous incarnations of modernist urban planning, particularly a utopian belief in technology and a self-proclaimed rationality as the solution for all urban ailments (Rabari and Storper 2014).

Urban sensors put in place a form of infrastructure-as-measurement that makes the city into enumerated variables and datasets to be managed in real time, to be anticipated through prediction and modeling, and to be correlated across separate infrastructural domains (Gabrys 2016). Considering that "that which is enumerated is also capable of becoming *automated*," urban sensors also point to emerging forms of urban regulation (Gabrys 2016; original emphasis). Jennifer Gabrys's work on programming environments (2014, 2016) provides a detailed critical analysis of urban sensing and its generative implications. Drawing on a Foucauldian governmentality framework, she uncovers how environmental sensing technologies put in place new modes of governing, with implications for both urban politics and forms of subjectification. The resulting environmentality, "the distribution of governance within and through environments and environmental technologies" (Gabrys 2014, 30), recasts who counts as a citizen. Members of the public themselves turn into environmental sensing nodes, articulating their citizenship through their engagement with data and monitoring practices. In this biopolitical formation, power operates not so much through disciplining subjects or governing populations, but by establishing environmental conditions. Drawing on Deleuze's concept of the *dividual* (the fragmented and divided self who emerges from a data-driven logic), Gabrys argues that sensors create *ambividuals*, distributed "ambient and malleable urban [sensor] operators that are expressions of computer environments" (Gabrys 2014, 43; see also Monahan and Mokos 2013).

For Gabrys, digital sensors mark the "becoming environmental of computation," where environments are not simply the background for sensing technologies but are produced *with* and *through* sensors. Based on the premise that environments and technologies are co-constitutive, Gabrys's detailed account illustrates how digital sensors and the data they collect do not simply describe preexisting conditions but make up new environments altogether. The sensor does not objectively detect external phenomena, but rather constructs a collective subject that enables "interpretive acts of sensation . . . articulating environmental change and matters of concern" (2016, 32). Sensing here is not only about collecting data, but about redistributing locations, agencies, and processes of sensing, creating an animate environment. These arguments lead to three key questions: What is the nature of the city that is being co-constructed through sensors? What types of infrastructural environments are being created as the city is sensed? What does the resulting urban embodiment of information look like, and what are the implications of such an ontological formation?

To answer these questions, we critically examine the role that sensors play in enabling the capacity of the Urban OS to dis- and re-assemble urban circulations through processes of datafication. As urban processes are distilled into immaterial data packages (chapters 2 and 3)—or, in other words, sensed, known, and captured in a computational format—the city and its parts are selectively rebundled into new configurations, systems, and functions. Data, as the source material for such recombination, operates as a common currency that enables the coming together of several urban flows or processes into new urban configurations. Transport flows sensed through GPS-enabled buses, for example, are reconstituted with spatiotemporal capabilities, resulting in new real-time temporalities (and "accuracies") in the city. Energy flows sensed through smart meters become embedded with information on consumption times and needs, enabling resource environments that are responsive to shortage or abundance and unlocking new forms of peak load management. Pedestrian flows along commercial streets, sensed through the signals emanating from mobile phone devices, are embedded with details about people's country of origin, allowing the system to distinguish between tourists and locals and through this activate modulated, fragmented, and targeted marketing environments. Resonating with Gabrys's line of argumentation, what is at stake is not only a new epistemology of the urban, or a way of knowing the city. Rather, this is about an ontogenesis of infrastructural operations: a way of conceptualizing the operationalization of urban infrastructural flows as productive and relational, not only through the flow's obvious capacity to connect the spaces and bodies it encounters, but also newly made up *of* and *through* relations— thus giving birth to a new nature of place and flow. Drawing on the notion of intelligence incarnate introduced in chapter 3, we argue that through the act of digitally sensing, information gives urban flows new functions, meanings, and corporealities.

Making the City Actionable

The experience of Barcelona illustrates broad shifts in urbanism resulting from an engagement with sensor technologies. Barcelona's Smart City initiative, a flagship program of Mayor Xavier Trias (2011–2015), fostered a

Figure 4.1
Municipal Wi-Fi provision and experimental environmental sensors mounted in a
lamp post opposite the *Mercat del Born*, Barcelona. *Source:* Andrés Luque-Ayala and
Simon Marvin.

range of public-private partnerships advancing digital innovation. Both
the municipal government and private sector partners have experimented
with sensing technologies and their incorporation in a variety of networked
infrastructures (figures 4.1–4.3)—illustrating how urban ecologies can be
selectively and carefully incorporated into digital monitoring and control
capabilities. Not all digital-sensing initiatives in the city are linked to the
official Smart City project, but sensing has emerged as an important and
distinctive dimension of Barcelona's version of computational urbanism.

Sensing technologies have significant implications for urban governance, and sensor makers in Barcelona are well aware of this. As one of
them points out, "The moment in which an extensive space, such as a
city, which has a number of square kilometers, [is made] into a system that
is not disconnected . . . it transforms governance." As in many other cities, the most common driver behind the use of urban sensors in Barcelona is the search for efficiency and optimization in service provision. This
desire to achieve financial savings gives sensors a privileged place within

Figures 4.2 and 4.3
Parking sensors developed by a Barcelona start-up and tested in the city center.
Source: Andrés Luque-Ayala and Simon Marvin.

emerging forms of austerity urbanism (cf. Peck 2012; Pollio 2016). Sensor makers in Barcelona argue that by measuring urban processes, sensors will unlock unlimited potential for operational improvement and bring cities into the twenty-first century—since without sensors, a city is "like a factory [where] processes are being managed as it was done in the 1900s." This is a straightforward principle, discussed by another sensor maker with reference to the linkages between processes of optimization and budgetary savings: "If I can have information about all those systems, in principle, I would be able to manage them better. And if you can manage them better, that has economic implications. . . . The first step is the use of technology for efficiency in the city."

There is some evidence to support these claims. A pilot project in nine of Barcelona's parks paired sensors for humidity and environmental conditions with the remote control of irrigation. An investment of €23,000 saved 25 percent in water consumption, an annual estimated saving of €425,000 (Ajuntament de Barcelona 2015). Waste management sensors developed by Urbiotica, a Barcelona-based company focusing on wireless sensor networks and their applications for cities, have been piloted in the city to measure waste levels in trash containers.[3] These connect every twenty minutes via the cellular network to a centralized management platform, where an algorithm determines whether the container needs emptying. Combining near-real-time data with historical information, sensors and algorithms work together to make predictions that can be used to optimize collection schedules and routes (Urbiotica, n.d.). Technology commentators claim that waste management sensors could save Barcelona up to US$4 billion over the course of ten years (Miller 2014), as well as provide additional benefits associated with reductions in labor use, traffic congestion, pollution, and noise.

City OS and Sentilo: Aligning the Logic of Sensing with the Urban Context

Two interrelated initiatives seeking to generate impact at a citywide scale stand out, both of them developed through the leadership of Barcelona's Municipal Institute of Informatics (IMI). They are Barcelona's own Urban OS, known as City OS (figure 4.4), and Sentilo (http://sentilo.bcn.cat/; figure 4.5), the city's sensor and actuator platform. City OS[4] is a comprehensive information system for the city, in which sensors connected to a sensor

**Ajuntament
de Barcelona**

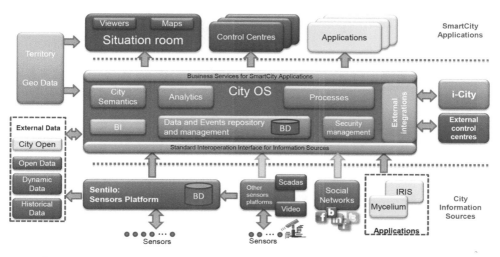

Figure 4.4
The Barcelona City OS, with the Sentilo platform at the bottom-left corner. *Source:*
IMI-Barcelona City Council.

platform (Sentilo) operate as a way of understanding the pulse of the city
and acting on it. It is described by the municipality as an open system
integrating "all the current municipal information systems—local population register, taxes, permits—with the new public management systems—
mobility, energy, resilience, noise—and also with the systems of private
service operators and suppliers—water, energy—and all the public players—
social, cultural, education. . . . City OS will be integrating the most technical systems that Barcelona has developed over the last few years" (City OS/
Ajuntament de Barcelona, n.d.). For the team of engineers behind City OS,
a city is a complex system; such information system should be aimed at
generating a model of reality that reduces and simplifies the city to data and
processes. In their view, the design of the database, a foundational aspect of
the system (see chapter 3), starts from the material reality of the city. The
latter is seen as a collection of entities and people; described as "something"
that has citizens, territories, and processes, this approach resonates strongly

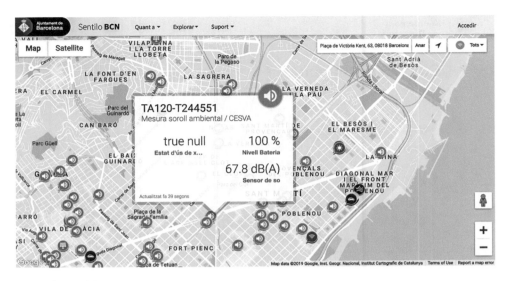

Figure 4.5
Screen capture of the Sentilo Platform as of November 2019. *Source:* http://sentilo
.bcn.cat/.

with particular coding languages such as object-oriented programming (see chapter 2). In view of these engineers, City OS extracts a model of the city's material reality and makes it into a "virtual" model made of data, aiming for a model of the city as a whole and not as individual pieces with limited relation. The objective is for the City OS to become a detailed classification of the city, fed via inputs in the form of data collected through sensors, public utility operations, or other sources. The ultimate aim is the establishment of an information system that connects to a physical reality and through this supports the work of urban managers and other practitioners: "That is our work as computer engineers: we do this model, implement it, and then others, those responsible for providing services, operate it."

An important component of Barcelona's City OS is an open-source sensor and actuator platform called Sentilo. Based on the principles of openness and interoperability (Ajuntament de Barcelona, n.d.), Sentilo agglomerates the data generated by a variety of municipally and privately owned sensors.[5] Through it, the ecologies of Barcelona (air quality, CO_2 emissions, noise, precipitation, temperature, humidity, and wastes, among others) become subject to microspatial monitoring and re-assembly into specialist ecosystems. Launched in 2014, by 2017 Sentilo had been linked to over seventeen thousand sensors and had processed over 1.5 billion data items. It provides a centralized and homogeneous way of managing and distributing the data generated by sensors and other software/hardware devices distributed across space. Sentilo is aimed "at anyone from the IT world interested in contributing to the expansion of the 'Internet of Things'" (Sentilo, n.d.). It operates via a system of subscription and publication: instead of responding to individual data requests, those interested in a particular dataset subscribe to it and the platform automatically delivers the data when it is available. Sentilo gathers and distributes information on three types of processes: measurements (including data on temperature, humidity, flow, occupation), alarms (alerts for conditions of disruption or outliers), and actuators (signals to prompt the initiation of a control mechanism). The latter results in an ability to send orders via the platform, enabling a two-way communication between urban processes on the ground and the city's administrators.

Implementing Sentilo required a realignment between the logic of sensing and the specificity of the urban context. Within IT circles, data at the city level is commonly seen as highly dispersed across space and therefore low density. This played a key role in defining the shape and form of urban sensing in Barcelona. Instead of operating through a small number of sensors providing large quantities of information, sensing in the urban context was imagined around a large quantity of highly dispersed sensors providing limited and specific types of information. In the early days of Sentilo, popular supervisory control and data acquisition (SCADA) systems were rejected as the technology of choice on the grounds that they were too expensive due to their high-precision and intense energy requirements, characteristics associated with their high speeds and low latency (the time interval between physical change and information relay).[6] During the development of Sentilo, engineers found that low latency was not a key requirement in urban environments; instead, depending on the specific function they served, sensors might only be required to relay information once per hour (a good example being sensors within waste collection bins, one of Barcelona's exemplary uses). The classic protocols of the internet (e.g., HTTP, IP, API, and RESTful) appeared to offer an appropriate technology for the city's network architecture, given their simplicity and widespread usage. Internet protocols operate with popular programming languages such as Java, making the required knowledge easily available. Network architecture and the need to scale a sensor system to an entire city also played a key role. Whereas SCADA systems are commonly based on architectures in which all sensors talk to a single point, wireless sensor network (WSN) technologies offer a more decentralized information architecture in which sensors communicate in network mode. This appeared well suited to the distributed and low-density nature of urban information. Considering the maintenance regimes of urban infrastructures, engineers also envisioned a system that would make low energy demands on the battery of sensors, significantly extending each sensor's useful life to a number of years before replacement would be required.

Reproducing common narratives of objectivity and impartiality within digital urban technologies (see chapters 2 and 3), the makers of Sentilo told us that sensors add neutrality to urban operations, as they simplify the display and use of preexisting urban information. Their interpretation of neutrality is specifically linked to notions of transferability, openness, and interoperability. Sentilo's principle of operation is that the data generated by a particular municipal department does not belong to the department itself (e.g., the transport agency or the waste management agency) but to the city as a whole, so it is transferable between different systems. This means that sensors are a transversal and common element across different municipal agencies and, in some cases, between agencies and members of the public. The view is that they allow for the data generated to be used in a holistic and horizontal way to produce a variety of urban insights. The makers of the platform claim that this allows the development of urban solutions that, beyond vertical chains (i.e., bounded by the specific remit of a single municipal agency), function in horizontal ways (i.e., across different agencies and services). Sentilo also separates the software of control (located in the platform) from the internet-enabled objects that collect data (such as the city's sensors or the urban infrastructures associated with them, such as light posts). This enables the phased incorporation of new sensor objects over an extended period of time (e.g., over the course of various city administrations or procurement cycles) without having to transform the platform itself.[7] Critically, it establishes a formal separation between the management of urban processes and the ownership of urban assets. Digitally enabled urban assets or infrastructures, such as light posts or irrigation points, do not necessarily need to be owned or directly managed by the agency responsible for lighting or irrigation. This fragmentation between ownership and operation has implications for underlying modes of service delivery, materially underpinning the possibility of public-public, public-private, and private-private associations or partnerships.

CITI-SENSE and the Smart Citizen Kit: From Activism to the Political Economy of Data

Beyond the world of city management, activists argue that urban sensors are a powerful force for the democratization of society. In Barcelona, several initiatives have mobilized sensing devices toward citizen involvement, participation, and, at times, political activism. At Barcelona's Institute for Global Health (ISGlobal), for example, the CITI-SENSE project developed and tested air pollution sensors that are small enough for citizens to carry with them, opening the possibility for citizens to operate as mobile and real-time measuring stations that could, in theory, complement the official city measuring stations. This citizen science initiative aimed to establish citizen observatories and develop community-based environmental monitoring systems that "empower citizens to contribute to and participate in environmental governance, to enable them to support and influence community and societal priorities and associated decision making" (CITI-SENSE, n.d.; see http://barcelona.citi-sense.eu/). Another popular example of the mobilization of digital sensors in the context of claims that generate or expand citizenship is the Smart Citizen Kit (https://smartcitizen.me/), which emphasizes the possibility of political activism and advocacy through citizen-owned digital sensors (figure 4.6). Developed at the Barcelona FabLab and marketed to individuals and organizations around the globe, this is a microsensor aimed at providing personalized (dwelling and neighborhood scale) readings for air quality, humidity, temperature, light, and noise. The sensor communicates via Wi-Fi with a web-based platform that agglomerates hundreds of readings through open data, geolocation, and crowdsourcing technologies, with the aim of providing a form of collective (nonstate and noninstitutional) citizen-sensing capability (figure 4.7).

For projects like the Smart Citizen Kit, citizen *sensorship* stands in direct opposition to citizen *censorship*. In their marketing for the project, the kit's manufacturers emphasize the central role of sensing in a political drive toward transparency and citizen involvement, and in opposition to the suppression of information flows. The kit, described to us by the project's founder as "a way of making visible the invisible," aims to make the public

Figure 4.6
Various prototypes of the Smart Citizen Kit. *Source:* Andrés Luque-Ayala and Simon Marvin.

more aware of environmental conditions in the city. Advertised as an "open source technology for citizens' political participation in smarter cities" (Smart Citizen, n.d.), the Smart Citizen Kit also embraces the openness and transparency logics characteristic of the IT world (see chapter 3). It was initially funded through crowdfunding campaigns, via Kickstarter and the Spain-based Goteo, and it uses Arduino-compatible hardware (open-source microprocessing boards that can be manufactured and distributed by anyone) alongside a range of environmental sensors. The system's design files are also open source and have been developed collaboratively through the GitHub platform (a web-based repository popular among coders and developers, commonly used to host and develop open-source software projects). For the developers of the project, citizen sensorship is a way of empowering citizens through technology. It means "that the citizen has the tools to capture . . . data about the city; or they can aggregate the data to a larger database and contribute to understanding various phenomenon in the city that are invisible to our eyes, or where the citizen can monitor a specific issue [that is affecting him/her directly]. . . . What is important is to increase options for citizen participation via technology."

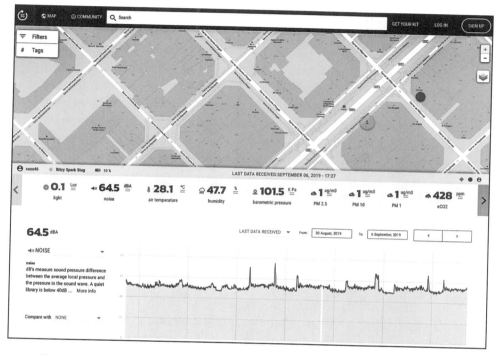

Figure 4.7

Screen capture of the Smart Citizen Kit platform, showcasing one single sensor's reading parameters (from left to right: light, noise, temperature, humidity, barometric pressure, and pollution [PM 2.5, PM 10, PM 1, and eCO2]), and a chart for a week-long noise reading. *Source:* https://smartcitizen.me/.

Within activists' circles, the citizen sensor is not relevant solely (or even primarily) as a sensing device. Its value comes from underpinning a citizen movement that raises questions about the quality of the city's environment and the effectiveness and legitimacy of institutional environmental monitoring regimes. Developers and users are acutely aware of the multiple limitations of these small-scale and do-it-yourself (DIY) sensing systems, many of which result from the experimental and precarious quality of components, the limited current state of technological development, and issues of sensor calibration, all of which lead to inexact and unreliable readings. But, in the activists' view, what matters is not the accuracy of the reading but the wider debate generated around the very act of reading. With well-known critics of digital urban systems praising the Smart Citizen Kit and similar technologies for their ability to involve the public in an emerging data-based urban science (Townsend 2015), and scientific journals such as *Nature* reporting on the citizen sensing movement as an inexpensive measure to fill future gaps opened by cuts in science funding (Austen 2015), the citizen sensor seems to be here to stay. Along with 3-D printers and spatial/social media, the sensor is an exemplary member of a wider family of technologies that make up the *DIY citizen*, a term used within digital fabrication movements to capture the political agency of a public that involves itself in designing and making the world (Ratto and Boler 2014; see also Smith 2015; Smith et al. 2016). Here, while the sensor serves to enact a notion of citizenship, citizenship itself displaces the sensor as the object of the design process (Lanzeni 2016).

However, a recognition of the broader political value of sensors must also consider their political economy. Citizen sensing mobilizes not only a politics of the environment, but also a politics of data—one that operates through raising awareness of the political economy of data production. Citizen sensing thus points to the tensions at play in a world where citizens are continuously producing data, yet have little ability to own or control this highly lucrative form of production. Responding to this, one of the developers of the Smart Citizen Kit expressed to us the view that citizens are already an urban infrastructure of data production, and the kit simply redirects agency and relocates the means of production and action within the hands of citizens. The Smart Citizen Kit, then,

> helps to generate awareness of the idea that we can be data producers; and that we are already . . . through sensors, we can generate data that belongs to us . . . The "citizen as producer" underpins this idea. Right now we are slaves of data. . . . We have ceded certain rights to corporations for such data to be used, and that data is generating value . . . but we don't see anything of such value. . . . Given the computers in our pockets, right now we are infrastructure. Our search patterns and movements are known and are being used. The objective is to embrace this idea of being infrastructure, but in a conscious manner.

This leads us to a simple yet powerful insight: the mobilization of sensors in the city, often justified as a means to achieve efficiency, to open new modes of urban action via actuators, or to reimagine citizenship, rests on assumptions around the collection of data as a form of value creation that enables further infrastructural interventions. With the public recast as a data producer and embroiled within larger infrastructural systems, both data and sensing quickly emerge not only as objects of political value, but as ways of generating monetary value. Sensing infrastructures are not simply about feeding broader data-based systems that, in governmental ways, command the city through digital ways of knowing (e.g. via supporting real-time rearrangements of traffic flows through crowdsourced navigation apps such as Waze). They are about new subject formations and infrastructural conceptualizations and, through this, about an emerging urban ontology through the Urban OS. Sensing infrastructures are about both being part of and becoming data-based systems of production (e.g., by generating data that, through social media or other means, creates and redirects marketing opportunities). In parallel to the infrastructuralization of citizens through the Urban OS (see chapter 7), the multiple nature of sensors juxtaposes the desires of openness and democratization with those of control and monetization. So it is to the wider question of economic value that we must now return in order to analyze the implications of sensors for urban governance and the emerging intersections between the infrastructuralization and monetization of sensing toward the creation of new urban economic circuits.

Digitizing Space as Value Creation: New Circuits of Commodification

Sensors both embody and enable computational urbanism's desire to create new forms of value via digital assets. This rationale exceeds those of operational efficiency, optimization, and political activism and suggests that sensors bring about a change in financial flows and value generation in cities. In this sense, sensors in the urban environment operate as a means of commodification. Our reading of the ways in which sensors transform value chains has been influenced by literature on financialization, the latter broadly understood as a practice of "establishing *the power* to effectively capitalize on future 'earnings'" (Ouma 2015, 227; original emphasis; see also Nitzan and Bichler 2009).[8] As a device for monetizing the urban, sensors and their platforms involve the mundane and the everyday in the creation of new asset streams, "usually through a process of aggregation, which then—and only then—allows speculation to take place" (Leyshon and Thrift 2007, 98). This reading of sensors as urban infrastructures that enable the extraction of value from the urban environment is consonant with a number of other emerging analyses of digital platforms as forms of platform capitalism: the moment when capitalism "turned to data as one way to maintain economic growth and vitality in the face of a sluggish production sector" (Srnicek 2017, 6). It resonates with what Fields (2019) has termed, in the context of digital platforms in the city's rental market, *digital value grabbing*. The digital sensor platform, as a form of intermediation that creates a business model through its ability to link, is a device aimed at capturing value within a process of capitalization—"valori[zing] potential for monopoly rents, [and prioritizing] up-scaling and the direct and/or indirect extraction rent from circulations and accompanying data trails" (Langley and Leyshon 2017, 25).[9] Our analysis of sensors and sensing platforms in cities suggests that digital platforms do not only structure "'market encounters' in digital space" and "co-create value" with/between users (Langley and Leyshon 2017, 13, 17; see also van Dijck 2013). They also play a more ontogenetic role, by creating the possibility of the marketplace itself through engendering the raw material and bodies for circulation, exchange, and accumulation, and by fostering an environment where exchange and circulation can freely take place.

Critically, sensor networks and their platforms aggregate new asset streams in the city. Their ability to generate value relies on their capacity to reaggregate (rebundle) hyperfragmented streams and data points. They stand as the critical electronic dispositifs that enable an economy to be constructed through the existing ecological flows of the city. Sensing platforms enable datafication, encouraging the dis-assembly of urban flows and their re-assembly into potential assets. As an engineer working for a sensor design company describes, once "the citizen becomes a source of information," this information "is dispersed all over the city." In concentrating these dispersed and relatively infrequent data streams (at least when compared with the factory, office, or battlefield), urban sensor platforms overcome any problems potentially arising from the dispersed and mobile nature of urban habitation (and therefore, of urban information). They generate forms of value derived from the flow of data and its recalculation on top of the traditional value of the circulation itself (e.g., the circulation of energy or water). This is explained by the founder of a Barcelona-based sensor company that specializes in connected operational intelligence. Using sensors to detect pedestrian flows (monitored through mobile phones), the company found that tourists visiting certain popular areas walk slowly in one direction, spending more time looking at shops, and faster on the way back, as they have seen the shops already. Based on this information, he argues that advertisements should be more expensive in the first direction of pedestrian flow, since people are likely to spend more time looking at them. In his view, the real value of sensors lies in the possibility of monetizing the data that they generate in the context of infrastructural and urban flows: "That is the key. . . . We can monetize secondary value. We are creating an economy on top of infrastructure. And what we saw was that sensors were the enabler for data capture towards the creation of such economy."

We heard a similar view from one of the directors of Barcelona's Smart City initiative, for whom the Sentilo platform underpins the possibility of both the city as a marketplace and a marketplace for cities: "We arrive [at] the idea that Sentilo was not a platform for Barcelona but a platform for cities . . . a framework that aligned the different datas with the different applications. All this data in one platform let us build something like a marketplace of cities. . . . If we put all this data in the concept of an operating system, with an iOS or Android for cities, everybody, all companies, can deploy a good solution not only for Barcelona, but for London, for Manchester . . ."

This is not about technourban transformation, but about a change in financial flows and value generation in cities. The digitization of Barcelona's flows and infrastructures, conducted through sensing, allows the development of new urban services by third parties (neither the citizens who generate the data nor the municipality that owns the platform). The resulting Urban OS, like Apple's iOS or Google's Android, is designed for private sector players to develop digital applications that, running on the city's data, make the city into a marketplace (see also chapter 5). This urban marketplace is simultaneously local and global: apps serve local needs but are transferable across urban contexts; algorithms operate in a local context yet generate market insights of global value; and an urban computational architecture (or, in the words of many practitioners, a *smart city architecture*) can easily be lifted from one city to another. In the view of the director of another sensing company in Barcelona, "value chains are currently being defined in this space." Within the emerging ecosystem, and underpinned by the sensing capabilities of the Urban OS, ICT providers, utility companies, technology developers, and urban strategists are rapidly advancing strategic market positions while experimenting with new data-driven business models.

Urban sensing, then, can be viewed as an emerging infrastructure that generates information points through and across other infrastructural processes. It provides an additional layer of spatialized digital assets that reflect and reconstitute more traditional urban infrastructures, creating geolocated points of data that circulate through a digital platform and can be recombined as marketable services or insights.[10] To an extent, this is the intensification of preexisting (and now familiar) trends around the monetization of public flows via IT-enabled strategies for measuring and monitoring. Referring to this as the *pay-per society,* as far back as 1989, Vincent Mosco spoke of the ways in which ICT technologies were enabling the micromeasurement of electronic space to achieve an increase in profit and control (Mosco 1989). Service provision became attached to small-scale time intervals that allowed charges per data unit: pay-per-call telephony, pay-per-view television, and pay-per-bit of information. A more contemporary reading of the role of information in capital accumulation sees data mining as a form of extraction, with a political economy similar to that of mining and agribusiness. Here, "the pervasive penetration of extraction into spheres of human activity" operates through ways of acquiring and generating data, expanding the frontiers of capitalist valorization and further entrenching processes of financialization in our daily lives (Mezzadra and Neilson 2017, 194). What is critical now is the extension of *pay-per* logics from electronic to urban space and infrastructure, opening possibilities for a new infrastructure aimed at generating monetary value through what was previously either collective urban resources or nonexistent flows (in the latter case, pointing to an ontogenetic function within sensing). This is a change in the way in which both urban space and the city's ecological flows configure financial flows—the rise of a new set of calculable practices that engender, monitor, and monetize urban network and space.

Conclusions

Increasingly, sensor technologies are positioned as an urban inevitability; an obligatory passage point for the making of any and every form of contemporary urbanism. Operating as the material interface of computing techniques, sensors combine potential and action, embodiment and disembodiment. They ground the speculative nature of digital urbanism (cf. Leszczynski 2016) in the concrete reality of the city. They make urban infrastructures into a way of thinking the city, while also enabling the city to *think infrastructurally.* In the first instance, this is about ways of

knowing—an epistemology of the urban. Sensors, in measuring, agglom-
erating, and allowing for the recombination of data, reveal patterns and
insights that can be acted upon. As we are told by the founder of an urban
sensing company in Barcelona, "our behavior is very repetitive"; patterns
and insights are revealed "when you use this data of the city, and represent
it and put it together, as in a film." Yet beyond the representational dimension of this digital way of "seeing" the city, what is at stake is the primacy
of measurement and calculation as a way of knowing the urban.

However, sensing infrastructures are not just about a digitally based way
of knowing the city, but about new ways of being: infrastructural ontogenesis and ontology. Such ways of being include the human subjects that are
infrastructuralized through their capacity to sense and transmit data, a new
generation of infrastructures aimed at capturing value through dis- and/or
re-assembly, the formation of corporealities that become present through
different media and the datafied infrastructural flows through which data
is embodied in material substance. Embodying the confluence of urban
flows and data, sensors and their platforms are a function of the formation
of new corporealities. They mark both boundary and point of connection
among the digital, spatial, and material worlds of the city—a message illustrated by a Barcelona-based sensor maker, for whom "the border with the
territory is a small box: the sensor platform." Similarly, in the words of an
environmental activist using personalized sensors to track pollution, sensors "take the physical world to the digital world; they are like scanners,
that translate such invisible information into something visible" Ironically,
in this statement it is precisely the physical aspect of the city that is invisible. It is precisely this position at the boundary between flow and data,
city and digitality, presence and absence, that locates sensors in between
potential and action.

Sensed data, made manifest through techniques of visualization or by its
incorporation into financial spreadsheets, emerges as not simply as a representation but as a being. The sensor takes the material flows of the city and
makes them into bits that both move and recombine; a new configuration
of the flow that in turn enables digital action and, through that, all sorts of
previously unavailable material responses with political-economic implications. Sensors and sensing platforms enable the creation of a new urban
economy based on data flows. They operate through the hyperfragmentation of urban processes, where resources and other flows are quantified and

divided into small, standardized units of time and space, rendered in numbers that record a quantification of flow per second in a gridded coordinate location. The mathematical rebundling of urban experience allows its commodification, creating opportunities for fragmented pricing, marketable insights, or new methods of service delivery. In effect, this constitutes an intensification of trends toward the commodifying urban occupation and processes,[11] yet it changes how space in general, and the city in particular, enter circuits of finance and accumulation. This is powerfully illustrated in the quotation we used to open this chapter, from the founder of an urban sensors start up. This interviewee equates the business of sensing the city with that of real estate, noting the way that urban sensors are purposefully mobilized for "virtualizing value" toward an economy that is underpinned by electronic dispositifs; an infrastructure of "virtualization" toward capital accumulation. The sensor digitizes public space by transforming the material nature of both resource and flow (some would refer to this as virtualizing[12]), resulting in new infrastructural modes and materialities by which third parties can build applications that generate and transform value chains.

While traditional readings of urban sensing foreground narratives of efficiency, optimization, and citizen participation, we have complicated this narrative by illustrating how urban sensing is also about value chains. Urban sensing forces a standardization of ecological flows (a way of knowing), and through this, it bypasses local specificity in our understanding of ecological flows in the city. This standardization of ecological flows is a first step in making the urban into a marketplace. Sensing puts in place new infrastructural circuits, enabling monitoring, measuring, and monetization of both space and ecologies in real time, layering new circuits of exploitation over existing networks and infrastructures. In this reading, urban sensors are an attempt to render every dimension of life as not just actionable but exploitable. At stake is a reconstitution of common ecologies, as it enables the commons to be reconstituted as tradeable commodities. This is a form of commodification in which urban flows are actionable from the perspective of monetization and capital accumulation, resulting in novel ways of capitalizing urban flows. In this way, in the long run, digital sensors have the ability to fundamentally remake the material foundations of value generation in cities, relocating and complementing value from notions of land and labor to a more dynamic geography of flows.

5 Mapping: The Computational Production of Territory

with Flávia Neves Maia

My team is obsessed with understanding everything there is to know about the real world. And we want to bring that insight and understanding of the real world to people around the globe, helping them navigate, explore, and decide with confidence. . . .

We've not only brought maps online all around the world; we've also done things like help people experience corners of the planet that they might otherwise never get to see. . . . To build these sorts of powerful user experiences, we've had to also build out an incredibly rich and complex understanding of the real world. And it turns out that the underlying data that powers these consumer mapping experiences can also fuel some incredibly powerful enterprise use cases, as well.

—Jen Fitzpatrick, Vice President of Google Maps (Fitzpatrick 2016)

This chapter examines the politics of digital mapping, and its role in the Urban OS, by exploring the ways in which it reconfigures circulation, power, and territorial formations. Digitally powered mapping platforms, including Google Maps, Microsoft Bing Maps, MapQuest, and OpenStreetMap have become a ubiquitous computational feature of everyday life. However, while critical mapping scholars have argued for decades that maps are not, and have never been, neutral devices (cf. Harley 1988), the political and social assumptions embedded within the production and operation of digital mapping platforms are often neglected. We argue that digital mapping does not simply represent space. Operating as a calculative practice, digital mapping is productive of the political spatiality that characterizes territory. Drawing on Stuart Elden's notion of territory as a "rendering of 'space' as a political category" (2010, 810), we uncover the conjunction of digital mapping and the geoweb as a political technique that is remaking territory through a computational logic. Digitally mapping the city puts in place new forms of territorial control that are governmental, in that they operate via the freedoms and capacities of the governed, yet also unsettling preexisting forms of spatial sovereignty (cf. Foucault 2009). We render visible the political dimensions embedded within the computational logic of mapping, analyzing how digital mapping is mobilized in informal settlements—areas that, in many cities around the world, have never previously been mapped. The chapter unpacks the spatial politics of computational urbanism and its attempt to depoliticize territory, a particularly pressing issue in the context of the tension between inclusion and exclusion experienced by those who live in informal settlements in cities in the Global South.

The empirical focus of the chapter is on Google Maps and its Rio de Janeiro–specific project *Ta no Mapa*, which translates as "It's on the map." Like elsewhere, Google Maps here functions alongside other Google platforms such as Google Street View and Google My Business, forming a suite of technological tools that are rapidly influencing how populations worldwide interact with and conceptualize space. We examine the use of spatial media technologies for digitally mapping informal settlements, and critically unpack the claim that this is a mechanism for socioeconomic inclusion. We particularly challenge the contention that digital maps incorporate favelas into the rest of the city providing recognition, legitimacy, visibility, and even citizenship to inhabitants.[1]

In the context of Rio de Janeiro's favelas, often wrongly characterized as spaces beyond the sovereignty of the state, digital mapping advances a way of governing the city through an opening to digital and material circulations that enable the incorporation of population into broader economic territories. With both the state and the underworld operating through the power of death—through the police, militias, drug lords, and criminal networks—favelas are an active site of contested sovereignties (cf. Hansen and Stepputat 2006). They are a place where the means through which power operates shift in consonance with political interests, economic configurations, social arrangements, and, more recently, technological configurations of space. The redemptive claims made by those who are digitally mapping favelas indicate points of tension between different agents asserting or enacting forms of sovereignty, a process that nowadays is mediated through an emerging Urban OS. Providing a counterargument to redemptive claims around recognition, inclusion, and citizenship, we discuss how the interface between digital and urban worlds constructs territory (in its political sense) through economic incorporation. This is precisely one of the main ways in which the various computational logics of the urban are advancing specific configurations of the city, a move that reaffirms the growing importance of critically examining the role of digital urban technologies within urban studies.

The chapter is divided into four sections and a set of conclusions. The first section provides a conceptualization of territory as a political technique already always operating through calculative processes. This opens possibilities for an understanding of the making of territory via computational processes. A second section then introduces Google's Ta no Mapa project, describing the process by which digital mapping aims to transform urban circulation. In a third section, we focus on the emphasis placed on economic circulations and the mechanisms by which digital mapping reimagines favelas as spaces of consumption. The fourth section analyses the ongoing transformation of territory and its sovereignty by pointing to the tensions and changes associated with overlapping powers. By looking at the various powers seeking to exercise a form of sovereignty in favelas, from drug lords and the state's police to the new digital powers claiming the capability to suspend the exception of informality, this section examines the implications of taking the favela from a "pacified" to a "calculated" territory. Finally, we critically evaluate the political claim that digitally mapping urban informality acts as a mechanism for social inclusion. Instead, we argue that the use of spatial media for digitally mapping favelas plays an active role in generating the favela itself, by making it into a seemingly depoliticized space of consumption and, through redirecting information flows, incorporating it into global markets (a move consistent with the making of data-as-infrastructure that we examined in chapter 3). Google's intervention complicates existing forms of sovereignty, as the type of calculative tools that in the past made up territory and enabled its control are now mobilized by the corporate sector—rewriting the code that rules territory, reinventing ways of ordering space, and redefining social exclusion as economic exclusion.

The resulting urban geography, produced both materially and discursively *through* and *by* computational logics, reorders everyday life through new modes of knowledge production and the enactment of new forms of spatial regulation and control (cf. Ash, Kitchin, and Leszczynski 2018; Kitchin and Dodge 2011). In favelas, Google Maps establishes a way of governing through an opening to broader global and local circulations, while prioritizing economic over social or political forms of inclusion. The chapter closes by pointing to the role of the urban computational logic of mapping in enabling a shift in territorial powers from the nation-state to the multinational corporation, and the emergence of a form of power that relocates sovereignty with the agents who are fashioning global capital circulations. This points to the broader political-economic framing that underpins the various computational logics of the Urban OS.

We seek to move beyond understandings of informal settlements, or favelas in this specific case, as silenced or excluded from the urban. Rather, informal settlements operate visibly within the urban under a condition of exceptionality: far from being beyond state reach, these areas are produced by a sovereign power (Roy 2005; see also Agamben 2005). We take inspiration from postcolonial theory and urban studies scholar Ananya Roy, for whom informality results from the suspension of law in a given time and space by a sovereign power: the state. Informality is not the chaos that precedes order, but rather the result of such suspension. Here, it is precisely the capacity to impose or suspend a state of exception, as much as the ability to alter a condition of legitimacy or illegitimacy, that indicates a sovereign power at play. However, we adapt Roy's approach to suggest that the mobilization of claims around who has the capacity to determine, enact, or lift informality evidences a space of contestation, where the state is not the only power at play.

The Digital Calculation of Territory

Territory describes "a particular and historically limited set of practices and ideas about the relation between place and power" (Elden 2013a, 7). It implies a combination of spatial and political conditions. Considering territory offers our understanding of computational urbanism a particularly salient political angle, foregrounding the workings of power and the various ways of conducting conducts at play (cf. Foucault 2009). Territory is not a process exclusively associated with state power, but a broader (historical and geographical) category of political organization and political thought (Brenner and Elden 2009). Our work takes inspiration from a reconciliation of networked and territorial logics, which suggests that territory can be an effect of networked relations and a product of sociotechnical practices—a work in progress, identified and claimed (Painter 2010).

Political geographers have already provided insightful analyses of the ways that territory becomes imbricated in, and transformed through, digital technologies. Amoore's (2018) inquiry into territorial sovereignty and the cloud is concerned with the ways in which the digital puts in place new forms of perceiving and analyzing the world. Her understanding of the digital politics of territory moves well beyond an analysis of the bounded space of the sovereign intervention (the latter being a concern with who has the capacity to access or see data located in a particular geography, an approach that attends to territorial jurisdiction rather than territory itself; think of, for example, a problematization of the location of data centers). Rather, Amoore's analysis transcends the politics of geographical location and, building on Elden's (2010) analysis of territory, signals both digital processes and the algorithm as a "novel political space of calculative reasoning" (Amoore 2018, 12)—a move that has implications for how the digital map plays a role in the very making of sovereign territory and, through this, a politics of space.

For Elden, territory is the "rendering of 'space' as a political category: owned, distributed, mapped, calculated, bordered, and controlled" (2010, 810). Territory is "not simply an object" but rather a process, "made and remade, shaped and shaping, active and reactive" (Elden 2013a, 17). Privileging the coming together of legal and technical domains, territory is seen here as a calculative political technique, "a bundle of political technologies . . . [made up of] techniques for measuring land and controlling terrain" (Elden 2013b, 36). These include statistics, censuses, cartography, and (from our perspective) digital mapping. In this sense, territory can also be configured digitally. As Elden points out, drawing on Heidegger, technology here does not simply aim to denote a practical application (e.g., geometry, land surveying, or, for that matter, digital coding and geotagging), but rather a way of conceiving the world—or what, in our terminology, we refer to as a *computational logic of the urban*.

Territory, therefore, is both the effect of particular calculative practices and itself a calculative technique that finds a practical expression in cartographic forms—bridging computational (i.e., digital and algorithmic) and spatial (i.e., cartographic) calculations (see also chapter 6). Calculation, both numeric and spatial in orientation, emerges here as a territorial strategy involved in the production of space (Crampton 2011). Citing Hannah (2001), but also referencing Dodge, Kitchin, and Zook's (2009) work on space and digital technologies, Crampton suggests that three knowledges are required for the calculative making of territory: "sociodemographic census data; geodemographic; and fleeting, transactional records (what Dodge, Kitchin, and Zook 2009 called 'software-sorted space')" (Crampton 2011, 95). Through calculation, spatial politics and mathematical thought come together, joining quantitative and qualitative dimensions of the city while mobilizing a rationality "through which space is made 'amenable to thought' (Osborne and Rose 2004: 212)" (Crampton and Elden 2006, 681–682; see also chapter 2, with reference to the work of Osborne and Rose [1999] on the making of the city as a space of government and authority). The cartographic assessment of territory rests on the use of numbers, counting, and arithmetic procedures, pointing to the map not as a matter of knowledge, meaning, or representation but of calculation. It follows that the relevance of mapping for the making of territory does not lie in its ability to provide visual representations, but rather in the coming together of space and the database (Crampton 2011). In the context of Google Maps, what matters is not so much the visual image of the map on a computer screen, but the databases and calculative possibilities behind such visual representation.

Mapping Favelas: Recalculating the Point of Interest

Practitioners and academics have carried out extensive work on participatory mapping in informal settlements. This research often presents the involvement of residents in mapping sites of urban informality as a means of achieving a range of socially progressive goals. Advocates argue that participatory mapping, along with other forms of data collection that involve the community (e.g., local censuses, data collection on living conditions, photographic records), can be used as a tool for political advocacy and a mechanism to achieve greater inclusion (Livengood and Kunte 2012; McFarlane and Söderström 2017; Patel, Baptist, and d'Cruz 2012).[2] However, we identify a contrasting trend—namely, the enrolment of community-based agents and agencies in mapping projects led by ICT corporations (e.g., Google and Microsoft). This trend substantiates arguments around the corporatization of the urban via digital technologies (Söderström, Paasche, and Klauser 2014; Vanolo 2014), specifically through enabling the expansion of the frontiers of capital accumulation through the digital reconfiguration of space.

As digital urbanism encounters the Global South, spatial media technologies have been linked to participative mapping methodologies "to count, map, survey, and document life in informal settlements" (McFarlane and Söderström 2017, 318). These projects often start from the assumption that a lack of access to spatial information leaves residents "disempowered and unable to use information to solve problems" (Hagen 2011, 70). In Nairobi's well-documented Map Kibera, for example, mapping Nairobi's largest slum using digital technology is described as a form of *community information empowerment* (figure 5.1), a "resource that would harness [the community's] collective wisdom and intimate knowledge of Kibera, so [residents] could become the drivers of development" (Hagen 2011, 76). In the neighboring informal settlement of Muhimu, residents and foreign volunteers expect digital mapping to offer transparency and visibility as a step toward political recognition (Poggiali 2016). The resulting products are seen to offer "a unique opportunity to significantly improve the lives of the poor through an exploration of the best ways to link open information and deliberative development" (Donovan 2012, 103). Advocates of digital mapping in informal settlements see an increase in access to information as a powerful

Figure 5.1
Community mapping in Kibera, Nairobi. Photo courtesy of Map Kibera/Erica Hagen.

tool to advance claims to territorial recognition and service provision, supporting development efforts and contributing to a politics of emancipation.

In our view, urban informality is experienced, actualized, and reconstituted (spatially and politically) through its engagement with digital technologies. As digital geography scholars argue, nowadays, in an unprecedented manner, "coming-into-contact with spatial media is generative of spatiality" (Leszczynski 2015b, 746). Beyond traditional paper or GIS mapping, the use of spatial media and the geoweb combines "pervasiveness" and "ordinariness" in the spatial practices of everyday life. Resonating with Crampton's arguments around the nonrepresentational nature of the map, Leszczynski (2015) sees the enrollment of spatial media technologies in "voluntary" mapping as particularly significant given the change in emphasis from spatial representation to a purposeful attempt to share information in and about the everyday. These arguments build on previous research on volunteered geographic information (spatial content that is generated by users and voluntarily disseminated on the internet, also referred to as *VGI*), which has identified the value of an understanding of quotidian space, pointing to "what it can tell about local activities in various geographic locations that go unnoticed by the world's media, and about life at a local level" (Goodchild 2007, 220). For us, the academic literature on VGI provides valuable clues for advancing a more nuanced reading of the use of digital technologies and spatial media for mapping informal settlements. In considering VGI as a social practice, Elwood, Goodchild, and Sui (2012) asks questions that are of relevance for our examination of the political implications of digital mapping in favelas: What knowledges are included or excluded from VGI practices, how socially and politically significant are these knowledges, and how is VGI transforming practices of representation and the very epistemological politics of geographic information?

Ta no Mapa is one of a dozen projects that have emerged in Rio de Janeiro over the last ten years to map favelas. Involving residents in a variety of ways, often but not always through spatial media, these initiatives frame the act of mapping as a "first step" toward exercising "the right to the city [through] visibility and recognition" (Redes de Desenvolvimento da Maré 2012, 8). Mobilizing a common imaginary around the historic invisibility of favelas, mapping is seen as a form of territorial recognition: "the recognition of a place inhabited by people and their lives" (Redes de Desenvolvimento da Maré 2012, 13). Mapping favelas is also described as an opportunity for spatial resignification and legitimacy, and even a chance for residents to rediscover a "lost identity" (Brasil 247, 2014). Often presented as a tool for the incorporation of the (arguably disconnected) favela to the rest of the city ("to integrate Rio as a unified city," as one source puts it; Instituto Pereira Passos 2014), maps are seen as a means to showcase the positive side of favelas, through empowering residents as the main actors in the process of producing cartographic information.

Technology companies, particularly Microsoft and Google, have played an important role in driving such processes, reproducing narratives that position the digital map as a tool of urban integration and social inclusion. Microsoft's *Na Área* ("on the area"), developed in collaboration with the municipality of Rio de Janeiro, is described as "another step . . . to help integrate [these communities] to the rest of the city" (Microsoft 2014). Google's Ta no Mapa claims that locating favelas on Google Maps will provide visibility while helping to overcome systematic exclusion. For Ta no Mapa, the absence of publicly available digital data on favelas is a source of "huge social and economic loss." By consequence, it is claimed, the generation of georeferenced data about the favela could help reverse this situation (Google/AfroReggae 2014).

Ta no Mapa is originally an initiative by AfroReggae, a Rio-based arts and culture nonprofit organization with over twenty years of community-based experience in favelas. In 2014 the project starts to be developed via a partnership with Google, and advertised as an effort to "turn these data free areas into data full zones . . . the most complete economical and behavioural data ever gathered on favelas has created a virtuous circle where everybody wins" (Google/AfroReggae 2014). Putting favelas on the map, we are told, boosts the creative economy, community pride, self-esteem, identity, and a sense of belonging, as well as "rescuing citizenship" (AfroReggae 2014). The legitimacy of these informal settlements, and the right of their inhabitants to dwell in the city, is discursively tied to the digital map. As described by a project coordinator from AfroReggae, the digital map is "where everyone is . . . it is a recognition that you exist . . . [that] you are not a white spot on the map, that you are not out of the city." Using the marketing tagline "Breaking the wall between the favela and the city," the project trumpets its capacity to provide a new form of digital visibility. The idea of a "wall" separating city and favela refers to a physical separation in space, a digital wall resulting from an absence of data, and also a "wall of prejudice" separating favelas from the wider city and the world (Google/AfroReggae 2014). Such claims grant data (and its corporate managers) the power of redressing historical wrongs by establishing the new informational shape of inclusion and equality.

As of 2016, Ta no Mapa had collected data on twenty-five of almost one thousand favelas in Rio de Janeiro, including data on over ten thousand businesses. The mapping process, coordinated by AfroReggae, is carried out in each favela by teams composed primarily of paid local residents (four to eight "field agents") contracted specifically for this purpose. They work alongside an "office agent" based in the offices of AfroReggae, often outside the specific favela being mapped. Field agents work for between two and four months, mapping between ten and fifteen points of interest per day. Their work is sometimes interrupted by environmental risks (e.g., heavy rains, floods, and landslides) or episodes of urban violence (e.g., disputes between gangs and police). They use the Google Map Maker Mobile Buddy app, installed on a smartphone supplied by Google, to capture georeferenced data. The app works exclusively in English, consolidating it as the neocolonial language through which local and global spaces are joined to digital domains. It comes with a set of predefined categories that restricts the types of features that can be mapped.

Mapping a point of interest starts with taking a photo. The GPS function of the smartphone tags the photo with the appropriate geographical coordinates and stores this information in the app. At the end of the day, the field team uploads the information to the cloud, to be processed by the office agent into the Google Map Maker platform. This process opens a connection with Google My Business (which creates business listings in Google Search), as well as other Google platforms. As part of data processing, geotagged photos are cross-referenced against satellite images, and field agents are often called to pinpoint the exact location of any points of interest that have not been accurately georeferenced (at times, the smartphone's GPS fails to identify the correct location, particularly in favelas characterized by sharp topography and/or high building density). Once the map is completed, regional mediators with knowledge and experience of Brazil and Rio de Janeiro (who are not necessarily residents of favelas) revise and upload the data, working alongside a technical team based in Google's EU headquarters in Dublin. They are the final gatekeepers, validating, rejecting, interpreting, translating, and adapting local information to the Google

Maps format, despite the fact that some of them are not entirely familiar with the typical and idiosyncratic features of space in some favelas, such as different streets having the same name or the same street having different names.

We conducted participant observation at training workshops, which revealed the distance between the richness of favela dwellers' mental maps and the spatial simplification and standardization required by the global digital map. Participants frequently debated what a point of interest was and what type of information they should record. Historic sites? Small businesses? Catholic churches? Umbanda temples? Recommendations aimed at tourists about fare prices for mototaxi trips? Local infrastructure problems, such as open sewers? Or the symbolic landmarks that house collective memories of violence (such as the sites where memorable homicides occurred)? When a participant suggested that he would not map Umbanda temples, out of fear of prejudice, the project coordinator explained that, for Google, neither religion nor political orientation matter. Only information counts, such as the location of mototaxis, popcorn carts, football fields, and so on; a *point of interest* is simply defined by him as "whatever is interesting!" Yet he recommended that field agents should not register where a homicide occurred or mention local problems, such as open ditches or fly-tipping. Instead, he encouraged the team to map business and touristic sights. Paraphrasing a field agent working on the project, dealing with trash dumps is not their responsibility but the government's; their mapping work is designed to show outsiders what a favela has: beauty salons, bakeries, dressmakers, and so on (figure 5.2).

In wanting to erase differences, the favela is produced as homogenous and coherent, which works to reify the very walls that the digital map is claiming to break down—both glossing over and appeasing problematic social conditions in the name of economic incorporation. It would be hard to say that this is either a form of participatory mapping or VGI. Space is made through foreign languages, eyes, and hands; a spatial neocoloniality that aims to depoliticize space, translating the needs and means of the market but not necessarily those of local dwellers. Not only are favelas produced through this kind of mapping practice; this form of digital intervention operates through a very particular form of cultural power and capital which depoliticizes and pacifies core issues.

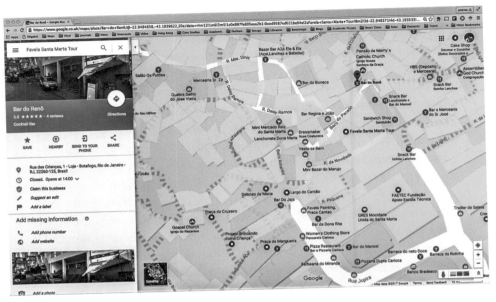

Figure 5.2
Screen capture of shops and restaurants at the Favela Santa Marta, in Rio de Janeiro, as mapped by Google Maps. *Source:* https://maps.google.com.

Beyond the Map: Opening City and Favela to Consumption

The digital territory resulting from Google's mapping of favelas is both calculated and mediated through the means and practices associated with code, software, hardware, spatial media, and other technological objects and domains. It is also imbued with the rationalities of its human and material mediators. This includes not only the computational logics embedded in spatial media, but the concerns and aspirations of Google as an informational corporation that promotes a reading of the world through digital forms of "location awareness." Previously, geographers have pointed to the ways in which digital mapping has the capacity to make everything calculable and monetizable and thus to open "new economic zones [to be] colonized for value extraction" (Crampton 2017, 42). In this section, we examine in more detail how the circulation of economic flows appears to be a central concern for Ta no Mapa.

In favelas and elsewhere in the city, being "on the map" is presented by Google as the key to commercial prosperity (see chapter 2). The company's business proposition transcends digital visibility (e.g., coordinate locations on a digital map). Rather, Google's offer focuses on shaping circulation, movement, and (commercial) decision-making in the material world through various types of digital immersion. A digital understanding of location awareness, achieved through spatial media, becomes a pillar of how Google intends to support business decisions, a world that Google describes as *beyond the map*. As Jen Fitzpatrick, the San Francisco–based leader of the company's Google Maps and Local team, explained: "In a connected world, location awareness can fuel all sorts of new and fun ways to interact with the things in our physical surroundings. That gives you a very brief taste of some of the many ways that we are seeing businesses build really game-changing experiences for their customers on top of our data and insights about the world. . . . In essence, we're helping businesses move beyond just visualizing the world, and helping them make major, real-world decisions. And at the center of it all is location, and this understanding of how the real world moves" (Fitzpatrick 2016).

Google's location awareness joins the digital realm to the material world outside the Google ecosystem, developing a series of relations that are key to the Urban OS. Specifically, it operates through the ability to share locational and nonlocational data, processes, and calculations with other internet-enabled devices and software, including users' smartphones, computers, and apps. As is the case with many other digital interactions, this occurs through application programming interfaces (APIs), the communication protocols between and across software components and operating systems. Google's location awareness APIs are provided to software developers beyond the Google ecosystem for the purpose of building "assistive and aware experiences . . . that bridge the physical and digital worlds . . . [they] simplify user interactions, provide assistance, and help users to better understand themselves" (Google Developers, n.d.). As with other digital calculative processes (e.g., algorithms; Amoore and Raley 2017), APIs are not neutral technologies but are charged with a political agency, resulting from the types of relationships they form and enable (Bucher 2013).

Location awareness is fundamental to the operation of the Urban OS. In its Google incarnation, it constitutes a calculative spatiality that prioritizes economic interactions. It takes material shape through a combination of three tools: Google Maps, local search capabilities, and Google My Business. In combining these, location awareness opens the possibility of a business-oriented spatial calculation that takes shape via three processes. First, it provides the user with a general sense of place and orientation. Second, it offers a targeted form of spatial knowledge around business transactions and/or forms of consumption. And third, it enables the incorporation of business locations and sites of consumption within an emerging and calculative sense of place. Google describes this as "an experience" occurring across local and global geographies, arguing that it helps people "navigate, explore, and decide" (Fitzpatrick 2016). It affords Google a complex and particular type of power: governmental in its ability to conduct conducts (cf. Foucault 2009) yet with strong overlaps with the sovereign forces that shape the circulation of capital and the nature of the relationship between subjects and territory.

Reimagining Favelas through a Digital Immersion

Building on Ta no Mapa, in the run-up to the 2016 Olympics Google launched a still more ambitious project, Rio: Beyond the Map.[3] It brings Google's Street View initiative to Rio de Janeiro's favelas, prioritizing a type of immersive experience that would operationalize Google's version of location awareness. Rio: Beyond the Map is an interactive web-based documentary that consists of eight interlinked 360° videos in Portuguese and English, portraying life in favelas through the story of their inhabitants (see Google, n.d.; figures 5.3 and 5.4). Foregrounding music, dance, sports, engagements with computers, and video games, favelas are portrayed as spaces full of life and creativity, where locals are working hard to make their dreams come true and, through this, to "put themselves on the map" (Google, n.d., video 7/8). Aimed at those who live outside favelas, and inviting them to step in for the first time, Rio: Beyond the Map intends to provide content for a previously "unchartered and mysterious part of the map" (Google, n.d., intro)—in a way that moves beyond the simple point-based representation of a digital map. "Favelas are not simply a place, they are a people. And to understand them, you must go inside and see for yourself" (Google, n.d., intro). In viewing favelas from the street level, viewers are invited to engage with the lives of those living there.

Rio: Beyond the Map mobilizes a narrative around the historic invisibility of favelas, positioning both business and the digital as the new nature of urban inclusion and visibility. In a video segment titled "Change Starts with Hello," Paloma, a favela resident, depicts the everyday invisibility suffered by residents in a way that demands a recognition of collective presence:

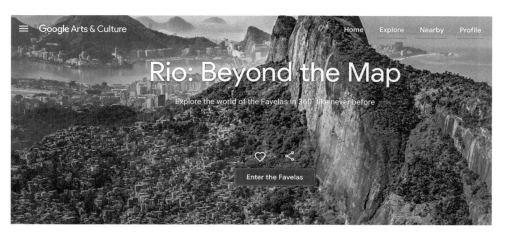

Figure 5.3
Screen capture of the opening screen of Google's Rio: Beyond the Map web documentary, with the legend "Explore the world of Favelas in 360° like never before." *Source:* https://beyondthemap.withgoogle.com/en-us/.

Figure 5.4
Screen capture of Google's Rio: Beyond the Map documentary, showing Google's Street View Camera mounted in a backpack and carried by a staff member of AfroReggae. *Source:* https://beyondthemap.withgoogle.com/en-us/.

"The favela is a blank spot on the map. Mail doesn't get delivered. Correspondence neither. It's as if we didn't exist. . . . This is a daily fight. We are saying that we are here, that we exist, that we are part of the city" (Google, n.d., video 2/8).

Paloma shares with viewers the story of her life, her memories of favela violence, her fascination with computer programming, and her surprise at becoming the only computer science student from a favela at the Federal University of Rio de Janeiro. Invisibility is discursively constructed so that it can be overcome via a digital presence. The web documentary explicitly links Rio: Beyond the Map to Ta no Mapa. Reproducing colonial narratives around light and darkness, it praises the latter as a project that "is somehow taking the favelas out of invisibility and throwing some light" (Google, n.d., video 8/8). This process of digitally mapping favelas is not simply described as a project about social inclusion but rather as a form of economic inclusion. "We're trying to map the most possible favelas, but with a focus larger than only inclusion. Also to show business" (Google, n.d., video 8/8).

Ta no Mapa's marketing material introduces favelas in decisively quantitative terms, foregrounding their unrealized economic potential given a lack of data. Promotional videos in English open with the line: "13 million people live in Brazilian favelas. Income in those areas totals 25 billion dollars. More impressive than these numbers is the absence of any others. Until recently, almost no data was available about favelas" (Google/ AfroReggae 2014). The posters and leaflets inviting favela residents to get involved in the project target small enterprises, emphasizing potential business benefits: "You are now on the map! Come for a breakfast and listen to experts to improve your business." Mapping teams are instructed to be particularly amiable and enthusiastic when engaging with local businesses, "developing trust and conveying the importance of gaining internet visibility for increasing sales" (Ta no Mapa 2015b, 3). After mapping a particular business, field agents encourage business owners to register with Google My Business, with the objective of "increasing the number of local entrepreneurs with global visibility" (Ta no Mapa 2015a, 3). They agree that one of the main purposes of the initiative is to allow outsiders, mainly tourists, to enter the informal settlement and consume the services and products available in the favela. A project coordinator taking part in a session at a mapping training workshop argued that the digital map will provide a valuable resource for outsiders "who want to come and stay in the favela. . . . If there is no information, they won't know . . . we are putting [this information] on the most accessed map on the planet." Yet the rare and sporadic media reports of tourists' deaths resulting from following some form of GPS navigation system (including the Google-owned Waze) into favelas are a reminder of the risks associated with navigating the city using only limited, digitally mediated knowledge—an artificial digital flattening of space that removes conflict and politics.

This mapping of favelas illustrates how computational urbanism operates in governmental ways in both formal and informal contexts, creating and maintaining urban flows and circulations rather than simply imposing the disciplinary spaces of surveillance (see chapter 7). Evidence collected by Ta no Mapa suggests that the digital map has impacted participating business: a survey of twenty-seven entrepreneurs in the favela of Vidigal, conducted six months after the project, revealed that half of participating businesses reported increased sales and customer visits. One in four had increased its number of employees, and "almost all considered that mapped businesses have greater chances for growth" (Instituto Data Popular/JWT 2015, 9). This governmental form of power, particularly amenable to the consolidation of neoliberal rationalities in those spaces where global capital has limited penetration, is aimed at opening favelas to broader economic circulations. Yet this is far from providing meaningful inclusion and/or citizenship for those who dwell there.

Favelas' Overlapping Powers: From Pacified to Calculated

The recent global interest in producing and sharing spatial data about favelas, slums, and other forms of urban informality should be read as a broader political reconfiguration of the relationships among informality, state, and city. This view transcends a simplistic reading of mapping urban informality as an unprecedented opportunity to support rights to the city for a long time denied—social inclusion, urban integration, citizenship, identity, and so on. The reconfiguration at stake both muddles and overlaps sovereign and governmental forms of power (cf. Foucault 2009). In making the favela into a digitally searchable space, new forms of calculating territory are enrolled and new techniques for governing local economies and circulations mobilized. As part of such process, new sovereignties come into being while others recede. As examined in this section, the digital making of territory in favelas runs in tension with the nondigital shape of territorialization.

Sites of urban informality, already information spaces, have always been ripe for encoding (cf. Leszczynski 2015b). In contrast to the narrative promoted by Google and its Ta no Mapa project, favelas in Rio de Janeiro are neither invisible nor marginal. Defying invisibility, they have always been at the core of the city's economy and politics. For some, the empty and disconnected cartographic representation of favelas (and informal settlements more generally) is a measure of urban exclusion (Brillembourg and Klumpner 2005; Gouverneur and Grauer 2008; Reyes Novaes 2014). For others, it represents an affirmative act of resistance to the colonizing practices of the state (Fabricius 2008; Freeman 2014; see also Varley 2013).[4] The marked attention to cartographic silences in academic and nonacademic readings of favelas—as either tools of knowledge, power, and domination (cf. Harley 1988) or as a deliberate resistance to domination—is rather simplistic, reifying a false dichotomy between formality and informality (Varley 2013).[5]

Favelas have been a spatial, social, economic, and political presence in Rio de Janeiro for over half a century, during which they have been subject to repeated political and economic interventions. However, contemporary attempts to govern and integrate favelas through digital code stand in sharp contrast to how sovereign powers have historically defined territorial control within them, and to the nature of their urban integration. Many of Rio de Janeiro's favelas, and particularly those located in hilly areas, have been controlled by local militias and drug trafficking networks since the 1980s. They provide favorable topographical and political conditions for the exertion of nonstate power: squeezed against the hillsides, overlooking the city, they provide strategic locations from which economic circulations can be overseen; their terrain, a maze of labyrinths and alleys, enables strategic blockages, hiding, and escape; their boundaries double as controlled borders, limiting access and establishing separation with the formally governed territory.

In 2008, the state government of Rio de Janeiro launched its Pacifying Police Units program in favelas (*Unidades de Polícia Pacificadora* [UPPs]), in what amounted to a conflict over sovereignty. Through a combination of military occupation, intense police presence, and interventions by social services, UPPs aimed at breaking the territorial control exercised by militia

Figure 5.5
Members of Rio de Janeiro's Pacifying Police Units program on patrol. *Source:* Agência
Brasil (ABr). Creative Commons Attribution 3.0 Brazil License.

and drug-trafficking networks, reinstating the formal authority of the state,
and interrupting well-established cycles of urban violence (figure 5.5). Academics and activists have criticized UPPs as a form of zero-tolerance policing and a colonizing intervention of the state, exposing residents to the
predatory aspects of capital (Freeman 2014; Swanson 2013). Others have
argued that they have enabled public service delivery and economic integration. Over 80 percent of the favelas chosen by Google and AfroReggae
for digital mapping were previously targets for UPP intervention. In the
language of the Brazilian state, they have been *pacified*. This illustrates the
extent to which the informational corporation, which through calculation
advances a governmental form of power, depends on forms of state violence to establish its regime.

The mobilization of spatial media in favelas illustrates the tensions
generated by the overlapping of computational code (a simplified configuration of space through digital calculability) and nondigital code (the

informal and unwritten rules that establish the operation of power and guide conducts in favelas). Whether advanced by the state, by militias and drug-trafficking networks, or by Google, altering the nature and function of territory, terrain, and border is not without obstacles. Each one of these stakeholders attempts to impose, or at least entice, their codes. The change comprises not only technologies but also ways of thinking about territory and population, as well as novel mechanisms for calculating them. Despite the "pacified" status of favelas selected for digital mapping, conflicts around territorial power provide both context and substance to the mapping exercise—illustrated by the troublesome nature of access to the sites to be digitally coded, the required nuanced knowledge of such sites, and the rationalities of resistance against the digital map. Previously, in the context of UPPs, scholars have identified local resistances to mapping in favelas and the extent to which this "significantly increase the knowledge and hence the power of outsiders" (Freeman 2014, 18). In the case of Google Maps, some residents fear that the digital map will bring with it forms of exposure, eviction, or displacement, and would prefer to be left out. Dwellers speak of the value of not being on the map as a way of avoiding the impositions of a calculative territorial sovereignty, such as taxation, or maintaining beneficial forms of irregularity, such as informal and unpaid connections to the electricity grid.

The way that favelas function through multiple, overlapping, semi-mundane, and context-specific unwritten codes, like elsewhere in the city, highlights the complexity of the nondigital location awareness that makes politics and everyday life. Here, residents are the only "sensors" (cf. Gabrys 2014) capable of reading the nondigital codes of space—how, when, and where to circulate. Their lived experience of place can hardly be translated into the stripped-down categories of the digital map. Terrain, as a particular three-dimensional reading of both the materiality of territory and its securitization (Elden 2013b), is of particular importance here. In hilly favelas, the vertical and volumetric nature of the space (cf. Graham 2016) means that only resident mappers have the intimate and nuanced spatial knowledge required to interpret urban form and translate urban materialities into digital code. Such forms and materialities include steep and interrupted alleys, informal rights of way across private spaces, shortcuts over roofs, and the microtemporal dimension of local political conditions, which allow some movements and flows and not others. In order to stand any hope of producing a digital map, the mappers themselves need to be born and raised locally. "This is the greatest *pulo do gato* ["trick of the trade"] of Ta no Mapa," explained a project coordinator. "We recruit people who know how to circulate in these places, who have a sense of danger, [and] a sense of how far they can go and where they cannot go." As residents, mappers can circulate freely; they understand the local codes of conduct and the unwritten rules and tacit spatial boundaries that mark the limits of what is allowed/not allowed to be placed on the digital map. Local and context-specific practices, such as the requirement to have the windows down when in a car, the need to avoid certain areas at certain hours of the day, and the knowledge to dress in keeping with the symbolic color codes of drug factions, do not translate into the Urban OS. Yet the digital map and its demand for calculative rationalities impose a numeric and simplified way of ordering space—one that, in favelas, is often absent: telephone numbers, postal codes, and even businesses' opening hours.

The economic incorporation of space through digital information flows that occurred in the Ta no Mapa project is highly political, not only because it advances a very specific and neoliberal form of political economy, but also because it effects changes to existing forms of sovereignty and the political calculation of territory. Digitally calculated territory transforms the relationship among citizens, the state, the private sector, and markets. This transformation demands a political-economic reading of both the emerging nodes of power that generate and own spatial information, and the platforms that enable data's recombination. Digitally calculated space *enters* production and consumption circuits and *through this* puts in place new political orders.[6] Linking the economic dimensions of digital mapping with political transformations in space, we argue that a new form of sovereignty is emerging from the control and regulation of spatial information: a digital empire (cf. Farman 2010; Hardt and Negri 2000). This upsets and deterritorializes traditional spatial forms, such as the nation and the state, while redistributing functions, processes, and powers traditionally in the hands of the state. The information space created by Ta no Mapa reconfigures the favela both as digital territory and market, becoming the new terrain at stake in the search for security. The market, envisioned by Hansen and Stepputat in their analysis of contemporary sovereignties as an emerging configuration of power, unfolds as a "magical and redemptive" (yet potentially "unpredictable and pitiless") sovereign force (Hansen and Stepputat

2006, 309); its power magnified by the calculative coming together of space and the digital database.

Conclusions

Urban big data and its computational analytics can only reproduce existing urban fragmentations and socioeconomic inequalities. The very materiality of poverty persists beyond the digital intervention, and the only certainty projected into the future is the characteristic unevenness of the contemporary city (Leszczynski 2016). Even within the favelas, digital mapping reproduces the unevenness characteristic of Rio de Janeiro, by focusing on favelas that are located within a short distance of tourist areas and that already have a greater economic integration with the city. In effect, the technology prioritizes the wealthiest informal settlements.

In translating their unique location awareness to digital languages and platforms, favela residents are presented as the main actors on a new techno-utopian path toward social justice, inclusion, and economic prosperity. Google and data are reified as the new powers capable of suspending the exceptions of informality. While the wall between favelas and the city is not broken, a gap is opened in order to secure calculability. Yet this is never meant to be the calculability of communities as a whole, nor of their deficiencies, complexities, and aspirations, but of their economic flows and businesses. Here, the coming together of digital mapping and the geoweb supports a form of governmental power, exercised through techniques of enumeration and spatial calculation, mobilized through the freedoms and capacities of the governed, and aimed at opening the favela to broader economic circulations.

There are three key implications of digital mapping for advancing an understanding of computational urbanism. First, digital mapping is an exercise in producing territory in its political sense. While the emancipatory power of digitally mapping the city and its sites of informality is in many cases undeniable (as both activists and academics have previously argued; Livengood and Kunte 2012; Patel, Baptist, and d'Cruz 2012), this is also a process that operates at multiple levels and that needs to be read in the context of contemporary processes of capital expansion and the enrollment of subjects, digital techniques, and computational logics in the creation of sites of accumulation and the reproduction of forms of inequality.

In the case of Google's involvement in digitally mapping favelas, what is at stake is not so much visibility and recognition, but rather calculation and the coming together of space and the database of economic flows. The chapter points to the importance of attending more to territory as a way of thinking about the politics of emerging digital urbanisms. In favelas, characterized by contested governing forms and conflicting and overlapping powers, digital mapping inevitably embodies particular forms of politics—which in turn have implications for how forms of exclusion and/or inclusion are configured in the city. Through digitally mapping favelas, Google Maps is advancing a project in which equity and social justice are achieved not so much through social inclusion and infrastructure provision, but rather through a calculative incorporation to a specific economic regime.

Second, the multiplicity of codes and ways of thinking shaping the politics of space can hardly be captured by a digitally based location awareness. The Urban OS is limited in its ability to account for urban processes, yet its reliance on calculative rationalities imposes a particular order in the city: a numeric and simplified way of configuring territory that is amenable to global economic circulations. This would not be the first time that, in reimagining the city, a techno-utopian dream backed by the logics of functional simplification fails to understand the role of local knowledges and the microsociology of public order, as encapsulated by Scott's analysis of Brasilia in *Seeing Like a State*. Yet as pointed out by Scott (1998, 37), "To codify local practices [is] a profoundly political act." The simplified form of location awareness of Google Maps, as mobilized in Ta no Mapa, has one aim in mind: to redefine social exclusion as economic exclusion and incorporate spatial value despite any obvious urban inequality.

Finally, just like statistics plays a key role in the making of a governable population, digital mapping plays a role in making the sites of urban informality into a new form of urban territory. Through digital incorporation, favelas become part of broader processes of governing characterized by the in-depth involvement of a multiplicity of global agents and their logics, from digital ICT corporates to financial flows. The challenges and contestations that the digital map experiences in favelas alert us against the fetishization of digital modes of planning, hinting at both a resistance to and the limits of the simplification and fragmentation of digitally enabled locational awareness. But beyond urban informality (beyond the favela itself), what is at stake in Google's digital mapping is the development of new forms of territorialization through digital calculation. Such use of spatial media represents the emerging form of making territory of the Urban OS. Through its calculative logics, the Urban OS reshapes territory, reshapes sovereignty, and reshapes the ways in which citizens engage with the sovereign powers at play, advancing a model where territory as a political space is constructed through digital-economic incorporation.

Here, in the digital making of territory, enabling or restricting flow and circulation appear to be the main currency at stake, the crux in the tensions between sovereign and governmental powers (cf. Foucault 2009). Digital tools are mobilized as the subtle weapon of the new powers to be. As such, the informational corporation (i.e., Google) seemingly works through governmentality. But, as discussed in more detail in chapter 7—also in the context of Rio de Janeiro—it would be a mistake to see the arrival of digitally enabled territorial powers as a battle between governmentality and sovereignty. Rather, these are entangled. The prioritization of "pacified" favelas in the digital reconfiguration of territory points to the role of state violence in clearing the way for corporate governmentality and, in doing so, the role of the state in engendering twenty-first-century forms of territorial sovereignty. This is a new and complex configuration of sovereignty; in the digital making of territory, it is the pairing of the spatial database with the gathering and control of information flows that concedes the ability to shape market configurations and capital flows, positioning the informational corporation as a linchpin in the recasting of the city as a space of market sovereignties.

6   Prediction: The City as a Calculative Machine

At its core, our idea allows us to anticipate and get ahead of problems before they begin, helping us to be a more effective, smarter government. This platform has the potential to fundamentally change the way cities operate. With data, we are building a new path for all cities in the 21st century.

—Rahm Emanuel, mayor of Chicago 2011–2019 (City of Chicago 2013)

In 2013, Chicago's SmartData Platform was selected by Bloomberg Philanthropies as one of five winners in its first Mayor's Challenge. Developed by the municipality as the world's first citywide, real-time analytics platform, the SmartData Platform was designed as an open software tool for use in any city whose administration wanted to use a combination of data and predictive analytics for decision-making. Rahm Emanuel, Chicago's mayor, believed the platform would transform how cities operate by giving them the capacity to make use of millions of pieces of data: "Residents will see services delivered earlier. They will see more targeted responses that will address a wide range of urban issues—from managing weather emergencies to scaling back traffic accidents" (City of Chicago 2013). Michael R. Bloomberg, then mayor of New York City, lauded the project: "Chicago's predictive analytics platform will help the Windy City—and other cities—harness the power of data. . . . [It] tackles an issue of growing importance for cities and companies alike" (City of Chicago 2013).

Both Emanuel and Bloomberg point to the significant impact that predictive logics can have on cities. In our view, their importance lies not so much in their ability to solve urban problems, but rather in the way that they advance a new epistemology of the urban, one characterized by the coming together of mathematics, time, and space. With predictive analytics, the data-driven city is reconceptualized as a calculative machine. This is a step change from the datafication logic examined in chapter 3, where transparency (e.g., open data platforms), visibility (e.g., data visualizations), and ease of use (e.g., the various interventions by civic hackers) were arguably the main drivers for the digitalization of the urban. By contrast, prediction involves a more explicit desire to rework both time and space in the city through calculation. Under this logic, *space in a calculative form* (specifically, as a numeric set of coordinate points) becomes the common denominator for all urban transactions. This translation of space into numeric common denominators is precisely what enables interoperability across urban domains and the possibility of calculating the urban across time—that is, predicting the city.

The very attempt at prediction involves rethinking how we come to know and engage with urban futures. It operationalizes a foreshortened temporal horizon, pushing decision-making away from the long term and strategic and toward the immediate and responsive. Engaging with prediction is fundamentally *preemptive* rather than preventive; it deems considering an "array of *possible* projected futures" and an incorporation of "the very unknowability and profound uncertainty of the future into *imminent* decision" (Amoore 2013, 9; our emphasis). The implication of this is that the future is not to be known and governed only through a long-term extrapolation of past statistical data (a common feature of planning), but also through working with uncertainty via short-term time frames that prioritize the immediate. Within predictive computational logics, rolled out in the context of big data (Aradau and Blanke 2017), what is at stake is not so much the strategic horizon of the future needed for city planning, but rather near-real-time decision-making. As such, urban prediction operates through the microhorizon of the future needed for urban operationalization. In this chapter, we will examine attempts to predict the city through calculative processes and the way these operate via a close coupling of time and space—more specifically, through the coming together of time sequences with a detailed fragmentation and parceling of space. The experience of Chicago points to an epistemology of the urban wherein calculation and the use of mathematical tools are the driving forces—an urban capacity constituted through a specific computational product.

A Short Genealogy of Prediction

As with many other computer applications, the history of predictive analytics is intertwined with both the history of military applications and that of cybernetics. Within cybernetics, established in the late 1940s by Norbert Wiener following years of experience working on antiaircraft control systems, flows of information and flows of matter are conceptualized in identical statistical terms. Both are seen as "behaviours or events" that are "subject to predictive analysis" (Hookway 2014, 95). From the perspective of military defense, prediction is the key capability underpinning antiaircraft warfare—an essential calculation required for reaching a target that is moving over time. By its very nature, this is a time-dependent calculation, with very short temporalities attached to it. One of its earliest applications was the Kerrison Predictor, an automated antiaircraft targeting system based on an electromechanical analogue computer designed in the late 1930s at the UK's Admiralty Research Laboratory. This was followed in 1946 by the legendary Electronic Numerical Integrator and Computer (ENIAC), developed by the University of Pennsylvania for the US Army Ordinance Corps. Built to calculate artillery-firing tables, ENIAC was one of the earliest applications of digital computing (Atomic Heritage Foundation 2014; Haigh, Priestley, and Rope 2016). Both predictive analytics and the computers that were calculating them played a key role in the prediction of nuclear chain reactions within the Manhattan Project, the World War II research initiative leading to the first nuclear weapons.

Over time, the targeting capabilities offered by computerized prediction extended beyond military uses. From the 1960s onward, corporations and research institutions began the era of commercial predictive analytics, with applications including forecasting the weather, solving the "shortest-path problem" to improve air travel and logistics, and applying predictive modeling to credit-risk decisions.[1] Set within a context of evidence-based decision-making, data within predictive analytics came to matter in relation to decisions. Computer scientists and corporate leaders began to see predictive analytics as part of a wider movement to transform fleeting forms of decision-making into systematic and process-driven acts via "digital things that we can describe, store, evaluate, compare, automate, and modify at the speed required by modern business" (Taylor 2011, xvii). In retail, a technological confluence of prediction and big data was used by large supermarket and retail chains for targeting offers, managing inventories, and modeling trends in customer behavior—a process referred to in the industry as extracting business value from the data, drawing on the collection of data on customers' consumption patterns via loyalty schemes (Hirst 2008; Swamy 2011).

What is at stake in predictive analytics is the spectrum of possible relationships (i.e., the associations), rather than a direct causality between them—and the implications for decision-making attached to this ontology of association (cf. Amoore 2011). In contrast to *descriptive analytics* (which refers to linear calculations based on historical data) and *prescriptive analytics* (aimed at evaluating new ways of operating and achieving business objectives), *predictive analytics* is concerned with what-ifs, transcending both data and probabilistic future trends (Evans and Lindner 2012; Haas et al. 2011). In the process, the role of data itself is reimagined. As IBM researchers Haas et al. (2011, 1486–1487) explain, the statistical "focus on data is much too narrow and must be expanded dramatically. . . . By definition, data reflects facts or assertions of facts that are already in existence. . . . Data just lies passively. . . . But data alone—even with very powerful descriptive analytics— tells us about the world as it is, and was, but cannot tell us much about the world as it might be." Data within predictive analysis thus is proactive and nonlinear; it plays a key role in navigating a world of possibilities and uncertainties in order to access the as yet unmade future.

In the context of predictive analytics, data goes through a process of discovery, standardization, and aggregation in order to enable anticipatory decision-making.[2] Applications use a variety of statistical and analytical techniques to model future events or behaviors, from forms of regression modeling to more advanced models using neural networks and nonlinear statistical modeling (Nyce 2007). The attraction of these techniques includes the speed with which they can process huge volumes of data, their potential to produce more consistent and reliable forecasts than humans, and their ability to identify hidden trends and relationships (Finlay 2014; Nyce 2007). The critical issues, from our perspective, lie in the translation of these techniques into the urban context. What are the consequences of utilizing a targeted form of calculative decision-making, based on preemptive and anticipatory modes of knowing? How is a data-driven reconfiguration of time-space likely to affect the way we understand the urban, the planning process, and its temporalities? Can this new logic be applied to any domain of urban life and infrastructure, or does the predictive logic of decision-making have limitations that restrict its use to specific domains? In this chapter, we will attempt to answer these questions, drawing on empirical fieldwork that we conducted in Chicago, a world-leading site for the application of predictive analytics to city management.

Predicting the City

Predictive analytic tools underpin a change in decision-making processes, arguably positioning algorithmic decision-making and mathematical thinking as the new shape of evidence-based policy in the city. Those developing predictive tools for cities argue, that this is allowing cities to move "from a reactive mode of operation based on gut instincts to a proactive mode of operation based on mathematical models" (Appel et al. 2014, 172). Indeed, city administrators and urban practitioners are increasingly turning to techniques based on algorithms and artificial intelligence as ideal tools for knowing and intervening in the city, in part "because they are able to process huge amount[s] of uncertain, imprecise and incomplete data, and to find approximate solutions for problems that, otherwise, would be intractable" (Salcedo-Sanz et al. 2014, 243). Fueled by this desire to model all things urban using algorithms, the city and its infrastructures are increasingly becoming privileged sites for the application of, and experimentation with, forms of prediction. One of the earliest applications of predictive analytics in cities was traffic modeling, mobilizing a mathematical understanding of urban circulation (Microsoft 2011; Min, Wynter and Amemiya 2007). Increasingly, predictive analytics play an essential role within utility services. In the case of water and energy, for example, the rollout of smart electricity and water meters has incentivized the development of predictive models to forecast short-term demand for these services (e.g., Candelieri and Archetti 2014). But the use of predictive analytics in the city stretches well beyond infrastructures: in the City of Syracuse, New York, for example, IBM researchers working in collaboration with the municipality have developed tools to predict and preempt property vacancies (Appel et al. 2014), generating within the municipality a set of capabilities for the calculation of space across time, in effect allowing them to target the sites and mechanisms of both urban decline and vitality. Decisions based on prediction thus intervene in urban sites, preempting one series of futures and enacting another (cf. De Goede and Randalls 2009). However, this highly targeted approach to city-making has not been mobilized evenly across urban domains.

For over twenty years, city administrations and police forces have used predictive decision-making to fight crime and track "abnormal" patterns of behavior. Within a "globalizing and urbanizing 'battlespace,'" both at home and in hostile cities (Crang and Graham 2007, 803), prediction as a form of anticipatory seeing has played a critical role in the *making* of urban targets. Perhaps the most common predictive analytics application in cities, particularly in the United States, has been crime forecasting, through what is known as predictive policing. Software packages such as HunchLab and PredPol are marketed to local authorities to enable them to identify "where and when crime is most likely to occur enabling [cities and municipalities] to effectively allocate . . . resources and prevent crime" (PredPol, n.d., "Overview"). As with the logic of datafication discussed in chapter 3, the technology's wide market appeal lies in its claim to use empirical data objectively, in a way that is arguably "free from human biases or inefficiencies" (Ferguson 2017, 1114). PredPol, originally developed through a collaboration between the Los Angeles Police Department and UCLA, combines algorithmic calculations, historical event datasets, and machine learning to predict crimes, prepare heat maps, and recommend areas for patrol. "Predictions are displayed as red boxes on a web interface via Google Maps. Each box is a 150 ×150-meter square . . . [and the boxes] represent the highest-risk areas for each day" (PredPol, n.d., "Predictive Policing"). Prediction of this type inevitably alters a future that is yet to come. It brings into being a specific reality of policing: targeting and deterrence. According to a police officer in Los Angeles whose words are cited by PredPol as part of the company's marketing material: "We told [officers] to go into the boxes. . . . They may stay there for just 15 minutes to a half-hour and let people see them walking around the area. . . . Would-be offenders see the police activity and are deterred from committing a crime there" (PredPol, n.d., "Predictive Policing"). As early as 2013, over 150 police departments in the United States were reportedly using predictive policing (Bond-Graham and Winston 2013), including initiatives in Santa Cruz, California; Seattle, Washington; Atlanta, Georgia; Memphis, Tennessee; and Chicago, Illinois. Software companies like PredPol now claim a proven track record of crime reduction.[3]

Critiques of predictive policing abound. The industry claims not to use personal information about individuals or groups of individuals, thus "eliminating any personal liberties and profiling concerns" (PredPol, n.d., "Proven Crime Reduction Results"). Civil rights activists disagree, arguing that predictive policing results in targeting not only high-risk zones but also high-risk individuals (Townsend 2015; Ferguson 2017; Selbst 2017). Critical geographers accuse the technology of racial bias, arguing that it refreshes and extends preexisting modes of racialized police profiling (Jefferson 2018). For Jefferson, whose research focuses on Chicago,

> predictive crime mapping further entrenches and legitimizes racialized policing as it (1) rearticulates police data sets as scientifically valid and (2) correlates those data with other geocoded information to create new rationalizations for controlling racialized districts through differential policing practices . . . the Chicago case illustrates that predictive crime mapping does not incur more precise applications of police force but rather legitimizes the widespread criminalization of racialized districts . . . Precrime maps garb the epistemologies of racialized policing in a scientific veneer, by mobilizing the language of spatial statistical analysis and data analytics to bolster city officials' rationale for using differential police surveillance and control in Black Belt and latinx districts. (Jefferson 2018, 1, 11)

As in many other cities, the history of predictive analytics in Chicago began with its police department (the Chicago Police Department, or CPD). Since the late 1980s, the CPD has been innovating with forms of matching computerized mapping and crime data for the purpose of devising strategies to respond to crime (Maltz, Gordon, and Friedman 2000). In 1995, the CPD implemented a system for displaying crime data known as the Information Collection for Automated Mapping (ICAM). ICAM was a user-friendly system running on Microsoft's Windows 95 and MapInfo 2.0 software that enabled police officers to print maps and tables showing the most frequently reported offences in a specific area of the city (e.g., police districts, sectors, and beats; O'Neil 2011; Rich 1996). The system has been "celebrated by officials for pinpointing hot spots of criminal activity at unprecedentedly spatial resolutions" (Jefferson 2018, 5). In the early 2000s, ICAM gave way to the Citizen and Law Enforcement Analysis and Reporting (CLEAR) system. Developed in partnership with the Oracle Corporation, CLEAR consists of a large GIS database of crime reports and offender records, among other data (Government Innovators Network, n.d.; Skogan et al. 2003). CLEAR now provides the data-driven foundations for a range of policing functions within the city.

In 2010, the CPD launched its Predictive Analytics Group, under the leadership of Brett Goldstein, a graduate of the University of Chicago's Graduate School for Computer Science. Goldstein joined the CPD in the mid-2000s and, after a period working on the beat, he started to combine his computer science knowledge with policing. Working on the streets of Chicago led him to ask questions about how he could "'design a computer model that could replicate' an officer's intuition" (Flock 2011; see also Howard 2015). Shortly after, his experience in dealing with data and databases and developing a predictive analytics strategy for the CDP propelled him to city hall. In 2011, Goldstein was appointed by the recently elected mayor, Rahm Emanuel, as the city's first chief data officer (CDO), after which he became the city's chief information officer (CIO), and then the commissioner of the city's Department of Innovation and Technology (DoIT).[4] Goldstein's progression through these newly created roles suggests the increasing importance accorded by Chicago's city administrators to his data-driven work.

Calculating Chicago: Operationalizing Urban Sciences

"We have a history in Chicago of operationalizing urban sciences," one of Goldstein's successors in the role of city CIO tells us in an interview. For over one hundred years, Chicago has been a hotspot of theoretical and applied urban knowledge. From the times of Jane Addams at Hull House (1889–1963) through the Chicago School of Urban Sociology (broadly speaking, 1920s–1960s), Chicago has been an object of study for the contemporary urban condition as well as an urban laboratory to test emerging ideas about the city. Here, scholarly knowledge about the urban has found routes into social reform, while also shaping how the very idea of the city—as a spatial abstraction of global purchase—is imagined and dealt with.

As smart city narratives began to dominate the world of urban planning, academic institutions in the vicinity, such as the University of Chicago, the University of Illinois, and Northwestern University, started offering graduate programs and postgraduate degrees on the application of computational analysis to urban planning.[5] Working in parallel with research centers such as the Urban Center for Computation and Data (University of Chicago/Argonne National Laboratory), the Center for Data Science and Public Policy (University of Chicago/Carnegie Mellon University), and the

Mansueto Institute for Urban Innovation (University of Chicago), these scholarly initiatives sought to mobilize ICT knowledge, data, and computer science to inform day-to-day decision-making in the city and to advance sustainable modes of urbanization. Brett Goldstein, a computer science graduate from the University of Chicago, is both a product and a developer of this landscape and a key figure in the application of predictive analytics to Chicago itself. At the start of his career, a key question for Goldstein was how to predict crime using not just data from past criminal events, but other information—such as 911 calls (the North American phone number set aside for accessing emergency services). He believed in the interoperability of urban processes across temporal and spatial sequences and, through that, in the possibility of identifying patterns that cut across different domains. In practice, this led to the somewhat counterintuitive claim that you did not need direct knowledge about crime in order to predict it. As Goldstein explained to us, "You'll talk to lots of other people in the field who will say 'you need to understand the subject matter and you need to sit down and hear people's stories' and all of these things—that wasn't me." In removing the need for sector-based expertise in order to achieve meaningful insights, Goldstein was going against established ideas about how urban processes operate and how knowledge about them should be accessed.

In the resulting urban computational system, prediction is not bounded by epistemic disciplines: it emerges from the calculative coming together of space and time, creating patterns that transcend any specific domain. Taking inspiration from epidemiology, by 2010 Goldstein had rolled out a system that predicted "when and where people would get shot or killed." Critical to this was the ability to predict through proxies, avoiding crime data. "I believed in sort of the purity of the math behind it," explained Goldstein, "where . . . there are polygons, there are vectors, there are segments, and if you understand the interoperability in the temporal spatial sequencing of the events, you're able to really apply prediction." Under this model, bounded disciplinary and professional knowledges no longer matter because the model uses indirect data. Its primary skillset is mathematical.

WindyGrid: An Emerging Bricolage of Hybrid Informational Ecologies

After he was appointed Chicago's first chief data officer, Goldstein took the knowledge he had developed in the police department to city hall. He set out

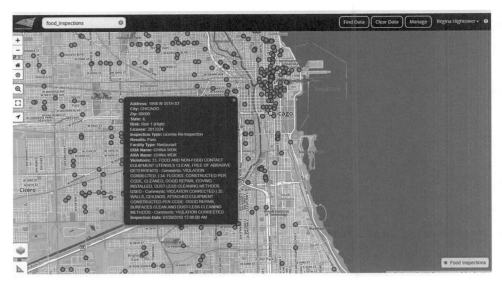

Figure 6.1
Screen capture of Chicago's WindyGrid interface, following a user query on food inspections. Taken from the WindyGrid online manual. *Source:* City of Chicago (https://webapps1.chicago.gov/windygrid/). Creative Commons Attribution-ShareAlike 4.0 International.

to develop WindyGrid, a computer application aimed at situational awareness and incident monitoring in real time. It combined GIS mapping, the city's key databases (e.g., 911 and 311 call records, building information, licenses and permits, etc.), social media feeds (e.g., Twitter), and a range of other software tools (Thornton 2013). WindyGrid (figure 6.1) was initially developed for the Chicago 2012 NATO Summit and more recently reconfigured as an open-source package by the name of OpenGrid (City of Chicago 2015; Thornton 2016). Discussing the early days of the platform, Goldstein recalls: "My responsibility was to ensure that we could determine what went on at any given place and at any given time during NATO. With a new Mayor, large-scale event, 'Black Block' [*sic*][6] expected and various threats coming in, this was very important" (Goldstein 2015, 7). As Goldstein explained:

> WindyGrid consumes all of the spatial data available, lifting information from the base and creating a so-called "large spatial index." In any given area, it became possible to find responses to queries as diverse as the number of police cars active, the sources of the Tweets being sent out, the identities of those using 911, etc.

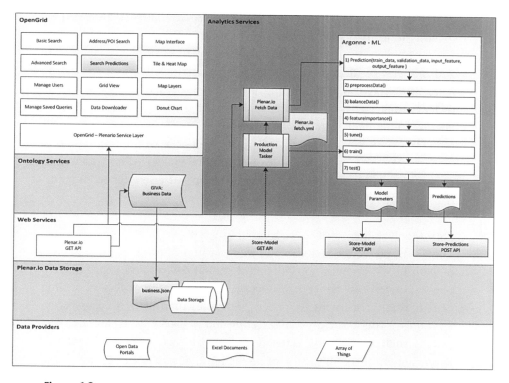

Figure 6.2
Information architecture diagram of Chicago's SmartData Platform. *Source:* City of Chicago/Smart Chicago Collaborative (via GitHub: https://chicago.github.io/ smart-data-platform/).

and making the needed predictions, for instance, on where rats would likely to be seen or where an outbreak might occur. All of this was achieved using open resources and entailed extraordinarily low costs. It is a system in which we take great pride. (Goldstein 2015, 7–8)

Critically, WindyGrid allows access to the city's predictive analytics application, Chicago's SmartData Platform.[7] Like many other digital platforms, Chicago's SmartData Platform was developed in collaborative ways using GitHub.[8] The SmartData Platform is described as a user-friendly system that "helps automate predictive analytics for use within cities and display it without requiring a background in data science or statistics" (City of Chicago 2017). Within GitHub, the application is illustrated with an image that is not unlike the various graphic illustrations discussed in chapter

2. It shows a novel bricolage of hybrid informational ecologies working together to form a type of Urban OS (figure 6.2). The platform "grabs data from multiple city systems which allows users to explore in a single map and provides predictions to help cities operate efficiently and *proactively*" (City of Chicago, n.d.; our emphasis). Indeed, proactivity is a theme in wider journalistic coverage of the system: "The intention is that the Smart-Data platform will shift city management away from a reactive model towards a proactive approach. The predictive power of the tool resides in its ability to analyze relationships in the data at a speed and on a scale not previously possible, helping Chicago to optimize services of all kinds" (Garnier 2014).

Rats! Mobilizing Predictive Analytics in City Hall

The use of predictive analytics in urban settings illustrates a fundamental tension in the mobilization of computational devices and logics for city-making: a contrast between claims of fundamental change and a range of remarkably consistent processes that rather than being transformative reproduce forms of sociospatial targeting and well-established logics of control in search of efficiency. As the quote from Chicago's mayor at the start of this chapter illustrates, the use of predictive analytics is seen by many as a transformative new path for cities. Yet for those who are involved in mobilizing predictive analytics at the street level, this is about operational efficiency. As a former chief data officer of Chicago noted: "When the mayor was elected the first time [in 2011], part of his election strategy was around being data driven. . . . When you translate that into operations, that pretty much means applying data to become more predictive in city services, and you can sort of apply that to almost any city service. . . . Our focus is on how can we drive day-to-day decisions that either improve the quality of life for residents or improve the efficiency of city operations."

Predictive analytics' entrance into City Hall (i.e., beyond the police department) evidences how this computational logic is not about structural transformation but about enabling the city's everyday. The initial uses of the predictive analytics applications developed by Chicago's Department of Innovation and Technology (DoIT) have centered on mundane processes: food safety violations, lead poisoning, the identification of black markets for cigarettes, and rat infestations (City of Chicago 2018). Working together with the Department of Public Health, for example, DoIT identified nine variables associated with food safety violations (including previous violations, nearby sanitary complaints, and length of time since last inspection) and produced an algorithm that generated a list of restaurants likely to breach safety standards in the near future. This work changed the order in which inspectors carry out restaurant visits, targeting those flagged by the algorithm. Media reports state that the prediction "found violations 7.5 days earlier, on average, than the inspectors operating as usual did" (Spector 2016). The work on lead poisoning is also about targeting, with the Department of Public Health, DoIT, and the University of Chicago's Center for Data Science and Public Policy working together on the identification of homes where children and pregnant women were at risk of being poisoned by lead paint (City of Chicago 2018).

An algorithm for predicting rat infestations, developed by DoIT in collaboration with the Event and Pattern Detection Laboratory (EPD Lab) at Carnegie Mellon University, uses thirty-one different variables to predict where rodents will appear. The data used comes primarily from citizen reports to 311 City Services (the city's telephone-based system for nonemergency requests) and includes things like the accumulation of garbage and broken water pipes. As the CDO behind the application explained: "Every single night we run that [data] through a series of algorithms to predict where we think rodents are going to be within the next seven days" (Chicago Architecture Center 2014). In an interview, he described how a combination of historic datasets and near-real-time events (311 calls) are a sound predictor of an increased number of rat-related calls: "We have a wealth of data from our 311 system. . . . We have about thirteen years of data in that system, so it's a wealth of information about the city and we've used it through a lot of our analysis. . . . Almost through just playing with that, the data engineers detected certain patterns that seemed to indicate a relationship that to us looked like we would be able to predict that we were going to get a call about a rat infestation prior to the call coming in."

This interviewee makes no claims about the algorithm replacing human knowledge. Rather, the city's new predictive capabilities complement years of knowledge, experience, and intuition already present within city hall staff. When DoIT contacted the Department of Streets and Sanitation, the latter was initially skeptical about the ability of an algorithm to replace the accumulated understanding of the streets gathered by rat baiters over decades of work. However, the deputy commissioner of the Bureau of

Figure 6.3
Baiting rats in Chicago. Photo courtesy of Leif Johnson.

Rodent Control was surprised by the accuracy of the system: "To me it works. . . . It helps us because we are getting ahead of an issue before it gets worse," she explained. At the time of fieldwork, between twelve and sixteen crews of rat baiters were working in the city on a daily basis, one of which was dedicated to sites identified through predictive analytics. The deputy commissioner explained that she had noticed a reduction in 311 calls associated with rat problems and that she believes that this reduction is partly linked to the predictive analytics work. In the context of rat baiting, one of the most mundane operations of the city (figure 6.3), an emerging predictive knowledge uses correlational logics for targeting purposes, mobilizing mundane unknown futures into city-making. This is also, at times, a contingent knowledge, with the key markers of prediction often identified in rather serendipitous ways. Chance still plays a role.

The City as a Calculative Machine

The transmutation of the urban into a combination of data and mathematical equations opens a window into a different understanding of time-space in the city, alongside interoperability across a range of urban domains. Despite claims about the transformative nature of Chicago's predictive analytics platform, what such systems do is often very mundane, concerned with everyday services (e.g., rodent control, environmental services) and the short-term temporalities associated with immediate events (e.g., knife crime, food safety violations). As a general rule, the sciences of prediction operate better in time intervals closer to the present, foregrounding short-term horizons. From meteorological to economic forecasts, the longer the time frame for the prediction, the greater the degree of variability, uncertainty, and error. Inevitably, rethinking time in the city through prediction locks the analyst into a short-term outlook. This, in practice, takes the form of operationalization and a focus on the immediate, affecting the system's ability to advance long-term perspectives and strategic transformation. A relevant consideration is that the logic behind the knowledge produced by prediction is not causative but correlative; it is a calculus that "does not seek a causal relationship between items of data, but works instead on and through the *relation* itself," based on "an unknown value that comes into view only through its association with other unknown values" (Amoore 2013, 59; original emphasis).

Urban predictive analytics systems, we argue, are marked by the calculative recombination of space and time. We discuss this through references to WindyGrid and the work of Chicago's first CDO, Brett Goldstein. There are five interrelated steps involved in operating the city as a calculative machine. The first is *a numeric and calculative understanding of space, alongside its recombination with time*. Data points (e.g., transactional databases) and polygons (e.g., spatial databases) allow for calculations (e.g., large-scale multivariate analysis). Space in a calculative form, via spatial coordinates within a GIS system, becomes the common denominator for all urban transactions, enabling interoperability across urban domains. It brings together the various databases of the city, mobilizing them toward a predictive system. In the words of Goldstein: "You have like a 911 system, a police [database], permits, licenses, you name it; and then maybe you have some sort of data warehouse or data-mart and you have all this data . . . you look at the rows of data and what's a common denominator through all these? Their coordinate systems . . . all the data pipes in and you build a massive spatial index."

In conjoining transactional urban data and the map, this way of engaging with GIS prioritizes the database over forms of representation (see chapter 5). Jeremy Crampton has previously identified this in his analysis of the territorial politics of spatial calculation. Crampton builds on Foucault's (1970) *The Order of Things* and Heidegger's (1966) *Discourse on Thinking* to point to the dangers of this "machinization" of the state (see also Hacking 1990). For Crampton, the issue at stake is not only a way of knowing, but the extent to which this determines a way of being—where "to be, is to be calculable": "The danger is that we already approach the world in a predetermined, calculative manner; where to be, is to be calculable: 'This calculation is the mark of all thinking that plans and investigates. Such thinking remains calculation even if it neither works with numbers nor uses an adding machine or computer. Calculative thinking computes. It computes ever new, ever more promising and at the same time more economical possibilities' (Heidegger 1966, 46)" (Crampton 2011, 94).

Only types of spatial experience and relations that are amenable to calculation and can be captured within the fragmented logic of data (see chapter 3) can play a role in this emerging form of urban knowledge. The coming together of the algorithm (as a mathematical calculation) and space, in combination with sequential time variables, underpins the possibility of prediction. Predictive logics break time into a series of sequential units (T1, T2, T3, etc.) that function as small, knowable, and quantifiable increments in the condition of an unfolding event (the numeric distance between T1 and T2, between T2 and T3, between T3 and T4, etc.). As previously mentioned, the greater the timeframe, the greater the uncertainty: accurate prediction requires time to be controlled and maintained close to the original point of inception (T1), privileging short-term interventions and a focus on the immediate over long-term planning.

Second, urban prediction relies on *a conceptual fragmentation of the urban*—where both the space and time of the city enter the calculative system only through small and disaggregated units or discreet fragments (see chapters 2 and 4). Behind the possibility of calculating and predicting the city lies the idea of *microgeographies*. This type of spatial-numerical analysis, particularly popular within criminology, relies on fine-grained modeling and small scales (cf. Weisburd, Groff, and Yang 2012). Microgeographies are about mobilizing a grid-based understanding of the city as an aid to algorithms for the purpose of calculating urban events. In the case of Chicago, the idea of microgeographies leads to the very name of the original predictive analytics tool, WindyGrid. *Windy* evokes the environmental conditions of Chicago (famously called the Windy City), while *grid* evokes the small-scale spatial abstraction required for predictive knowledge. The city is seen as a spatial abstraction in the form of a numeric grid where all events have coordinates associated with them.

The third consequence of the urban computational logic of prediction is that it effects *a transformation in the forms of knowledge (expertise)* that matter. With the city seen as a computational entity, mathematical expertise alongside technical GIS knowledge becomes a driving force behind emerging forms of urban knowledge. Once space and time have been fragmented into standardized units, the engine of knowledge production is the algorithm: "It's a whole new way for a city to do things. . . . If you're going to make a prediction in my grid, there's some algorithm that drives it, there needs to be underlying mathematics that do it. . . . Algorithms are at the heart of it. . . . The brains are the algorithms. . . . And the brains do everything from offer up ideas to answer questions," Goldstein tells us. "The math that drove the rats [analysis] was remarkably similar to the math that predicts the homicides . . . algorithmically." For the predictive logic of urban computing, whether it is homicides or rats doesn't matter. What matters is calculating a point within an adjacency matrix associated with a targeted behavior. For those involved in developing the prediction system, the different and multiple data sources involved provide an "enormous amount of ability to create equations for outcomes"—equations that can be repurposed across a range of urban domains in order to achieve different outcomes. Expertise on urban issues, while retained, is seen as a form of intuition that could and should be codified. Once nonurban experts achieve access to models underpinned by mathematics, they are in a position to become the new urban experts.

Fourth, urban prediction is about *targeting and microcustomization*. The analytically integrated city operates through a range of forms of targeting, originally derived from security domains (from military approaches to policing and criminology). Establishing an analogy with bodily disease, Goldstein suggests that prediction opens the possibility of "tailored" or targeted approaches: "15 or 20 years ago if you got cancer, how did we treat it? We treated the whole system, you would have blank radiation, you would have chemotherapy. Now it's all about tailored focal treatment. It's the

same thing in government . . . you have customized policy approaches."
Yet the specificity of this approach to the city has significant political and
social implications. As Louise Amoore argues in her study of the role played
by predictive algorithms in identifying potential terrorists at international
border crossings, the computational logic of prediction allows the imposition of partial and fractured exceptions, creating "differential degrees of
inclusion or exclusion" (Amoore 2013, 8). At the city level, such technology
may be used to understand, control, and govern neighborhoods in differential ways, not only reproducing and entrenching the characteristics of particular urban spaces, but potentially discriminating against neighborhoods
with "undesirable" profiles.

Finally, within this configuration of the urban, *the possibility of ask-*
ing questions is subservient to the predictive system itself. Predictive analytics
promises to uncover meaningful relations that would otherwise remain
hidden and unknown. The claim is that "advanced statistical data mining,
and machine learning algorithms dig deeper to find patterns that traditional BI [business intelligence] tools may not reveal" (Gualtieri, Powers,
and Brown 2013, 2).[9] Yet this creates a domain that is explicitly *not* known,
beyond that of straightforward uncertainty: the *causes* of patterns in the
data may remain unknown, as only the correlation is seen. What precisely
are the causal or associational relations that matter is, in view of the system,
an unknown, and this influences how we pose questions to the system.[10]
In addition, the scope of questioning is narrowed by the form of operation
of the system itself. As we argued in chapter 3, urban prediction relies on
datafication—that is, the quantification of all urban processes. This remains
its limit; anything that cannot be reduced to quantitative data is left out.
For many of those who embrace urban prediction, the limit is data. In strategic terms, the main limitation of the system is seen as the city's ability
to quantify things—often overlooking an inquiry into who is asking questions to the system or what are the right questions to ask. As those behind
WindyGrid themselves argue, within computational logic, such matters are
of secondary importance: "Question-asking is a sexier part of the job but
we still . . . it's kind of like worrying about the paint on a house when
you're still building the foundation. If you don't build a really smart and
good foundation to your house, your house will fall down." Data in the
computational city is teleological: seen as the foundation for analytics, its
assembly becomes a driver beyond and above its specific function.

Conclusions

Not every problem of the city can be solved through predictive analytics. We were reminded of this by the CDO of Chicago, who was acutely aware of the gap between the expectations created by the promise of urban predictive analytics and its potential to deliver results on the ground: "Every time we sit down with the mayor's office to look at priorities, the first thing out of their mouth is "we need you guys to look at tree trimming." And there is such a deep backlog [in tree trimming] that the only thing our data engineers could ever do was go out and help trim the trees! . . . They think predictive analytics is a bit of a panacea, [but] it doesn't fix every kind of problem. So they'll present us with something and when we explain that it's not something that can be addressed by predictive analytics, it is a little bit hard to explain to them."

This example perfectly illustrates the gap between the limitations of these methods and their perceived benefits: technology cannot yet perform all aspects of human labor and cannot therefore find creative solutions to problems caused by a lack of resources. There are multiple material issues that remain obdurately beyond technological solution: however accurately the computational logic of prediction may allow us to foresee events in the urban realm, it cannot produce the extra tree surgeons that the city needs! In practice, urban prediction is currently about creating opportunities for intervention at microtemporal scales that form part of wider efforts to operationalize the city. Additionally, however, computational prediction is reshaping expectations about how the city can and should function, reshaping the urban in its own image.

An important implication of urban prediction is that calculation becomes a dominant way of knowing and making the city. Prediction generates knowledge that can improve the short-term operational efficiency of an urban service, and in doing this it *tends to reproduce socio-economic conditions, rather than to transform them*. The limitations of a close temporal horizon effectively mean that the use of urban predictive analytics tends to reduce possibilities for significant structural change. It is not so much transformational as operational, with data-led mathematical expertise as an obligatory passage point in the production of knowledge about the city. Rather than responding to strategic priorities, the system itself searches for problems to be solved. This highly procedural way of knowing the city privileges mathematical reasoning and computational expertise, and it attempts to provide a standardized way of knowing the future, to the exclusion of other forms of knowing, such as experience, deliberation, emotion, embodied encounter, and language. The holders of mathematical and computational expertise become critical to this new urban science, as they decide the means and rules (and at times purposes) by which these systems are used. This is a change that is advancing the emergence of a new class of urban actors.

As the computational logic of prediction operationalizes the city, it also advances a particularly powerful way of seeing the urban context, with significant effects not only on decision-making, but also on the horizon of possibilities. Prediction prioritizes short-term questions around efficiency and optimization, at the expense of long-term questions about strategic intent and politics. Its numeric and calculative way of encountering the urban through mathematical expertise reduces what is seen to what is standardizable within a dataset. Its tendency to produce solutions that are specifically targeted develops a microcustomized way of approaching the city, based on spatiotemporal fragmentation and spatial differentiation. The diverse and varied experience of human encounter in the public realm of the city, as well as insights from non-data-based experts, are largely ignored, as systems capture only events that can be reduced to standard units of time and space: neighborhood, street, polygon. The predictive city, endlessly analyzing itself through a closed loop of data flow, prediction, and action, is therefore at risk of entrenching spatial inequalities while it locks down possibilities for wider and more significant forms of structural transformation.

7 Circulation: Maintaining Urban Flows under Turbulence

Not far from Copacabana Beach here is a control room that looks straight out of NASA. City employees in white jumpsuits work quietly in front of a giant wall of screens—a sort of virtual Rio, rendered in real time. Video streams in from subway stations and major intersections. A sophisticated weather program predicts rainfall across the city. A map glows with the locations of car accidents, power failures and other problems . . . what is happening here reflects a bold and potentially lucrative experiment that could shape the future of cities around the world. This building is the Operations Center of the City of Rio, and its system was designed by I.B.M. . . .

"I come from I.B.M. research. I'm attracted to large, complex systems," [the IBM executive] said. "Can you think of a system that is more complex than a city?"

—*New York Times* (Singer 2012)

In 2011, Rio de Janeiro opened the *Centro de Operações Rio* (Rio Operations Center, known locally as COR). Designed by IBM under the direction of the city's Municipal Informatics Company,[1] the COR is a metropolitan-scale control room that aims to integrate the work of a multiplicity of public and private organizations who manage urban infrastructures, deliver key local services, and provide emergency response. Remarkable for its dominant role within the public imagination, it has been ubiquitously showcased by media and technology corporates as an exemplar smart city initiative. The COR, an archetypical type of Urban OS, led IBM to develop a handbook to guide other cities in the implementation of similar technologies: the *IBM Intelligent Operations Center for Smarter Cities Administration Guide* (IBM 2012; figure 7.1; see also chapter 2). Both the handbook and the COR illustrate how an operating system for the city can constitute (and arguably operates

Figure 7.1
IBM Intelligent Operations Center for Smarter Cities Administration Guide (cover).
Source: IBM 2012.

as) a single off-the-shelf product—a vision that is different from that of the previous cases we have explored, which involved a bricolage of stakeholders and technological packages. In Rio de Janeiro, the COR's operations have significantly increased the visibility of urban infrastructures—a function of a close coupling between networked infrastructures and information technologies, alongside the establishment of new ways of seeing the city and its infrastructures through (digital and traditional) media platforms.

In this chapter, we examine the COR as a form of Urban OS, and the possible implications of this configuration for emerging forms of governmentality associated with smart technologies (Braun 2014; Gabrys 2014). We look in particular detail at the ways in which circulatory flow is conceptualized and managed in the computational city. Drawing on a Foucauldian unpacking of circulation as a "key instrument and target of governing processes" (Aradau and Blanke 2010, 45), we focus on the emergence of new forms of circulatory control through information technologies.

Building on the arguments developed in previous chapters, we are particularly interested in the way that the Urban OS undertakes a partial and selective rebundling of splintered networks and fragmented urban space. The COR can be understood as a form of metainfrastructure: a capacity that coordinates selected control functions of diverse networked infrastructures. In doing this, the COR reworks established forms of infrastructural visibility and invisibility—an empirical phenomena that allows us to revisit longstanding debates within STS and urban studies around infrastructural *black boxing*. Infrastructures, alongside their significant social and political implications (see chapter 1), invoke powerful images of stability, appearing "immanent, universal, [and] unproblematic" (Graham and Marvin 2001, 21; see also Hughes 1983). They possess an invisibility that leads them to quietly support the task at hand (Star 1999). Such process of gaining invisibility is referred to as *black boxing*, defined as a "(temporary) stability" that is sufficiently strong that "the controversies surrounding their adoption have to a large extent been erased" (Hinchliffe 1996, 665). Given this black boxed nature, infrastructures often disappear "almost by definition. The easier they are to use . . . [and] the bigger they are, the harder they are to see" (Bowker and Star 2000, 33). However, this ubiquitous invisibility shatters when they break down (Graham 2010; Star 1999), revealing the fragility and precarious achievement of stabilized infrastructure.[2]

In this chapter we argue that the COR, and by extension particular configurations of urban operating systems, operates through an "un-black boxing" of urban infrastructures, where the extension of control room logics to the totality of the city points to their fragility and the continuous effort involved in their operational accomplishment. It also functions through a collapse in relations of control—of the everyday and the emergency— which, enabled by the digitally led incorporation of the public in operational control, further raise public awareness of urban infrastructures.

However, control here is not seen from a military-inspired perspective that, via command-and-control logics, prioritizes domination (as exemplified by the work of Norbert Wiener, a perspective that influenced the original makeup of the cases examined in chapters 2 and 6). Rather, akin to the understanding of cybernetics developed by the prominent twentieth-century British cybernetician Stafford Beer, control in the context of the COR is more a function of self-regulation aimed at adaptation and ultimately survival.[3] Under Beer's approach, computer systems are positioned as the brain of the organization, and control rooms act as a primary interface between humans, computer systems, and society. Arguably, this configuration of urban computing is less influenced by military operations and more by concerns around business operations, as espoused by municipal informatics institutes (e.g., see chapter 4 for the case of Barcelona).[4] Combined, these characteristics point to a specific form of urban governmentality based on the need to continuously adapt to conditions of turbulence via the operationalization of infrastructural flows and the development of novel ways of seeing and engaging with the city and its infrastructures.

Besides operating as a macro-level urban infrastructure, the COR is also a control room. Like other control rooms, it is a key site that enables the city's infrastructural life by securing urban flows and maintaining the city's circulations. Existing literature on control rooms identifies two broad types: those established for the management of the everyday, and those, usually temporal, established for managing emergencies (Gordon 2012). Like infrastructure, control rooms tend to be invisible: they are enclosed and hidden environments, often subject to extreme security given their importance as control foci for network infrastructures (Coaffee, Wood, and Rogers 2009). Despite the primary role of control rooms for the functioning of infrastructures, they have been remarkably absent from academic literature on networked urban infrastructures (for exceptions, see Anderson and Gordon

2017; Mattern 2015; Silvast 2013). Instead, sociotechnical analyses of control rooms tend to be grounded in two largely disconnected fields: surveillance (where the control room is seen as a site constituting specific ways of seeing the city; see Boyne 2000; Graham 1998; Monahan 2007; Norris and McCahill 2006)[5] and workplace studies (which see the control room as a node of coordination, where the spatial and temporal gap between human and material participants is filled by technology; see Ikeya 2003; Lundberg and Asplund 2011; Suchman 1995).

An important aspect of the chapter is to foreground the intimate connections between control rooms, urban infrastructures, and infrastructural flows, a move that allows us to further elaborate on the transformation of this relationship through an engagement with urban operating systems. Control rooms, thanks to their continuous work in preventing infrastructural breakdown, responding to disruption, and overcoming interruption, play a key role in the achievement of infrastructural black boxing. Through this, they are essential for "the continuation of what has become normal" (Gordon et al. 2014, 10). Developing a broader understanding of agency within control rooms, previous research points to the way they function as "an ongoing yet situated practical accomplishment" (Gordon 2012, 119). Capacity to act in and through the control room is not limited to individuals (staff members) or technology but achieved as a dispersed and relational effect involving human and nonhuman agents. Thus, the accomplishments of the control room require continuous effort; from the viewpoint of the control room, infrastructure is never invisible or stable, but rather visible, unstable, and always at a point of breakdown (Gordon et al. 2014). But what happens when a conventionally hidden control room, through its engagement with digital technologies, is opened to the city and reconfigured as a metropolitan object capacity-capability for the management of the city's infrastructure?

The COR in Context

Rio de Janeiro's COR "operates 24 hours a day and 7 days a week, interconnecting the information of several municipal systems for visualization, monitoring, analysis and response in real time" (Prefeitura Rio de Janeiro 2011, 14). The initial idea for the system dates back to April 2010, when the state of Rio de Janeiro experienced a traumatic rain event that resulted

Figure 7.2
Rio de Janeiro's Operations Center (COR). *Source:* Andrés Luque-Ayala and Simon
Marvin.

in widespread flooding, hundreds of landslides, fifteen thousand homeless
families, and the loss of over two hundred lives. The city of Rio de Janeiro,
the state's capital, was significantly affected. Its main roads were flooded,
public transport collapsed, power, gas, and water supplies were disrupted,
and commercial activity paralyzed. Shortly after, the city's mayor enlisted
the help of IBM to create a facility that could provide rapid responses to
urban emergencies and disruptions while constantly feeding information
on the conditions of the city to public agencies and to the public.

The COR (figure 7.2) was designed to function both as an operations
center (managing the city's everyday) and an emergency response center, two processes that, according to an IBM engineer involved, utilize the
"the same approach and the same actors, players and technologies." It
overcomes issues of institutional isolation through a digital architecture
and physical colocation that facilitates communication while maintaining the specialized knowledge and experience of each municipal agency

Figure 7.3
The COR's control room. *Source:* Andrés Luque-Ayala and Simon Marvin.

and organization involved. All agencies and organizations involved remain autonomous, maintaining their own control room, operative systems, and response protocols. However, the COR provides both an overarching computational capacity and a physical location where horizontal integration of urban flow maintenance can be managed, coordinated, and regulated. In its main operations room, formally known as the control room (figure 7.3), staff members from different agencies share and access a broad range of information about the state of the city in real time while also dispatching responses and allocating resources. Here, through a mapping platform built over systems developed by Google Enterprise, the COR visualizes key resources and disruptive events as they happen, from vehicle collisions to power outages. Its screens constantly provide views and visualizations of the city and its operations (e.g., weather patterns, public transport movements, and even the location of each of the city's municipal guards) through video images captured by over eight hundred cameras, maps, and points of georeferenced urban data.

Examining the maintenance of circulation in a city like Rio de Janeiro inevitably requires engaging with empirical and academic debates about the securitization of the urban. Drawing on an extensive body of work around surveillance and coercion, critical scholars have examined the role of circulation in securitizing the urban. They have pointed to the ways in which people and objects "are mobilized, monitored and filtered between fortified places" (Fussey 2015, 214; Klauser 2013, 2015), uncovering the ways in which such processes alter both the physical configuration of space and public perceptions of the city (Coaffee 2013). Undoubtedly, this is the case in Rio de Janeiro. Here, contemporary politics are shaped by crime and inequality (Kleiman 2001; see also chapter 5) and politicians often use local elections to mobilize issues of violence and security as a priority. However, the municipal nature of the COR means that its remit is limited to urban management. The COR coordinates some minor policing functions carried out by the city's Municipal Guard (e.g., parking and traffic management, environmental protection, and tourism support), but issues of crime prevention and policing remain outside its remit since responsibility for them rests at federal and state, rather than municipal, levels. City administrators and local law enforcement have, however, used the COR's functionality to secure and manage megaevents, particularly the 2014 World Cup and the 2016 Olympics, and those events have, in turn, fed into the development of urban security strategies and new infrastructures of urban control (Cardoso 2013). Such experiences have fed back into the everyday management of the city, establishing "temporary regimes of extra-legal governance that permanently transform [the city's] socio-space" (Gaffney 2010, 7; see also Coaffee 2015; Graham 2011; Fussey and Klauser 2015).

In our view, the division of policing functions in Rio de Janeiro (whereby policing rests at state and federal levels, with only limited functions at municipal levels) reminds us of the extent to which the role of urban operating systems in the domain of security needs to be understood within a framework that transcends debates around surveillance and coercion. Rather, this needs a framework that can deal with the broad and subtler ways in which power is exerted, covering "the range of technologies and power/knowledge epistemologies which regulate freedom as contingency through the principle of economy" (Dillon 2015, 48). As outlined in the previous chapters, our conceptual model of control is not confined to types of violence, coercion, and surveillance. Drawing on a Foucauldian interpretation of power as creative and productive of subjects, meanings, and interventions (Miller and Rose 2008; Patton 1998), we instead argue that the COR, like other configurations of Urban OS, operates in a governmental fashion—as a political technology that intervenes in the world by reshaping subjectivity from the inside (enabling freedoms), rather than imposing constraints from the outside (see chapter 1).[6]

Rio's COR: Governing the City's Everyday

Urban infrastructures are usually controlled through a complex patchwork of separate control rooms at a range of scales. However, the COR is unique in that it brings the horizontal control of these networked infrastructures together in one integrated center. Technologically and institutionally separate networked infrastructures are brought together within a single domain of control, echoing what Collier and Lakoff (2015) have identified as a *system of systems* aimed at reducing risk and vulnerability. Such an emerging mode of infrastructural control via systems of systems (see chapter 2) is characterized by an organizational and material rebundling, where ICT platforms and the digital visualization of spatial data play an important integrative role. Broadcasting an image of an integrated city, the COR not only presents infrastructural operations to the public but also engages the public as a key component of the city's infrastructural operations. Here we provide an overview of the everyday functioning of the COR by focusing on three of its operational domains: its integrative capacity, its relationship with the media, and its interaction with the public via new media technologies.

Operational Rebundling toward Flow Maintenance

The COR is staffed by over four hundred people, working 24-7. They represent thirty-two municipal agencies (including waste collection, transport, health, social assistance, civil defense, and the city's meteorological monitoring agency), twelve private utility and service companies (including the bus companies, as well as Light, the privately owned company in charge of supplying electricity to the city), and a selected number of state-level agencies. "We focus on those organizations that are directly linked with citizens' well-being on an everyday basis," explained a COR director. The municipal agency with the largest number of representatives is the Transport Department (in Portuguese, the *Secretaria Municipal de Transportes*), and its cameras are linked to the COR's primary workload. As a director told us, "Since the major bottleneck of this city on an everyday basis is traffic, staff work mostly with the images of the cameras, showing the streets." Traffic flows during large events such as the World Cup are a priority, with COR staff preparing advance routes for the different sports delegations, determining closure points for the purpose of safety, and creating alternative routes for nonessential traffic. But these are not the only flows and resources that are visualized and monitored: energy provision, waste collection, and even social services are also mapped in real time. "We show the work of agencies, agents, and people. For us, for example, during New Year's Eve it is important to know where all the waste collection trucks are located, working all over the city, so that the city is clean at the end of the celebration," explained a staff member. He continued, "I can visualize the electricity transformers of Light and identify where there are power cuts in the city, which is crucial for the COR."

Integrating a large number of agencies means accessing a greater amount of information, the key currency that enables the COR to operate. Integration occurs through organizational and institutional arrangements, as well as spatial and visual arrangements and information flows. The latter take the form of spatial data (georeferenced location points to be mapped on a common GIS platform) and image exchange. "The [toll road] concessions send us their images, and . . . members of the COR analyze those images on a constant basis," explained a COR executive. But the operations of the COR do not rely exclusively on digital exchanges and integration: physical colocation plays an important role in sharing information. Three times a day, all agencies represented at the COR have a 15-minute meeting in which representatives from each agency report on any relevant incidents and on the actions they are taking to resolve them. "Nothing substitutes for direct physical contact," argued the director of the city's civil defense. The COR directly employs a group of coordinators who maintain the requisite links between different agencies, monitor progress on incident response, and, where necessary, put pressure on agencies to speed up response time. In describing the coordinators' role, the director of operations pointed to their previous corporate sector experience with logistical operations and control: "They come from the private sector. . . . They are highly trained, with experience in operating airports and aviation companies, and are now operating cities."

Infrastructural Journalism in the Everyday

Traditionally, the role of control rooms in the management and organization of infrastructural systems is not visible to the public, except in an emergency or following disruption (Graham 2010). Yet inside a control room, the fragility and potential instability of the infrastructure network is fully visible to the operators and constitutes a constant source of preoccupation for them (Gordon 2012). Conventionally, the work of maintaining, controlling, and reestablishing city systems goes unseen by the users of infrastructure. However, in Rio, the COR is unusually visible. Traditional and new media channels (from radio and television to Twitter, Facebook, and Instagram) have brought the COR to the city's collective attention, directing citizens' gaze to urban infrastructures. In this coverage, journalists represent the city's infrastructures in a way that stresses their precariousness and potential instability, showing, and simultaneously justifying, the constant work that is needed to maintain them. Rather than being invisible, the COR begins to shape the way in which the public views and imagines the city, opening its infrastructures to the public. Through its pervasive role in media representations of the city, yet still seeing and acting as a control room, the COR becomes a critical producer and communicator of knowledge about the city.

Hosting the media is part of the COR's strategy to establish a continuous two-way communication with the public, a move that allegedly aligns it with broader municipal, IT, and open government narratives praising transparency in local government (see chapter 3). In the words of one of the COR's directors, "This is a form of transparency in public service, and an explicit purpose of the mayor himself. Everything here is done in a very transparent way, with the media reporting from here twenty-four hours a day." This emphasis on transparency is embedded within the physical design of the building, with the press room located on an open balcony right above the control room, with a full view of its activities (figure 7.4). It is fitted with fourteen desk stations that are in permanent use by radio and TV journalists who constantly report on the state of the city and its infrastructure while also, at times, providing the COR with additional sources of information.

A brief account of a typical morning broadcast from the channel TV Globo Rio de Janeiro provides a snapshot of the COR's interaction with the media. Every weekday during the morning rush hour, Rede Globo, Brazil's largest TV network, broadcasts directly from the COR. Embedded within

Figure 7.4
The COR's press room. *Source:* Andrés Luque-Ayala and Simon Marvin.

a well-known breakfast show called *Good Morning Brazil* (*Bom Dia Brasil*), Rede Globo transmits periodic four-minute live segments of news with a focus on urban issues. The broadcast of the relay between the TV studios and the COR occurs in a highly performative manner through the use of a variety of visual techniques. Studio-based journalists report in front of a TV screen that displays maps and satellite images of the city, showcasing the issues discussed, and the show then cuts to a live link to the COR at moments when additional in-depth and up-to-date information is required. The announcement of the transmission relay starts with an aerial image of Rio de Janeiro, providing a bird's-eye view of the city, then rapidly zooms in on the COR. "With our map, let's go there, to the Operations Center, to establish contact with [our journalist] there," says the studio-based presenter, passing the baton to her colleague stationed at the COR (figure 7.5).

These daily broadcasts focus on the city's weather, transport conditions, emergencies, and other events likely to disrupt daily commutes and other urban flows. Journalists frequently interview high-ranking municipal officers to discuss various urban events, from changes in the cost of public transport to waste collection strikes. Working together, the COR and the

0m 10s. Studio based journalist provides digitalised bird's eye view of urban road layout and reports on average road speeds.

0m 40s. Direct connection with several COR's cameras is established and quality of traffic flows discussed.

2m 08s. Announcement of live link with COR. An aerial image pans over the city from above and zooms in on the COR.

2m 12s. Studio based journalist greets colleague based at COR, and engages in a short conversation about traffic flows.

2m 15s. With a live feed of the COR's main operations room in the background, journalist discusses key disruptions in the city and how the municipality is responding.

3m 20s. Back in the studio, additional live traffic cameras are presented and further information provided.

Figure 7.5

Analysis of six screenshots of a typical four-minute morning broadcast linking Rede Globo studios with the COR. *Source:* Andrés Luque-Ayala and Simon Marvin, based on a video transmission by TV Globo Rio de Janeiro.

media provide a highly visible platform from which they can explain the measures the municipality is taking in response to disruptions. Reporting directly from the COR's pressroom, with the control room in the background, TV Globo Rio de Janeiro provides viewers with a window into the heart of the city's operations, and from there to a multiplicity of urban sites. Journalists have direct access to the COR's data and can flick between the many traffic cameras or rain gauges integrated into its systems. During TV transmissions, the use of satellite imagery and bird's-eye views suggests the possibility of a distanced, all-round understanding of the city. This viewpoint frames the relationship between the COR and the public eye, creating an Apollonian gaze (Cosgrove 2003; see also Kingsbury and Jones 2009)— an illusion of total control.

The visibility of—and through—Rio's infrastructure is intertwined with the way the municipality invokes a principle of transparency and a mission around immediate response. The COR puts in practice a way of governing through visual domains (cf. Dean 2010; Otter 2008), reaffirming a mode of governing through infrastructure and exemplifying how technology and design play a central role in emerging modes of urban governance (Wakefield and Braun 2014). Authorities are both surveyor and surveyed, as the public is given the opportunity to experience the city through the COR: "The COR is the eyes of the population; for everything that happens here [in the city] we must give the best possible response in the quickest possible way," explained a COR director. The COR's limited emphasis on policing allows it to embrace a discourse on transparency in its management of the everyday; its open and integrated use of information allows it to construct itself as the vehicle by which transparency and accountability are achieved. Information is not only a path toward operational response but also provides an explanation and justification of disruption and response. Yet, as discussed by Dillon (2015, 40), "the more radically transparent modern rulers and the ruled become to demographic and digital knowledge, the more politically opaque . . . the world become[s] to rulers and the ruled alike." Several urban operations remain outside of the COR's control capabilities and are therefore also hidden from the public gaze—from the problematic sewer networks of the city and the sanitation crisis experienced by favelas within the *Complexo da Maré*, to the now defunct cable car system serving favelas in the *Complexo do Alemão*.[7]

Seeing the City through the COR? Involving the Public via Social Media
In addition to Facebook, Twitter, Instagram, and YouTube, staff at the COR regularly use two smartphone apps to interact with the public (figures 7.6 and 7.7). The first is Waze, a popular traffic-management app owned by Google. The second is a purpose-built app called Eyes of the City (*Olhos da Cidade*),[8] which is inspired by other popular urban apps that enable direct communication between the public and local authorities (e.g., FixMyStreet). Waze, with over six million users in Brazil (Machado 2013), combines a vehicle navigation system and social media. Like a traditional satnav system, it operates by providing an overview of the city's transport network, enhanced by real-time updates on traffic conditions generated via crowdsourcing. Waze maps hazards, congestion, accidents, and police

---

Figure 7.6
(a) Twitter and (b) Facebook (screen capture) feeds of the COR. *Source:* (a) Andrés Luque-Ayala and Simon Marvin; (b) Facebook.

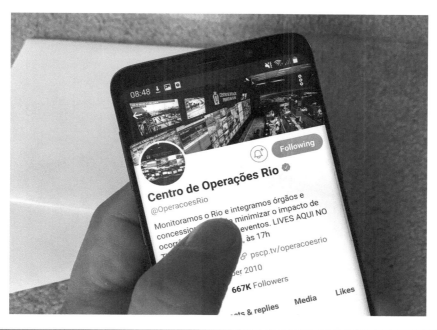

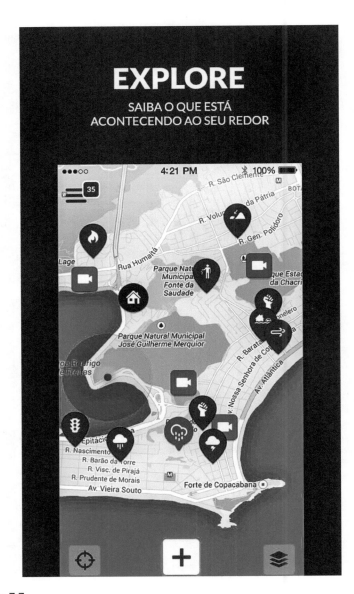

Figure 7.7
(a) Olhos da Cidade, the COR's own mobile phone app, and (b) use of Waze within
the COR. Photo courtesy of Prefeitura do Rio.

Figure 7.7 (continued)

presence, and provides updates on the average speed of roads. Since 2013, the COR has used it to engage with the public, allowing Waze users to have access to the different operational plans made by the municipality, such as road closures resulting from planned works or events, diversions, and other unplanned disruptions. In exchange, the COR receives over 750,000 daily alerts logged by Waze users, which allows it to identify and prescreen traffic disruptions. For example, the COR uses the density of Waze alerts to verify the accuracy and severity of possible traffic incidents (Prefeitura Rio de Janeiro 2014).

It would be easy to fall into the trap of reading the COR as a Foucauldian panoptic device that uses surveillance to multiply its eyes on the streets. Yet in line with Otter's (2008) critique of a reading of the history of urban vision and power as a history of discipline, the COR should not be interpreted as a panopticon that sustains disciplinary power; rather, it is a governmental technique of visibility. By engaging with citizens who voluntarily provide georeferenced data, the COR reinforces the creation of a different way of seeing and sensing the city (cf. Dodge and Kitchin 2013;

Goodchild 2007). At the launch of its partnership with Waze, the COR's director praised the value of crowdsourced information as "an important tool for the operation of the city. . . . The account of any occurrence outside the field of view of our cameras is a great support in targeting efforts and [provides] an improved time response to incidents" (Telesintese 2013). In a similar fashion, at a research interview, the city's chief executive of digital technologies celebrated the way that integration with Waze meant that citizens could be "100 percent part of the everyday life of the city. . . . In this way we go from 650 official cameras to over one million cameras; the more citizens use this technology, the more agile we can be." Yet the eyes that multiply are not only those of the COR but also those of the public. Waze alerts, uploaded by the public into the COR's system, illustrate the extent to which the citizen, through its ability to share real-time information about urban flows, becomes a functional component of the transport infrastructure being developed by the COR.

Rather than disciplining bodies, what is at stake here is a conduct of conducts; a way of governing population. The visibility accorded to infrastructure is expected to generate particular reactions, or conducts, in the public: changes in traffic routes, preparations for emergency response, avoidance of sectors of the city, or simply patience until services are reestablished. In making infrastructure visible and pointing to its weaknesses and breakdowns (congested roads, sites of accidents, power outages, weather incidents, etc.), the COR thus operates in a governmental fashion, "forming an internal feedback loop within the apparatus itself" (Braun 2014, 53). The digital reorganization of both subjects and infrastructures and the framing of the urban as a reality in need of urgent intervention (Braun 2014; Wakefield and Braun 2014)—two pivotal processes within the establishment of the COR—are an essential part of the material-spatial arrangements involved in this transformation in urban governmentalities. In transforming citizenship into citizen sensing, the public becomes a constitutive element of the emerging "urban computational apparatus" (cf. Gabrys 2014). Citizen sensors capable of monitoring environmental conditions "engage in the labour of being watched," passively collecting data while feeding a system beyond their control (Monahan and Mokos 2013, 286). In this configuration of the Urban OS, the public operates as a distributed perceptual system that expands the capabilities of the CCTV control room. In seeing the city through the COR, "the performance of smart urban citizenship occurs not by expanding the possibilities of democratically engaged citizens, but rather by delimiting the practices constitutive of citizenship" (Gabrys 2014, 45). Such a form of governmentality prioritizes productivity and efficiency toward sustaining dominant economic logics, while the recasting of citizens transforms them into mere operators.

Emergency Response and the Institutionalization of Permanent Emergency

Rio's unique and spectacular topography exacerbates the impact of extreme rain events. The city's seafront location and hilly nature mean that clouds regularly settle above the city. This humidity easily turns to rain on contact with colder winds from the north, which happens frequently over the summer period. Abundant stormwater currents are often blocked by the rising tides, resulting in recurrent flooding in low-lying areas of the city (figure 7.8). Extreme rain events, coupled with changes in land use that have reduced forest cover and absorption capacity, have increased the likelihood of landslides, a phenomenon that particularly affects the 20 percent of

Figure 7.8
Floods in Rio de Janeiro in 2016. *Source:* Agência Brasil (ABr). Creative Commons Attribution 3.0 Brazil License.

population living in the city's favelas given that many of these are located on mountainsides and hilly areas.

On Monday, April 14, 2014, four years after the rain events that marked the birth of the COR, we were carrying out fieldwork for this chapter when a weather forecast predicting several hours of moderate but sustained rain led to the COR declaring a state of alert for the city. From early in the morning, as the rains started to fall, TV Globo Rio de Janeiro journalists reporting from the COR were building a sense of anticipation, providing viewers with detailed weather forecasts for the different neighborhoods of the city. The COR's control room served as the backdrop for live interviews with municipal officers and COR staff members, who described the municipal response that was underway, alerting the public to the possibility that an early-warning system in risk locations could be activated and explaining what to do in case of evacuation or floods. The broadcasts emphasized the preparedness of the city via a coordinated response: "All municipal agencies have already met today; some of us spent the night here and we are ready. The teams have been alerted, and those who spent the night here have also expanded their shifts" (COR's director, as interviewed by TV Globo Rio de Janeiro, April 2014).

Since the dramatic rain event of April 2010, Rio de Janeiro has taken significant steps to build preparedness and emergency response. As the director of the city's Civil Defense explained, the COR is the site for the coordination of responses, the location where "all directors of key agencies go to . . . take decisions." In 2011, the municipality prepared a detailed plan of the areas that were prone to landslides, alongside an emergency plan for extreme rain events (Prefeitura Rio de Janeiro 2011). A municipally owned meteorological radar provides images to the city's own weather agency, Alerta Rio, headquartered at the COR, as well as up-to-the-minute information on the specific location and intensity of precipitation over the city (figure 7.9). This is complemented by satellite imagery, as well as data generated by a network of over 130 rain gauges spread across the city and connected to the COR. The city's strategy for emergency response also draws heavily on community involvement, particularly in the many favelas located in areas prone to landslides. The Civil Defense has established a Community Alert and Alarm System for Heavy Rains, operated by local networks of community leaders and volunteers trained to support evacuation efforts (known as *Núcleos Comunitários de Defesa Civil*): an early-warning

Figure 7.9
Screen capture of the COR's website relaying live images generated by the city's meteorological radar, May 2014. *Source:* http://www.centrodeoperacoes.rio.gov.br.

system based on sirens, available, at the time of our fieldwork, in over one hundred communities at-risk. When a state of alert is declared, the system also sends blanket SMS messages to all registered users warning them about hazardous weather conditions, and targeted messages to community leaders and volunteers with requests to organize and prepare their communities.

Over the course of the following forty-eight hours, TV Globo Rio de Janeiro, radio broadcasters, and the COR were in constant contact with the public, reporting the changing weather conditions in the city on an hourly basis (figure 7.10). Viewers were constantly reminded that the city was in a state of alert, yet the broadcasts portrayed a situation that was under close monitoring and control. The public was provided with a clear understanding of both the city's vulnerability and of its preparedness via a broad infrastructural system of emergency response. By Tuesday morning, news anchors were reporting on the disruptions caused by the rain (road accidents, fallen trees, localized flooding) and the immediate response of municipal agencies to restore the city back to normality.

Figure 7.10
Screen capture of TV interviews with COR staff members discussing emergency response actions, April 15, 2014. *Source: Bom Dia Brasil,* TV Globo Rio de Janeiro.

News anchors would make constant references to the COR as the site from where the emergency was being managed; citizens were urged to stay alert, and those living in high-risk areas were asked to prepare for the possibility of evacuation. Using digital mapping techniques and 3-D renderings of the city, news anchors described the city's ecological conditions and also informed the public about the infrastructural tools used to develop such knowledge (especially the network of pluviometric stations distributed across the city and way that the rain gauges work). On that occasion, after hours of deliberation and in order to avoid affecting the credibility of the COR in the eyes of the public, it was decided not to proceed with an evacuation.

Echoing the work of Grusin (2010), where a sense of anticipation is inbuilt in contemporary media operations, the mediated viewing of both the COR and Rio de Janeiro's digitally integrated infrastructures modulates the public's attention. It anticipates the event through a state of alert and builds everyday expectations ahead of the emergency. This "mediality," concerned with modulating the public's affect and aimed at generating a response, acts as a technology of government. Within the COR, the everyday is seen in a state of permanent emergency; urgency is the paradigm driving action. The focus is always the moment, and the aim an immediate response. For staff members, working at the COR is a constant exercise in solving problems in as close as possible to real time. "We work very much on top of what is happening at the moment!" explained a COR directive; "it is a daily exercise in how to solve problems." Framing urban flows as a matter of civic rights, the COR's focus is maintaining the city's flow, its movement, its circulations. Even when the disruption is explicitly political—for example, in the anti–World Cup demonstrations of 2014—maintaining circulation as an operational requirement takes precedence over the very politics that are being made manifest. Despite this, flow maintenance is presented as value-neutral. "We don't want to get into the issues of the demonstrators, whether they're right or wrong," said the COR director in an interview with the *Guardian* (Frey 2014). "For us it's about the rest of the city being able to maintain their routines. We communicate the situation to citizens, and keep the city flowing around the interruption."

The emergency response capabilities, applied to the everyday, rest on a preparedness based on specific forms of logistical control, forecasting and anticipating at the municipal level. In the case of the COR, these are applied specifically to the interface between urban conditions, infrastructural flows, and the city's ecological cycles. This is a logic that extends beyond the COR itself and applies to the broader emergency response systems in the city. A logic of preparedness is embedded into the population via community training programs, evacuation simulations, and mobile communications. The integration of the public as a functional component of the infrastructure also occurs through the deployment of technologies of visibility, enabled by digital technologies, ICT and media involvement, narratives of transparency, and the generation of new viewpoints. New media such as Facebook, Twitter, and smartphone apps establish bidirectional communication between the COR and the public, providing a constant stream of information back to the COR. The COR foregrounds a particular understanding of the city as a space of logistical operations, reducing it to a set of procedural steps within a contained and manageable environment. "The city is a building with six million inhabitants," said the COR's director of operations, referring to the key role played by his staff—highly experienced in operations and logistical systems. "If you know about operations, you will adjust to [operating] here."

Conclusions

Scholars have argued that governing the contemporary world is increasingly an urban endeavor (Braun 2014; Magnusson 2011). Key global processes that are rapidly transforming the world, such as climate change, economic crisis, and the rapid advancement of digital technologies, find significant expressions in cities. Reciprocally, the city is increasingly seen as a primary site of experimentation and intervention, with new modes of governance that incorporate crisis as ubiquitous and disaster as inevitable (Hodson and Marvin 2009; Wakefield and Braun 2014). We argue that the COR illustrates a modality of the Urban OS that is focused on turbulence and its modulation (cf. Cooper 2010). This signals an emerging mode of urban governance in which governing occurs not only through the material (infrastructural) capacities of the city, but also through digitally expanded capacities that modulate time and space while also constituting of new ways of knowing, seeing, acting, and being. The maintenance of circulation plays a key role in overcoming turbulence, modulating fluctuation yet letting things happen, "so that, by connecting up with the very reality of these fluctuations . . . the phenomenon is gradually compensated for, checked, finally limited, and . . . cancelled out" (Foucault 2009, 37). In the context of the coming together of digital systems and urban infrastructures, and within this configuration of urban operating systems, what we see in practice is the constitution of the governing milieu at the crossroads of technology and crisis (Braun 2014; Gabrys 2014; Halpern et al. 2013; O'Grady 2013).

Rio's COR provided an early global template for an emerging digital urbanism. It pilots a particular, but transferable, example of a technology-driven approach to urban integration and control, decidedly influencing how other cities engage with digital technologies, from Curitiba (Prefeitura de Curitiba 2015) to Glasgow (Davies 2014). Through the COR, Rio has also advanced an archetypal, technologically based model of urban resilience, enrolling the Urban OS in the design and development of disaster-risk-reduction strategies and adaptation-driven responses to climate change (see Rockefeller Foundation, n.d.).[9] As a type of Urban OS based on an urban computational logic of circulation, the COR has inaugurated a regime of urban governmentality based on the transmutation of technologies, techniques, and rationalities previously developed for the corporate and logistics sectors. The COR generates new understandings of the city, representing a novel mode of urban infrastructure that is largely based on the partial and selective digital rebundling of networks and urban space.

The COR seeks to integrate two underlying spatial logics. The first is a network logic of logistical control, initially developed in the context of corporate management and integration (discussed in chapter 2) and further expanded within the logistics sector, particularly within the aviation, transportation, freight, and distribution industries (Cowen 2014). These systems are designed to provide real-time, efficient, and effective circulatory flow management under conditions of disruption (political unrest, delay/congestion, adverse weather conditions, and technological failure). They embody particular governing dimensions, tending to reduce agency to procedural effects and to simplify relationships into cross-functional transactions. The second is the nodal logic of the control room, more present in the control of commercial spaces like sports stadiums, shopping centers, and office complexes. This provides a form of territorial control with a mix of flow, safety, maintenance, and incident control. The Urban OS brings together these network (the infrastructure that commands flows) and territorial (the node of control) logics in a new set of techniques and practices for circulation and flow maintenance in the city.

The experience of the COR speaks of the possibility for urban operating systems to make emergency into a major mode of urban existence, and preparedness a mode of urban governance (in line with Collier and Lakoff 2015). The COR is distinctive in the way that it seeks to integrate different modes and rhythms of control that are often separated in conventional typologies of control rooms, bringing together the maintenance of everyday operations and the challenges of dealing with exceptional and emergency situations. It seeks to combine continuous and pervasive twenty-four-hour monitoring of infrastructural network conditions *and* to develop intermittent and discontinuous responses to events that require special control measures to be applied. Echoing the *turbulent worlds* described by Melinda Cooper (2010),[10] such horizontal extension of network and nodal logics across urban infrastructures represents a particular form of operational rebundling aimed at guaranteeing flow maintenance under unpredictable, unsettled conditions.

The extension of such control room logic to the totality of the city is indicative of the emergence of infrastructures into everyday life and public view, something we describe as the *un-black boxing* of infrastructures through digital technologies. This is advanced by the close coupling between crisis response and everyday forms of management, and by media representations of the city and its infrastructures as an ongoing practical accomplishment. The latter reveal the fragility of infrastructural systems, their unstable nature, and the extent to which they require constant work in order to deliver services, which also justifies the ever-alert, ever-on logic of the COR. This signals a departure from dominant forms of infrastructural configuration, problematizing our understanding of infrastructure as stable and black boxed (Graham and Marvin 2001). At stake is, first, a collapse in relations of control of the everyday and the emergency; and, second, the transformation of the relationship between infrastructures and the public, where the public no longer operates as the final receiving end point of the infrastructure network but as an essential functional or operational element. Both processes lead to enhanced levels of awareness of infrastructure and its operations. New logics of infrastructural visibility, alongside the generation of new modes of engaging with infrastructure, denote a different set of capacities and ways of doing.

We need to distinguish between exposure of infrastructure and its management in the way described above and forms of infrastructural "white boxing," in which open-source platforms actively empower citizens to change operational systems (Corsín Jiménez 2014). Far from being progressive and emancipatory, the very visibility provided by digitized and mediatized infrastructures creates new invisibilities. The city's infrastructures are not actually coextensive with the COR; the control room integrates only certain flows and provides only limited and partial public access to these. As the COR directs the city's gaze to particular urban sites and processes, others, both digital and nondigital, go unseen. Social and political analyses of the digitalization of the everyday point to algorithms as an emerging form of black boxing, characterized by an ability to develop forms of social ordering hidden from view and inaccessible decision-making procedures (Gillespie 2014; Rouvroy 2012; see chapter 6). In this sense, the un-black boxing of the city's infrastructures is only partial. Such a novel digital and mediatized infrastructural condition begs asking questions about the rationalities and emerging modes of black boxing that underpin the new forms of urban control embedded within urban operating systems and the forms and types of publics that engage with it (e.g., whether this "smart Rio" works for all or only for a few, a matter of particular relevance in a city where infrastructures historically have been experienced in differential ways, functioning for some while operating in a permanent state of disrepair for others). Is the metropolitan control room, by providing an illusion of movement and action, being used materially and discursively to sidestep attention from critically required interventions?

In developing new ways of experiencing the city, and in un-black boxing infrastructures, the Urban OS brings about an operationalization of the urban, a direct response to what Foucault termed the primary problem of the city—one of circulation. What is at stake is the ability of the city to secure the required exchanges for the reproduction and maintenance of its economy (Foucault 2009). If maintaining flow is seen as an ideal form of urban operation, it is important to recognize that the priority flow is not only the material flow of resources (waste, traffic, water, power, etc.), but also the configuration of information as a key urban resource—one that also needs to keep flowing (see chapter 2). Constant information flow is the new nature of the city, the milieu that has to be created. In a world increasingly governed through a collapse between infrastructure and the environment, where natural processes are not to be stopped but allowed to occur (Braun 2014), the Urban OS naturalizes flow and, through this, the urban imperative of efficiency and productivity.

In being offered the viewpoint of the control room, the citizen, rather than a political subject, becomes an operational component of the infrastructure. Braun draws on Agamben (2009) to argue that these new urban apparatuses (from resilience urbanism to the smart city) "represent the 'eclipse of politics,' that is, the triumph of 'oikonomia' or 'management' as a pure activity of government that aims at nothing other than its own replication" (Braun 2014, 61). The form of governmentality established here, in which the city is managed like a logistical enterprise, does not question the established social or economic order. Instead, it seeks to ensure their maintenance without changing organization, ownership, or orientation. The incorporation of the public within both urban operating systems and infrastructures occurs primarily from the perspective of operationalization. As such, the political agency of the citizen recedes, contributing to what we have described as a digital hollowing of the polis.

8 Resistance? Civic Hacking and an Operating System for Urban Occupation

No resistance as workers backed by 7,000 police clear out community that lasted 75 days, and hardcore protesters wait patiently to be arrested. The occupied site in Admiralty was cleared without resistance or any visible scuffles yesterday in a police operation that was described by a watchdog as "smooth and peaceful." Last night, authorities were still working to return blocked roads to the way they were in late September before the "umbrella movement" for democracy erupted. The colourful tents that once lined Harcourt Road—the busiest in the city centre—the creative banners and artworks that enlivened the space, the assorted chairs and beds, and the people who were behind it all—were gone after a day-long operation by police and bailiffs. . . .

The clearance ended the 75-day lifespan of a vibrant community equipped with a supply station, study area, workshop, and first-aid centre. The operation started officially at 9am, when about 50 workers, several bailiffs and lawyer Paul Tse Wai-chun—representing company All China Express—descended on the site and notified protesters about their enforcement of a High Court injunction granted to the cross-border bus operator. Tse warned protesters that resistance would leave them liable to contempt of court. The workers then started the demolition process, breaking the cement that glued barriers to the road surface at four locations. . . . Everything that the protesters once treasured, but was in the way of the officers, was eventually crane-lifted onto trucks. At least 10 trucks were working to remove the materials. . . . And in just a few minutes, a supply station and workshop that was once covered by another yellow umbrella was reduced to a pile of debris.

—*South China Morning Post* (Chan et al. 2014)

The end of the Hong Kong Umbrella Movement was based on a high court order obtained by a bus company to reopen infrastructural connections through protest sites (figure 8.1). Over the course of seventy-nine days, the

Figure 8.1
Hong Kong's Police clear roads in the Admiralty site of the Umbrella Movement
(December 11, 2014). Photo courtesy of the *South China Morning Post*.

three protest sites of Admiralty, Causeway Bay, and Mong Kok immobilized critical transport communications along key strategic routes through the city—seriously disrupting economic activity and the infrastructural rhythms of everyday life. Like many other contemporary protest movements, Hong Kong's Umbrella Movement provides an example of the ways in which ICT and digital platforms are reshaping the nature of political protest. Local protesters employed a bricolage of digital systems, some proprietary, others created by civic hackers specifically for the movement. They used these to organize themselves and to communicate, both with each other and with a much wider international audience. However, those participating in the Umbrella Movement also needed more conventional forms of infrastructural support, such as water, logistics, shelter, and waste removal, in order to sustain their occupation.

In this chapter, we examine the Umbrella Movement's mobilization of a variety of digital systems, platforms, and technologies to support urban protest and to operationalize protest sites, and we interrogate the configuration of an Urban OS in the context of resistance. We draw on a conventional conceptualization of resistance as "organized opposition to a particular configuration of power relations" (Hughes 2019, 1)[1] to explore the role of computational logics in forms of urban protest that are characterized by spatial occupation, flow disruption, and the creation of contested urban spaces. Our aim is twofold. First, we want to examine how digital technologies are being repurposed by political movements, in this case providing an operating system to enhance communications and coordinate the everyday logistics necessary to maintain an occupation. Second, we seek to identify the key tensions and critical contradictions involved in thinking about forms of Urban OS aimed at supporting contemporary forms of political protest. In particular, we assess the balance between the protesters' use of a loose, collaborative, and multiplatform infrastructure of digital systems and their continued reliance on the more traditional, nondigital infrastructural configurations of the city, such as energy, water, logistics, and waste flow management. This leads us to question the somewhat grandiose claims often made about the emancipatory potential of digital technologies, drawing attention to the critical limitations of digital tools to support grounded, material, and sustained modes of resistance.

Empirically, in this chapter we delineate the wide collection of digital technologies used by protesters in Hong Kong's Umbrella Movement, considering both digital platforms and systems that preexisted the occupation (e.g., Facebook, WhatsApp, Firechat), as well as platforms purposefully designed for the occupation itself. We investigate linked groups of civic hackers in Hong Kong and Taipei, as there are important connections between Taiwan's Sunflower Movement (March 18, 2014–April 10, 2014) and Hong Kong's Umbrella Movement (September 28, 2014–December 15, 2014). In both protests, organizations involved in digital activism deployed a suite of digital tools to more effectively manage and coordinate both communications and the everyday logistical requirements of occupation—an Urban OS that, as we demonstrate, operated alongside more traditional (yet pop-up) water, energy, waste management, logistics, and other infrastructural facilities aimed at supporting the occupation on the ground.

In contrast to the configurations of Urban OS examined in the previous chapter, the prodemocracy protests of 2014 in Hong Kong and Taipei illustrate a different sociotechnical configuration. In Hong Kong, civic hackers developed a digital platform that, operating in real time, shared information about the protest (e.g., police presence, media coverage, maps, levels of provisions) and sought to support the coordination of issues of logistics and supply chains. Developed with the support of Taiwanese civic hackers, this platform was arguably a new digital infrastructure of urban protest. Like other cases described throughout the chapters, this is a system designed to provide infrastructural coordination and governance at city scale (see particularly chapters 2 and 7). Yet there are three significant differences. First, Hong Kong's Urban OS for resistance was made of a complex and heterogeneous bricolage of stakeholders, digital practices, and existing and new technologies that were continually (re)assembled, repurposed, and revised. Second, it was produced by protesters themselves, who embraced a role as logistics coordinators and technology providers working in coalition with a range of actors within civil society. Third, the prime motivation for the Hong Kong protesters was to enable new infrastructural circulations that sought to *disrupt* (rather than *optimize*) conventional urban flows. The resulting Urban OS was aimed at supporting capacity for the immobilization of parts of the city's road network and its economy.

However, we seek to avoid making grandiose claims about the significance of this Urban OS for resistance within the Hong Kong Umbrella Movement. Instead, we argue that it played a relatively minor role in the movement when compared to other, nondigital forms of knowledge, flow, and expertise. The chapter locates the analysis within the wider literature on the links between digital technologies and occupy movements around the world and discuss the benefits and pitfalls of digital technologies in support of urban protest. We show the extent to which, despite the support of a range of digital systems, the occupation in practice relied to a large extent on social and physical networks operating in and around the protest site—both in person and through the traditional material flows of the city rather than via digital processes for coordination. The emerging digital operating system of occupation showcased a range of vulnerabilities inhibiting its operations, from being highly sensitive to issues of trust and susceptible to monitoring and surveillance from security forces, to a frailness associated to a lack of other resource flows, particularly energy. The chapter thus is about both alternative mobilizations and the very limits of digital interventions, foregrounding a condition wherein the rhetoric of transformation associated with digital urbanism coexists with the limits imposed by the materiality of the city (understood in its more traditional sense).

Computational Technologies Come to the Aid of Protest

December 2010 saw a spike in political unrest in cities across the globe. That month marked the beginning of the Arab Spring in Tunisia, a series of protests that quickly led to the ousting of President Zine El Abidine Ben Ali. By February 2011, the unrest had made its mark in Egypt, with protests in Cairo's Tahir Square bringing an end to Hosni Mubarak's regime. Over the course of two years, the Arab Spring produced two civil wars and the overthrow of six governments. In May 2011, thousands of inhabitants of Madrid took to the streets to protest against austerity measures, kick-starting the 15-M Movement. In New York City, Occupy Wall Street (OWS), started in Zuccotti Park on September 17, 2011, inspired a wave of Occupy movements in over thirty-five other North American cities. Despite their many differences, all of these protests have one thing in common: they rely heavily on social media and new digital technologies.

New ICT tools and digital technologies are reshaping modes of political protest in significant ways. Social media platforms (e.g., Twitter, Facebook, YouTube, Weibo, WeChat, and blogs) have helped to define "a new global protest politics" (Bennett 2003, 143). They enable a form of collective action that mobilizes rapidly, underpinned by nontraditional information flows and an ability to form broad and loose social networks despite weak social identities (Bennett 2003; Bimber, Flanagin, and Stohl 2005). Although some critics argue that the role of the internet in political activism is overstated (Gladwell 2010; Morozov 2011), since the early 2000s new ICTs have complemented face-to-face interactions in support of political protest (Juris 2005; Nielsen 2013). Writing in the context of Egypt and Tunisia, for example, Howard and Hussain (2011) argue that social media provided those interested in democracy with an appropriate set of tools for building networks of supporters, organizing and mobilizing direct action, shaping public debate, hosting political conversations, and spreading the word across international borders. Twitter played a major role in Occupy movements, allowing messages to be rapidly circulated to a "geographically dispersed, networked counter public that can articulate a critique of power outside the parameters of mainstream media" (Penney and Dadas 2014, 74;

see also Tremayne 2014; for an analysis of the role of Facebook, see Gaby and Caren 2012). Scholars argue that the additionality that social media offer for political protest lies in its impact on the mobilization of people: a more effective gathering of crowds via what is known as *aggregation*. As Juris argues, social media's advantage lies in "getting large numbers of individuals to converge in protest at particular physical locations. Rather than generating organizational networks, these tools primarily link and help stitch together interpersonal networks, facilitating the mass aggregation of individuals within concrete locales through viral communication flows" (Juris 2012, 267; see also Molnár 2014 on flash mobs). The role of social media and new ICTs in prodemocracy movements is of particular importance in authoritarian regimes, it has been argued, as they enable information flows that escape the control of the state by mobilizing a trusted network of friends (Howard and Hussain 2011; Tufekci and Wilson 2012).

Of course, the use of ICTs and digital technologies in support of protests also has limitations and contradictions. People's agglomerations at protest sites are often ephemeral, leading only to temporary mobilizations (Conover et al. 2013; Juris 2012). The dependence on platforms leaves protesters vulnerable to the corporations that control them and to state agents with the ability to limit or survey them (Etling, Faris, and Palfrey 2010; Morozov 2009; Palfrey, Etling, and Faris 2009; Penney and Dadas 2014). Such tools also create the risk of excluding those who have no internet access or social network profiles (Nielsen 2013). Finally, digital records create traceable vulnerabilities (Juris 2005), potentially leading to legal action against platforms themselves, as well as their users (Howard et al. 2011). Fuchs (2014) has analyzed social media use in the Occupy movements and identifies conflicted feelings and a strong awareness of contradiction in protesters' use of commercial (corporate and privately owned) versus alternative (self-managed and commons-based) social media. Given these limitations, it is not surprising that some critics have asked "whether or not the internet can bring about a new form of political activism" (Fenton 2008, 233; see also Fenton 2016).

Beyond social media and digital technologies, a missing dimension in the analysis of networked infrastructures within contemporary forms of political protest is an examination of the role of life-support services in maintaining occupations: water and energy networks, waste management, shelter, and food, as well as education and health. An exception is the architect Reinhold Martin, whose work reflects on the requirements of urban occupation within the built environment, including infrastructural services. Reflecting on the Occupy Wall Street movement, Martin charts the ways in which protesters struggled to deal with a series of physical and material issues, from winter weather and spatial organization to shelter provision, health services, and all manner of infrastructure services. In his view, police and municipal authorities sought to push life on the site into a "permanent state of emergency," making repeated attempts to clear the encampment on account of its lack of "hygiene" and removing electricity generators after classifying them as "fire hazards." In response, the protesters developed a kind of improvised expertise, drawing upon long-standing lessons from movements resisting the destruction of public housing and denouncing the inadequacy of health services and education, developing a "model of how to live, both in microcosm and macrocosm" under adverse political and weather conditions (Martin 2011). Similarly, Michael Ralph, academic and activist in a range of Occupy activities, has shown the extent to which traditional infrastructures are not simply vital for the occupation, but also a material and symbolic means for a "society of mutual aid" to emerge both within and outside the occupation site (Bauer and Ralph, n.d.). Ralph argues that these infrastructural responses challenge neoliberal urban priorities, while Martin concludes that such responses might provide models of possible worlds offering new forms of shelter and living together. Unfortunately, these transformational understandings of infrastructure did not prevent authorities in New York City from removing Occupy's Zuccotti Park encampment on the grounds that it posed a threat to health and safety. This chapter seeks to add to these debates as it investigates the tensions between different forms of networked infrastructure and the limitations of digital systems in support of political protest.

Transnational Hackers and the Digital Infrastructures of Resistance

Like with other urban protests of the last decade, social media and digital systems played a role in supporting the 2014 prodemocracy movement in Hong Kong. In late September of 2014, various student and civic organizations in the city started protesting against Beijing's decision to limit universal suffrage in Hong Kong. The previous month, the National People's Congress Standing Committee (NPCSC) of China had established a set of

Figure 8.2
The Admiralty protest site in Hong Kong, December 2014. *Source:* Andrés Luque-Ayala and Simon Marvin.

proposed reforms to the Hong Kong electoral system, ruling itself as the nominating body for candidates aspiring to the position of Hong Kong chief executive. According to the rule, the chief executive would be appointed by the Central People's Government following a popular vote on a narrow list put together by the NPCSC. Many of those living in Hong Kong saw this a direct threat to free and fair elections and as a loss of autonomy and democratic freedoms. This gave birth to the Umbrella Movement and its occupation of three sites within the city (Admiralty, Causeway Bay, and Mong Kok; figure 8.2). The movement linked various organizations with similar aims, including Scholarism, the Hong Kong Federation of Students, and Occupy Central with Love and Peace.

Social media was key for the circulation of information about the protests and, through this, the mobilization of (and coordination between) protesters and organizations. Researchers at the Chinese University of Hong Kong suggest that digital media, by providing a platform for online alternative media and through their ability to connect social activists and critical journalists, contributed significantly to the formation of a counter-public that was favorably inclined toward democracy and critical toward both the Chinese and Hong Kong governments (Lee 2015; Lee, Chen, and Chan 2017; Lee, So, and Leung 2015). Hong Kong boasts a high-quality digital infrastructure, with strong 4G broadband cellular network coverage in nearly every corner of its urban area and around seventeen million mobile phone subscribers (about 2.3 subscriptions per inhabitant; Dingle 2014; GovHK 2016). This everyday and everyplace connectivity is complemented by one of the highest average broadband speeds and one of the highest fixed broadband penetration rates in the world (Chun-ho 2017; Economist 2016; King, n.d.). Unsurprisingly, this enabled protesters to use digital spaces as active and privileged sites for advancing their cause. As reported by the online media news outlet Quartz, "The Umbrella Revolution, may be the most high-tech protest ever, using wireless broadband, multimedia smartphones, drone film making, mobile video projectors, and live streaming video to communicate and to broadcast their cause to the entire world in real time. The victor in this conflict will be determined by who holds the streets, and who rules the digital space" (Lih 2014).

Indeed, the Umbrella Movement led to an explosion of digital activity and social media accounts. A sample of Hong Kong residents across various age groups showed that Facebook was the third main source of news about the protest, following Television Broadcasts Ltd. (TVB) and the independent and prodemocracy newspaper *Apple Daily*. Of those who used Facebook to access news, 62.1 percent supported the movement, compared to 37.9 percent who didn't (Lee, So, and Leung 2015). Between September and December 2014, Facebook pages related to the movement proliferated, offering communication platforms to hundreds of social causes that supported the occupation—with titles as diverse as Teachers in Solidarity with Student Strike, Umbrella Parents, Non Standard Civil Servants, Fluid Occupiers, Umbrella Groupbuy, Police Violence Database in Umbrella Movement, and the Umbrella Movement Visual Archive. The *Wall Street Journal* reported over 1.3 million tweets about the protest over its initial days, from September 26 to October 1 (Pope-Chappell 2014). YouTube became a popular platform not only for circulating news and footage of the occupation, but particularly for the circulation of music videos and protest songs in its support (Rühlig 2016). Surveys of protesters indicate an "empowering effect of digital media," pointing out that those who "engaged in digital media activities more frequently were involved in the movement more deeply: they spent more time in the occupied areas, were more likely to have mobilized others to participate, and were more active in both frontline activism and support provision" (Lee and Chan 2016, 17).[2]

Instant messaging was particularly used by protesters. Their favored platform was the Facebook-owned WhatsApp, but they also relied heavily on the cloud-based instant-messaging app Telegram, which they argued possessed better encryption capabilities. At the height of the protests, media outlets reported that the messaging application Firechat was being downloaded over one hundred thousand times every twenty-four hours (Dingle 2014; Grasty 2017; Meyer 2014). Firechat avoids the internet and does not rely on external Wi-Fi or 3G/4G mobile networks. Instead, it provides peer-to-peer connectivity via Bluetooth or the internal Wi-Fi capabilities of mobile phones, creating highly localized and temporary *mesh networks*. This means that Firechat can continue providing communication capabilities when mobile networks are down, which frequently happened during the protests, when thousands of protesters were out on the streets using their mobile phones at the same time.[3]

Developers produced a number of purpose-built apps and games for the protest. Google Play hosted applications such as To Praise/Compliment Hongkongese Police, which matched a police agent's ID number with their name so that users could "praise the police whenever [they] want" (figure 8.3). The Yellow Umbrella app, one of many social aggregation engines, provided real-time updates by gathering Twitter hashtags or RSS feeds from key organizations involved in the protest. A smartphone game with the same title locates cartoon-like protesters behind barricades, reliving the events of the evening of September 28, when police fired tear gas at protesters (figure 8.4).[4] A digital art project, *Stand by You: "Add Oil" Machine*, crowd-sourced messages of support from around the world via a purposefully developed website. The project projected these messages onto a large wall on the Admiralty occupation site in order to inspire those resisting there (figure 8.5). By the end of November, *Rolling Stone* magazine reported that over thirty thousand messages from seventy countries had been displayed (Kreps 2014), including messages from Peter Gabriel and Pussy Riot, among other celebrities.

Figure 8.3
Screen capture of the To Praise/Compliment Hongkongese Police mobile phone app, as advertised in Google Play in December 2014. *Source:* https://play.google.com.

Figure 8.4
Screen capture of the Yellow Umbrella smartphone game, as advertised in Google Play in December 2014. *Source:* https://play.google.com.

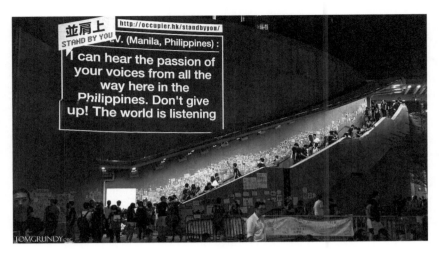

Figure 8.5
Crowdsourced messages of support to the Umbrella Movement, displayed by *Stand by You: "Add Oil" Machine* on the Admiralty site, Hong Kong, October 2014. Photo courtesy of the *Hong Kong Free Press*.

Hacking across Taiwan and Hong Kong

In late September 2014, as the occupation movement in Hong Kong took shape following a night of tear gas in Hong Kong's Admiralty district, civic hackers in Hong Kong and across the world began putting in place a digital communications infrastructure for the protest. They drew on work and practices developed by Taiwanese civic hackers six months earlier during the Sunflower Movement (a protest against a free trade agreement between Taiwan and China; figure 8.6). Grouped around a loose organization called g0v.tw (https://g0v.tw/en-US/), the Taiwanese hackers already had experience with organizing a basic digital infrastructure for resistance. They livestreamed the occupation of the Taiwan Legislative Yuan and coordinated information sharing and crowdsourcing in support of the protests (Daybreak Editor 2017; O'Flaherty 2018). They developed basic technical support for the movement, enabling internet connectivity and Wi-Fi and coordinating online updates. Most significantly, they mobilized the Hackfoldr platform (hackfoldr.org) in support of the protest, providing a template for *g0v.today*, a purpose-built digital platform in support of the Sunflower Movement. In this way, created by one of the founders of g0v. tw and originally designed to "organize many dynamic documents before

Figure 8.6
Occupation of Taiwan's Legislative Yuan, as part of the Sunflower Movement in Taipei, April 2014. Photo courtesy of Ian Rowen.

and during [a] hackathon" (GitHub 2016), Hackfoldr became the basis
for a publicly accessible digital space that supported Taiwan's protest. The
g0v.today platform consolidated the multiple information and discussion streams developed by the protesters of the Sunflower Movement,
aggregated news and articles from international media, and provided
easy access to nearly twenty live video feeds streaming the occupation
(V. Chao 2014; Coca 2016; Jacomet, Hsuan, and Kao 2017; Roubini and
Tashea 2014).

Its developers describe Hackfoldr as an information aggregator software,
linking various types of digital documents and files from different sources
(from Facebook links and Google Docs files to video streams) in a single
platform. This is an important capability at times of protest and one that
quickly migrated from Taiwan to Hong Kong. As a Hackfoldr developer
involved in the Sunflower Movement told us: "When the [protest] happened in Hong Kong then it is natural; they started to use this software

to organize all the info; critical information like what's happening where, and do people need something somewhere, and then livestreams for every corner." When the Hong Kong protests began, civic hackers who had been involved in g0v.tw joined a group of counterparts in Hong Kong called Code4HK (http://www.code4.hk) to collaborate via the GitHub platform. Together, they created a digital platform for the Hong Kong protests, filling an immediate need for information flows. As one of the developers explained: "I was in [Europe] the night this happened. [The protesters] had to, in minimum time . . . have an accurate mapping of where actually the concentrated areas are, and what are the rumors and what are the facts."

In line with the values of civic hackers in other parts of the world (see chapter 3), there were arguably two key motivations for hackers affiliated with the Taiwanese g0v.tw to support Hong Kong's Umbrella Movement: transparency and connectivity. g0v.tw sought to provide an infrastructure of communication and deliberation, aimed at consensus building. Despite its direct actions in support of protests, the group publicly claims to explicitly avoid aligning itself with a given political position. For g0v.tw, digital communication is a basic infrastructure that cuts across political interests. The driving principle, in its view, was not to support the protest itself, but to support the *possibility* of transparency and communication, regardless of the political viewpoints at stake. The group viewed digital communication as a life-support service and positioned it as a type of neutral intervention, akin to humanitarian work. As one interviewee explained, this work could be used to help those protesting against the government, but also to assist those who are protesting against the occupation itself: "Because to us . . . communication is no less than, say, the right to medical support . . . [these are] people who work on communication freedom."

The today.code4.hk Platform: An Operating System for the Occupation

The collaboration between Taiwanese and Hong Kongese civic hackers led to today.code4.hk, a comprehensive online platform aimed at supporting the prodemocracy movement in Hong Kong (figure 8.7). The platform was primarily developed by civic hackers within Code4HK, a group that takes inspiration from the North American civic-tech organization Code for America, and whose motto is "Drive social changes by code." The today.code4.hk platform was a data and information portal that could

Figure 8.7
Screen capture of the home screen of today.code4.hk, December 2014. *Source:* http://today.code4.hk.

consolidate communications within a highly decentralized protest movement. Its objective was to provide both protesters and the public with information so that they could deliberate and make informed decisions. In the
view of its creators: "We try to get all kinds of information sources together,
so that people can decide when they should go, and where they should go,
and what kind of support [to provide]." This almost naïve desire for neutrality underpinned by communication and information freedom fully aligns
with common narratives within the IT world assigning a special power to
transparency and open data flows (chapters 3 and 4). In practice, however,
it is a position that drives attention away from the specific political aims of
the protest and acknowledges the difficult conditions within which such
hackers operate in the context of the relationship between mainland China
and Hong Kong. Still, today.code4.hk aimed to be an operating system for
the occupation so that the protest could be (temporarily) stabilized as it
sought to disrupt conventional urban circulations. It achieved this through
a digital and open-source style of infrastructural management, providing
a control network that could support information and logistical flows in
locations where this was previously absent. This allowed new demands to
be matched to supply and created new distributional channels to support
metabolic flows in and out of protest sites.

The today.code4.hk platform is an infrastructure of connectivity and logistical coordination; a system of systems made of various interconnected platforms, which operate thanks to the crowdsourcing of information flows. Through an ecosystem of digital platforms, it works as an operating system to coordinate supplies, services, and information flows to and from the space of the protest. All platforms involved in today.code4.hk are open source—from GitHub, the original coding platform that enabled civic hackers around the globe to cooperate, to Google Sheets and Google Maps. The system also makes direct use of Gitter (a chatroom popular with developers; https://gitter.im), TimeMapper (http://timemapper.okfnlabs.org), and Hackpad (a web-based collaborative text editor).[5] To distribute information, today.code4.hk could redirect users to various livestream channels (e.g., via livestream.com) or social media accounts. Through a combination of cloud-based computing, the segmentation of functions, interconnected media content, and spreadsheets, folders, and subfolders, the protest site is conceived through the lens of a computer system. Open source, open access, and open data—as the practical expressions of narratives around openness and transparency—underpin the functioning of this mini digital city.

Figure 8.7 shows the home screen of the final stabilized package. The Hackfoldr interface, in the left-hand column, allows the system to consolidate in a single screen a range of data streams and information flows. The opening screen focuses the viewer's attention on four key functionalities, each represented by a purpose-designed icon: video live streaming of protest sites, live occupation maps, news, and requests for supplies for the protest. The video live streaming section was linked to feeds from both traditional and independent media, while the maps section connected to Google Maps displaying the boundaries of the protest sites and relevant annotations, including the location of local rest stops, supply centers, health facilities, protesters, police, and others (figure 8.8). The news function was based on the open-source web mapping application TimeMapper, developed by the Open Knowledge Foundation, which provided a user-friendly and detailed summary of older and more recent news about the protest, mapped in both time and space (figure 8.9).

Behind the main interface lay a Google Sheets spreadsheet listing hundreds of URLs. These linked to websites and to digital repositories housing key information for the protest (figure 8.10). These included Hackpad

Figure 8.8

Screen capture of the Google Maps interface of today.code4.hk from December 2014, showing a range of facilities and police presence at the Mong Kok protest site, making a call to users to keep updating the map. Text on the bottom-left corner, translated from Mandarin: "Please help update the police force, road closure, traffic arrangements, first aid station, material station, shelter, toilet, garbage collection point, etc. Thank you!" Translation of key: *Demonstration area/police line of defense:* disbanded, police line, occupied area, small police presence, other/no data; *Supplies, first aid, rest and recycling stations:* emergency, support point, material station, recycle bin; *Others:* convenience store, magistrates' court; *Water machine/toilet:* WC, drinking fountain. *Source:* http://today.code4.hk.

documents with titles such as "Resistance Must Knows," report forms to be used in case of arrest or injury, and links to social media accounts offering free services and support to protesters (e.g., via Facebook), alternative and mainstream media outlets, and key Instagram and Twitter accounts. The information was functionally organized by folders that collated resources in one place: news and broadcasting, video channels, Facebook organizations, police and violence monitoring, boycott campaigns, arts initiatives, sports activities, educational activities, and even recommended shopping practices, among others.

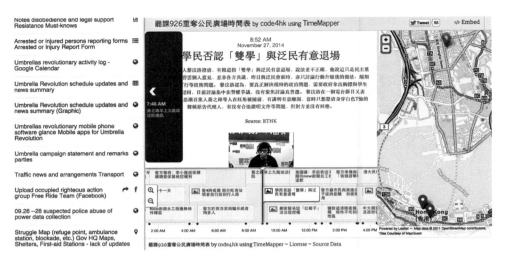

Figure 8.9
Screen capture of the TimeMapper interface of today.code4.hk, providing a historic account of key events mapped against an OpenStreetMap base, December 2014. *Source:* http://today.code4.hk.

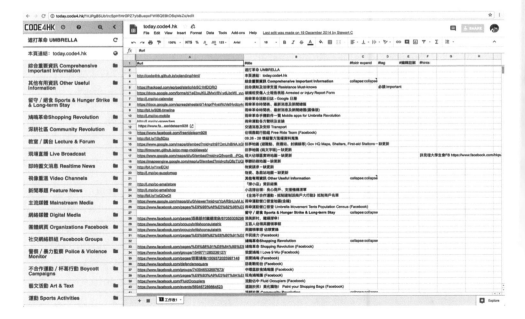

Figure 8.10
Screen capture of a Google Sheets spreadsheet listing URLs linked by the today. code4.hk platform, December 2014. *Source:* http://today.code4.hk.

The final key functionality of the platform, dealing with flows of supplies, was designed to organize the logistical and infrastructural requirements of the Umbrella Movement. It identified needs and directed the provision of water, food, tents, health supplies, and other material resources, as well as services such as legal and medical expertise. In the words of one of the creators of the system, "We need to know . . . how to distribute, how to use the resources, how to allocate how many people in this place, and how many people in [each protest site]; some kind of communication [system] for people to join the campaign." Through a form of collective, open, transparent, and decentralized intelligence, this digital logistics structure sought to broadcast protest needs to the wider population, asking for inputs of material resources and specific expertise at particular sites. It also sought to identify specific resource stations to gather these resources and to monitor stock and recirculate surplus between resource stations to better match needs. This modulation in the circulation of resources, matching supply and demand over time and space (amounts, excess/shortage), substantiates a desire to develop an ability to intervene at points of crisis (i.e., when under pressure from the police), either materially or informationally.

The entire system, as an open-source platform for logistical management, worked via crowdsourced information, offering anybody the ability to access the master documents and add information or make requests. We are told by a member of Code4HK, "The first version was . . . just a simple spreadsheet. . . . People kept editing it, they got their own thoughts, [and] at some point it becomes a chatroom." It evolved incrementally over time, gaining complexity as more people used it. The same principles applied to the digital maps of the occupation, which were updated by volunteers in Google Maps and built over preexisting open data sources (e.g., government sources).

Transparency and openness within the platform were not seen simply as passive ideological principles, but as an active defense weapon. In the words of the platform's creators, "All the things are open, that's why people get into [the system]. . . . We should keep this group open because that is our biggest tool, our biggest weapon to fight back . . . because if we keep everything open people know what we did and what we didn't." Yet such openness made the resulting Urban OS vulnerable to attack. Over the course of the occupation, the content of the logistics feature of the system was deleted on various occasions, and conflicts over its content eventually led to careful moderation by the system's creators.

Overall, despite playing an important role in raising the profile of the protest, digital infrastructures were significantly constrained in their ability to support the occupation on the ground. As we shall see in the next pages, the strength of the occupation came from a rather different way of mobilizing networked infrastructures.

Life Support: The Material Obduracy of Urban Occupation

The everyday experience of protesters across all sites revealed the materiality of protest and its engagement with a broad range of traditional infrastructures. Despite the sophistication of today.code4hk, it became clear to us during fieldwork that the digital platform was not really used systematically or consistently by protesters. At the occupation sites we never met any protester using the platform. A number of protesters who knew the protest sites well and were significantly involved did not even know of its existence. Our queries about it were met with puzzlement and surprise, at times followed by a positive statement about the extent to which such a type of system would indeed be useful.

When it comes to urban technologies, it was not so much the digital infrastructures that made the Hong Kong Umbrella Movement stand out, but its onsite infrastructures of occupation and the high level of social organization achieved via face-to-face encounters. At the time, a number of media commentators noted that the protesters were using highly effective on-the-ground organizational, logistical, and infrastructural systems. "Though nobody is in charge, Umbrella Square and the two other tent communities run as well as anything else in this city of 7.2 million," reported *Time Magazine* (Barber 2014a). Similarly, Reuters described how "teams of volunteers pick up rubbish and litter, even sorting it for recycling. Supplies of food and water are organized in neat stockpiles along the edges of the main traffic arteries in the center of Hong Kong. And the demonstrators, who are blocking key roads, obediently part for ambulances and emergency vehicles" (Lague, Pomfret, and Torode 2014). The movement put in place improvised yet sophisticated (and, at times, experimental) systems for logistics and resourcing, sanitation, recycling, food provision, first aid, and energy provision. Using planning and decentralized control practices, they covered all the main elements of life support needed for an extended occupation of the city. The Umbrella Movement thus reconstituted the city within protest sites, creating a mirror image of the very urban world it was trying to disrupt. It was effective at providing the infrastructural support necessary to sustain the immobilization of the city. This infrastructural response, achieved with little recourse to digital systems, generated the necessary capacity to ensure that material resources and metabolic flows of energy, food, and extraction of wastes could be provided to support the occupation—in other words, a type of support needed to overcome the material hardships associated with temporarily occupying public space and maintaining the protest for seventy-nine days. Examining these more material forms of infrastructural response in detail sheds light on the significant limits that digital infra- structures face when supporting extended occupation. Central to this is the vulnerability of digital systems to a lack of other resource flows (particularly energy) and the importance of informal and face-to-face contact in coordi- nating infrastructural resourcing and service provision.

Parasitic Infrastructures: A Microcosm of the Host City

To recap, despite the occupation's intent to disrupt the city's flows, its pres- ence depended on a range of infrastructures that enabled life support for those protesting. For the protest to achieve success, it needed to replicate, in ad hoc and improvisatory forms, the support systems of the city, often working with existing systems in the infrastructural landscape of Hong Kong. Critically, this meant that protesters often stretched preexisting infrastructures to gain material support for their targeted acts of immo- bilization. In this sense, their response had a parasitic quality: it had to develop adaptable, transient, and exploitative relationships with existing infrastructure, forcing it to work for them. To achieve this, they used forms of interception, substitution, distribution, intensification, cleansing, and logistical coordination.

The Umbrella Movement focused on three historically and symbolically important sites in key areas of Hong Kong: the dense, traditional market area of Mong Kok; the business and government center of Admiralty; and the high-end shopping district of Causeway Bay. In each of these sites, protesters disrupted transport infrastructure, immobilizing circulations through demonstrations that became more obdurate as they constructed tented cities, surrounding them with barricades to prevent their removal by the authorities (figure 8.11). Over time, they produced a form of temporary urbanism, creating a spatially and socially organized space serviced through

Figure 8.11
Tented city at the Admiralty site of Hong Kong's Umbrella Movement, December 2014. *Source:* Andrés Luque-Ayala and Simon Marvin.

a complex arrangement of material infrastructures. Sites were characterized by the following sociospatial features (figures 8.12–8.15):

- Protesters occupied road space and footpaths at the ground level, using existing footbridges to position banners and as temporary stages for meetings and events.

- Protesters created extensive tented areas and other temporary structures that were used for a range of activities: domestic and sleeping spaces, study spaces, areas for storing and distributing resources, recycling points, first aid zones, locations providing legal advice, and even art and educational spaces. These were carefully managed through mapping, occasional sequential numbering, and standardized spatial layouts.

- Protesters enclosed the perimeter of the occupation sites with barricades, protecting themselves from eviction by the police and security forces, yet also allowing some degree of entry and egress for their fellow campers, visitors, and representatives from the media. This also allowed the operation of resource supply chains and the removal of wastes.

Figure 8.12
Tent numbering system, tented city at the Admiralty site of Hong Kong's Umbrella Movement, December 2014. *Source:* Andrés Luque-Ayala and Simon Marvin.

Figure 8.13
Map of the Admiralty protest site at the exit of one of the city's Mass Transit Railway stations detailing key infrastructural facilities, December 2014. *Source:* Andrés Luque-Ayala and Simon Marvin.

Figure 8.14
Admiralty site of Hong Kong's Umbrella Movement, December 2014. *Source:* Andrés
Luque-Ayala and Simon Marvin.

Figure 8.15
Student library at the Admiralty site of Hong Kong's Umbrella Movement, December
2014. *Source:* Andrés Luque-Ayala and Simon Marvin.

These forms of temporary urbanism were critically dependent on infrastructure flows and networks. Reliable municipal electricity networks provided light via the traditional street-lighting system, while nearby shops allowed protesters to use their electricity for the purpose of charging laptops and mobile phones. Small electricity generators provided crucial electricity for powering the protests' sound systems. A network of water fountains, carefully mapped by protesters, provided drinking water. A preexisting network of public restrooms gained a new relevance in the context of the protest, becoming an effective strategy for sanitation. In some cases, protesters had access to public showers and organized volunteer cleaning rotas, and even free toiletries. Access to toilets and showers was supplemented by sympathetic local businesses, shops, restaurants, and nearby residents. Protesters arranged the removal of wastes and litter as part of an explicit strategy to ensure that the site was kept clean and tidy, and even organized recycling points (figure 8.16). First aid stations provided basic medical support. Legal advice stations were staffed by volunteers with legal knowledge, providing advice on what to do if arrested by the police, while study centers aimed at high school students enabled teenagers to continue their studies. For a short period of time, mail could be delivered to tents, as some of the tents were carefully numbered and marked on a map.

Finally, activists developed a decentralized yet highly sophisticated logistics strategy, with abundant and largely autonomous supply stations distributed across protest sites. These stocked and distributed tents, camping equipment, drinking water, packaged food, plastic cups, kitchen rolls, and so on (figures 8.17 and 8.18). These supplies were dispensed for free, according to need, to anybody who asked. Established ad hoc by many of the organizations supporting the protest, these resource stations functioned in a fairly organic way. There was a level of communications between them, with the *China Daily* reporting that different groups of volunteers "coordinate with nearby stations via runners, redistributing water, food and materials to where they are needed" (Chui 2014).

All of these material resources and flows were required to stabilize the blockage and interruption of the city's critical infrastructural transport flows in the occupied areas (cars, buses, and trams, as well as road-based distribution and logistical systems), largely bringing flows and many aspects of economic life to a standstill. These tented cities were described by a journalist at *Time Magazine* as a "microcosm of the city that hosts it," with the

Figure 8.16
Recycling station at the Admiralty site of Hong Kong's Umbrella Movement, December 2014. *Source:* Andrés Luque-Ayala and Simon Marvin.

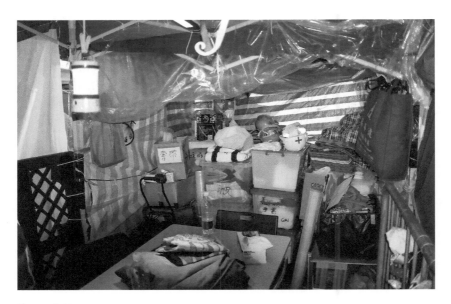

Figure 8.17
Resource station at the Admiralty site of Hong Kong's Umbrella Movement, December 2014. *Source:* Andrés Luque-Ayala and Simon Marvin.

Figure 8.18
Resource station at the Admiralty site of Hong Kong's Umbrella Movement, December 2014. *Source:* Andrés Luque-Ayala and Simon Marvin.

exception that it had no form of central command (Barber 2014b). The occupation sites clearly had many of the features of the existing sociomaterial character of Hong Kong: shelter, education facilities, services, and infrastructure. Like with many other functions in the protest, coordination among volunteers would involve a mixture of face-to-face conversation and social media messaging, particularly via WhatsApp and Telegram, but never the sophistication of a digital platform of platforms such as today.code4.hk.

The Limits of Digital Protest

Shortly after the beginning of the protest, the *frontline* developed: a core of protesters whose presence was more permanent than sporadic and who played active roles in creating and maintaining the barricades that sheltered protest sites from the police. For them, onsite communications did not occur by digital means. As one protester explained to us, the main communication tool for those with a permanent presence onsite was "a whistle . . . otherwise we would be walking." Cycle couriers who could deliver messages quickly within a protest site were also popular. In the view of the same interviewee, on the "frontline you don't rely on that much of technology." Partly, this was a matter of logistics; anybody staying within the protest sites for twenty-four to thirty-six hours or more experienced problems with mobile phone technology: short battery life, clogged 4G networks at critical times, and serious concerns about digital surveillance. Communications at the frontline were based instead on face-to-face contact, building on the trust that developed through relationships of friendship and camaraderie formed within protest sites.

The frontline also proved to be unreceptive to attempts to roll out digital practices on site. A group of civic hackers opened a technology-based tent, the Tech Tent @ Harcourt Road, within the Admiralty protest site. Familiar with the broad context and network of today.code4.hk, the hackers' objective was to create a space for onsite coding, bringing digital skills and practices to the occupation (figure 8.19). After securing an independent energy source (an electricity generator purchased over the internet through crowdsourced funding), they sought to create a public Wi-Fi hotspot by

---

Figure 8.19
Screen capture of the (a) Facebook page and (b) announcements of the Tech Tent @ Harcourt Road, November 2014. *Source:* https://facebook.com.

Tech Tent @ Harcourt Road
🔒 Closed group

About
Discussion
Chats
Members
Events
Photos

Search this group

Shortcuts

Joined ▾   ✔ Notifications   ➤ Share   ⋯ More

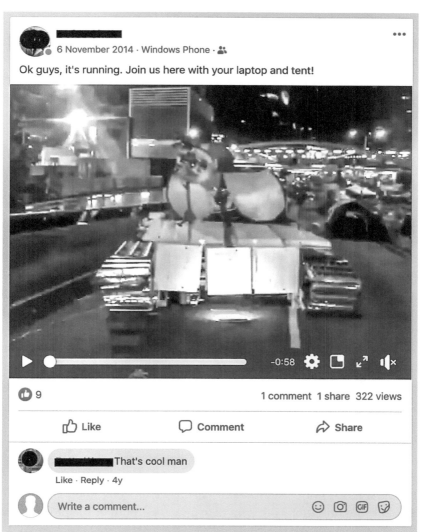

6 November 2014 · Windows Phone · 👥

Ok guys, it's running. Join us here with your laptop and tent!

▶   ───────────────────   -0:58 ⚙ 🔲 ↗ 🔇

👍 9   1 comment   1 share   322 views

👍 Like   💬 Comment   ➤ Share

That's cool man
Like · Reply · 4y

Write a comment...   🙂 📷 GIF 🏷

sharing (tethering) the internet connection of a mobile phone connected to the 4G network. "There's nothing much [we need]; a generator, we need power, we need internet, that's all the things we need for [an] IT person to work," said one of the organizers. Yet, the Tech Tent operation lasted no more than a couple of weeks. Using a mobile phone to supply internet connectivity to a laptop proved impractical as Wi-Fi "takes up your battery. Batteries are very important for us to communicate. When we are arrested for anything, we need a mobile phone to make calls to lawyers. . . . So, we need to reserve the battery." Mobile phones would also play a role in communicating with friends and family outside the protest. As a result, for those spending long periods of time within the occupation site, prioritizing how to use the batteries of their mobile phones was a necessity. Furthermore, the 4G connectivity available onsite was not robust enough for working on the cloud, significantly impeding any type of coding work. This was to be expected given the fact that the mobile network regularly clogged up due to the large concentration of protesters and visitors using it at the same time. "The internet kind of dies when you have like a few hundred to a thousand people sitting in the same location. So the internet infrastructure wasn't that strong to support everyone using the internet."

Finally, heavy rains damaged the electricity generator, which was difficult to run anyway, given that gasoline had to be smuggled in, a risky operation as the site was often surrounded by police. Even before the breakdown of the generator, our interviewee had come to the conclusion that there were more urgent and practical uses for energy than laptops, such as providing a hot drink or recharging phones so that protesters could call family and friends. In his words, "A few days were actually very cold; people were actually thinking that with a generator they can boil hot water, which is what other people think is more important and some people think that they need to charge a phone . . . they have families, they need to call back home and say they're still safe . . . At the beginning I didn't think of the generator to be used this way, but I changed my idea."

Conclusions

Digital technologies undoubtedly play a significant role in enabling contemporary forms of protest. As the experience of Hong Kong has shown, digital communications can help raise awareness both of the protest itself and of the political cause it advances—at local, national, and international levels. This can mobilize global support for a form of spatially bounded occupation. Digital communications via social media were also key in supporting the aggregation of protesters, organizing existing groups, and enticing unknown strangers to commit to a common cause. As the Umbrella Movement turned into an occupation, digital communications still played a role in supporting the coordination of activities among protesters, despite obvious shortcomings associated with the fact that such technologies enable forms of monitoring and surveillance from security forces.[6] To some degree, digital flows facilitated the material flows needed to sustain the occupation. This occurred primarily through social media channels, messaging services, and platforms such as Facebook, Twitter, WhatsApp, and YouTube. Operating in tandem with other nontraditional media (including games, purpose-built apps, and a range of specialist platforms), this digital ecology can be seen as an emerging Urban OS for protest: a bricolage of digital operating systems that are used to support a political cause.

However, as we have argued, the role of digital technology in enabling protest can be overstated. Digital systems in contemporary political protest need to be qualified and read within specific spatial contexts and operations. They cannot be understood as operating outside of the material realm of the city but are instead intertwined with the material conditions of specific protests in specific sites. The immobilization advanced by contemporary forms of occupation relies on physical bodies on the street, and from that perspective it depends on the various forms of life support that enable living on the streets. This is the material obduracy of urban occupation. The recent hype about the role of digital tools within contemporary forms of protest can be flawed, as the immobilization advanced by forms of occupation relies primarily on material infrastructures and flows and not digital ones.

As illustrated by the failure of today.code4.hk, the specialist platform created for the Umbrella Movement, in practice the occupation relied to a large extent on social and physical infrastructural networks operating in and around the protest site. Digital technologies, subject to constant interference and interception, proved to be brittle, hackable, vulnerable, not particularly secure, and, most importantly, overly reliant on basic flows of limited resources, such as energy. It was the remobilization of the traditional material flows of the city in support of the protest, rather than any form of datafication or digital coordination, that sustained the protest for seventy-nine days. However, to be clear, we are not trying to propose or endorse a simple dichotomy of digital versus material infrastructures, whereby the power of digital systems stop as they encounter the material world. Protesters were never trying to produce an exclusively digital or an exclusively material intervention. Rather, it's the way digital and material infrastructures intertwine—both productively and imposing limitations on each other—that is interesting. In creating relationships between the two, the protest draws attention to a politics of infrastructure that the computational logics of the Urban OS often hide.

Perhaps it is not ironic that, in the specific case of the Umbrella Movement, it was eventually a court order in support of a bus operator that reestablished the status quo. Here, the maintenance of urban circulation (see chapter 7) took precedence over the political right to protest disruptively. On December 1, 2014, Hong Kong's high court ruled in favor of the All China Express bus company, allowing bailiffs "to 'request the assistance of police' where necessary in order to clear the [protest] site" (ABC News 2014). For the court, the occupation infringed on the public's right to use the public highway in a lawful, legitimate, and reasonable manner: "No one can possibly claim a monopoly of using the public highway in total disregard of the interests of his fellow citizens, no matter how honorable or noble his cause may be. That is so even if the right to demonstration or assembly as guaranteed by the Basic Law is engaged" (High Court of the Hong Kong Special Administrative Region 2014). Ten days later, on December 11, the clearance process began at the Admiralty site. A temporary infrastructural logic of occupation and resistance was swept away, legitimated by a logic that saw the continuation of urban circulation as paramount. This "more-than-digital" circulatory politics in the city reminds us that those who define the priorities of infrastructural flows, and those who have the ability to meaningfully reshape them in the metropolitan context (turn on/off, disrupt, filter, etc.), hold an important political power.

9 Conclusion: The Urban OS as a Political Technology

Any objects or persons can be reasonably thought of in terms of disassembly and reassembly. . . . No objects, spaces, or bodies are sacred in themselves; any component can be interfaced with any other if the proper standard, the proper code, can be constructed for processing signals in a common language. Exchange in this world transcends the universal translation effected by capitalist markets that Marx analyzed so well.

—Donna Haraway, writing on the informatics of domination (Haraway 1985, 81–82)

Over the last eight chapters, we have explored the Urban OS in detail, looking at the way that it engages in processes of datafication, sensing, mapping, prediction, and circulation management, and also its reinvention for the purpose of resistance. The Urban OS that emerges from our study is much more than a single, commercial software product. It is a logic of control that aims to fragment, re-assemble, and recalculate the city and its material infrastructures. It comprises a diverse set of evolving computational ecosystems, which often share an underlying approach to urban problems, a range of objects and practices (from sensors and control rooms to hackathons and open platforms), and a variety of stakeholders (including businesses, public organizations, IT professionals, civic technologists, data activists, and community groups, among many others). Together, these make up a sociotechnical process that reshapes the city in a way that transcends the aims of its makers. In doing so, it advances a particular configuration of the city primarily focused on the possibility and practice of calculability, based on the digitization of urban flows and on transmutations from logistics, corporate, and at times military domains to urban contexts. The city is reenvisioned as a simplified and integrated space of functionality, capable of constant reengineering and reconfigurability. This IT-inspired reading of the world sees the city as analogous to a digitally enabled corporate enterprise, with complex, uncoordinated, and disconnected systems of systems in need of integration and coordination. All of this is aimed at enhancing efficiency, modulating turbulence, and ensuring predictability.

From the outset, we sought to understand how the Urban OS acts as a political technology, changing the ways in which cities are governed. We drew inspiration from history, using the works of Joyce (2003) and Otter (2007) to build on the idea that the earlier, nineteenth-century development of urban technologies (networked infrastructures) embodied a new way of governing the urban. Arguing that this remains the case in our contemporary cities, we explored how the Urban OS is changing existing configurations of power and governance. Using Osborne and Rose's (1999) suggestion that forms of governing are territorialized thorough diagrams of power, we argued that the Urban OS is a diagram that imposes a new set of power relations on the city (cf. Deleuze and Guattari 2004). The diagram, as a postrepresentational analytical device, works as an abstract machine, producing a new kind of reality. It "does not function to represent, even something real, but rather constructs a real that is yet to come, a new type of reality" (Deleuze and Guattari 2004, 157). Like previous urban diagrams, such as the nineteenth-century sanitary city (Rabinow 1995) or the twentieth-century zoned city (Holston 1989; Scott 1998), it imposes ways of conceiving and governing the urban.

Our analysis shows how the Urban OS, functioning as an emerging diagram of power, inscribes particular ways of seeing the city—framing relationships and anticipating a changed material future through remaking connections and disconnections. We united this insight to a series of concepts drawn from Foucault, particularly governmentality, to identify the manifold transformations that are occurring at the interface between digital technology and urban worlds, demonstrating how logics of thought become embedded in technical means (cf. Dean 2010) in order to create an indirect mode of rule. While many scholarly accounts of the effects of digital technologies in cities foreground their disciplinary and surveillance dimensions, for us, a wider governmentality approach opens the possibility to analyze digital urban technologies as a subtle mechanism of power—one that operates "through the freedom or capacities of the governed" (Dean

2010, 23), enabling a "government *through* and *by* technology" (Otter 2007, 578; original emphasis).

Our broad motivation in writing this book was to understand how these forms of digital technology are reshaping urban governance and whether—and if so, how—they are transforming urban flows. We therefore undertook an in-depth empirical analysis of the role of urban operating systems in a range of contemporary cities, with a view to abstracting out the logics and rationalities that their techniques deploy. There were three sets of core objectives associated with our aims.

First, we wanted to understand where the Urban OS has come from, to provide a historical and material account of its emergence. This involved revisiting computational systems originally developed outside the urban context but which operated as antecedents to urban applications; and, in examining the resulting transmutation, looking at the frictional effects of what is contested or resisted.

Second, we wanted to examine the ways by which this recasting of the urban, operating through an emerging logic of quantification and computation, not only advances specific ways of knowing the city but also remakes the city in particular ways. Our analysis shows the Urban OS as an onto-epistemological process of knowing and shaping the world through numeric and calculative ways of thinking, which, beyond simply advancing computation as a privileged form of decision-making, is generative of urban forms, flows, and processes. Quantification and computation enable the mobilization of new circuits of accumulation, woven through capital, land, and infrastructure via a process of datafication and digital control. It results in, among others, a new generation of human subjects that are infrastructuralized through their capacity to sense and transmit data, working alongside datafied infrastructural flows through which data is embodied in material substance. This inquiry involved looking at how and why selective elements of the urban context are dis- and re-assembled, as well as a consideration of the effects that this has in how power and politics operate within the city. The effect is reductive: the Urban OS is generative of a city that only makes sense if counted.

Finally, we wanted to examine the way in which the resulting computational logics of the urban depoliticize the city via efficiency and operationalization. This at times reproduces business as usual and prevents progressive urban transformations; at other times, it advances radical transformations toward the implementation of new logics of capital. When it comes to power, we argued, the Urban OS acts as a relay device, translating a mechanism of power into a function, in a way that collapses the boundaries between governing intent, techniques of action, and material technologies (cf. Deleuze and Guattari 2004; Knoespel 2001). The means of governing offered by the Urban OS thus soon becomes an end in itself, as the normalization of processes of datafication and circulation are quickly mobilized for the maintenance of the status quo. What we set to achieve here is an analysis of an emerging form of political economy for the city based on an encounter with the digital. We examine these three core objectives in more detail in the following sections.

The (Problematic) Making of the Computational City

Our starting point has been to reinsert the often-ignored history of the computational city back into contemporary debates about the "radically transformative" and "completely novel" digital or smart city. In chapters 1 and 2, contrasting popular narratives that foreground novelty and innovation, we were able to place the Urban OS in a much longer-run set of efforts by coalitions of state and corporate interests—spanning over sixty years—to subject the city to the discipline of computational systems. We charted how computers became a key tool for understanding the city from the postwar period onward, exploring repeated attempts to apply computational ways of thinking developed by the military to urban decision-making in US cities (Light 2002, 2003). Although initial efforts were relatively short-lived and failed to deliver on their promises, the eventual development of ERP technology in the 1980s for the management of corporate processes represents an important predecessor of the Urban OS.

The 2000s marked a new era, as IT corporates began to see cities as a destination market for their complex and costly computational products. In the emerging form of IT urbanism, computers have provided a powerful analogy for how we conceptualize and envision the city. As products originally developed to support digitally enabled corporations began to be translated into the urban context, city administrators began to see computation and calculation as a powerful, effective, efficient, and relevant decision-making mechanism for cities. Optimistic "smart city" narratives gained purchase across the world, as IT corporations, the civic tech sector, and cash-strapped cities argued that this technocratic way of viewing city management and development could provide a more efficient and effective means to manage the urban. This privileged and preeminent mode of configuring the urban context comes at the exclusion of other modes of control—social values, participatory perspectives, local knowledges, and even professional expertise, among others.

This book carefully subjects the totalizing and universal vision of the Urban OS to critical scrutiny. We contrast the vision of the integrated Urban OS provided by the producers of these computational products with the much more problematic and messy landscape produced by its partial and selective implementation in emblematic urban sites. In table 9.1, we compare the claims of the totalizing vision, set out in chapter 2, with the messy practice of the Urban OS, as revealed in chapters 3 to 8. This comparison reveals significant dissonances.

Our analysis has revealed that the Urban OS has largely failed to achieve the claims that its advocates have made on its behalf. It has not transformed the city into a totally unified and integrated entity; instead, digital systems put in place multiple limitations in achieving integration across the huge diversity of urban processes and domains that make up what we collectively experience as "the city." The Urban OS has not and cannot

Table 9.1
The Urban OS as a diagram of control: comparing vision and practice

(Totalizing) vision	Urban OS	(Messy) practice
Universal integration of the whole urban context	**System of systems**	Practice of selective/partial forms of integration
Unbundling of the city into homogenous layers	**Unbundling strata**	Partial practices and multiple sites of selective sorting
The urban CPU; single site of technically mediated control	**Control capacity**	Multiple sites of control through new technocrats
Single comprehensive and transparent data set for city advancing a neutral approach	**Data flows**	Multiple data sites of exclusive channels already imbued with ideology requiring a range of data production and cleaning practices
Comprehensive process of metropolitan dis-/re-assembly from one site	**Dis- and re-assembly**	Multiple sites of sociospatial selectivity and targeted dis-/re-assembly

provide a *single* site of technologically mediated control, and there is not a *single* dataset through which we can come to understand the urban. What has tended to happen is the development of a series of different but interoperable computational products, networked together into diverse ecosystems. These individual products are built through a range of practices and broader networks of knowledge and technology, in the fragmented and loosely connected actions of civic hackers (chapter 3); in the multiple companies and municipal agencies attempting to interconnect dispersed digital technologies such as urban sensors (chapter 4); or on the technoideological hotchpotch behind the various attempts to digitally map or predict the urban (chapters 5 and 6). Even in examples such as Rio de Janeiro's Operations Center (chapter 7), which initially looks like a comprehensive and all-encompassing digitally enabled control room, the resulting Urban OS is selective, focusing on particular flows and sites in the city.

The Quantified City: Knowing and Reshaping the City

We have shown that the many techniques and technologies of the Urban OS share ways of imagining and encountering the urban world. The underlying rationale for this process is the epistemic logic of quantitative calculation. We analyzed the process in detail through our examination of distinctive elements within seven urban computational logics: operationalization, datafication, sensing, mapping, prediction, circulation, and resistance.

The first, and perhaps most important, of these logics is *operationalization*, or the attempt to define urban variables through measurable factors. The resulting epistemology of the urban is calculative, numeric, tightly quantified, and highly standardized. The multiplicity of urban flows is broken into standardized units that are dictated by the need to regiment and divide space and time in datasets. The fragmented city, now reconceptualized as datasets, can then be recombined and reconstituted in new ways, a process that also opens the digital and material management of urban infrastructures to new forms of value and investment. Operationalization, examined in chapter 2, supports the workings of all of the remaining computational logics discussed in the book. This microtemporal and microgeographical fragmentation of flow into data points enables the precise targeting required for an informatics of domination. However, the claim that all urban flows and processes can be quantified, and in this way become commensurable, has implications beyond epistemology. The power of recombining urban processes and flows into new flows, processes, and bodies is generative of urban form and therefore ontogenetic. Recalling the words of Donna Haraway at the beginning of this chapter, the city has been technodigested, reconceptualized, and remade by this process, as the Urban OS engenders a new generation of digital/material infrastructures, both digital and corporeal, co-constituted through the affordances of each other: what we have termed, drawing on Michel Dillon's (2003) analysis of digital technologies, an *intelligence incarnate of the urban*; an onto-epistemic form of knowing that takes bodily form, and an urban infrastructure that is always already co-constituted with digital technologies.

Datafication: From Recombination to New Embodiments

Datafication, the becoming of data as the primary urban flow that underpins all urban computational logics, endows the Urban OS with a set of specific powers. In knowing and making the urban through numbers, the urban computational logic of datafication creates the potential for a new type of city: a city-in-formation that is always amenable to dis- and re-assembly, recombination, flexibility, and mutability. This is the city as a machine of interoperability. As we explored in chapter 3, through our analysis of open data platforms in New York, the Urban OS constitutes data as a key urban flow that underpins a new type of utility: data-as-infrastructure. The capability to render what was previously obdurate, hidden, or inaccessible as configurable and flexible through data is mobilized not only to overcome urban challenges (via optimization and efficiency), but also to create new urban materialities, economic circuits, and customized services.

What we see in the mobilization of data in the city is *"the translation of the world into a problem of coding"* (Haraway 1985, 83; original emphasis): the imposition of a common language that subjects city life to instrumental control. Here, heterogeneity is no longer (political) difference, but a prerequisite for standardization and thus a fundamental input for the establishment of a new mode of digital control. Datafication, as a form of translation, is inevitably a hegemonic practice, imposing a particular language and, through this, particular orderings and understandings of the world (Machen 2018). With data as the language of translation and the means for dis-assembly, re-assembly, investment, and exchange, the Urban OS puts in place a space where "particular decision choices are naturalized and the possibility for alternatives denied" (Machen 2018, 14).

A critical insight of our analysis of data-as-infrastructure is the embodied nature of urban data. As data lines flow in the city, arguably as binary/digital types of (im)materiality, they are reconstituted as urban flows encapsulating a multiplicity of urban materialities. Data and its urban footprint, as the primary flow of the contemporary information society, is not simply a digital and immaterial abstraction of urban processes and flows. As an urban flow, data has its own materiality. Its power comes not from its digital nature, but from its ability to materialize, attaching itself to material flows and through this engendering a new nature of flow. Electricity flows are no longer made of electrons; now they are made of electrons *and* data. Water flows are no longer made solely of water molecules, but water molecules *and* data. Transport and waste flows are no longer made of vehicles, pedestrians, refuse, and litter, but of these *and* data. This form of embodiment, as engendering intelligence incarnate, is related to the new (nondigital) materialities of data as much as to the emergence of "carnal" bodies in the city's infrastructures. Datafication in the city heralds a reconfiguration of the boundary between infrastructure and the public (as discussed in chapters 4 and 7), where people and organizations become an essential component of the infrastructure. From a "sensing citizen" and Waze's crowdsourcing of transport flows to the civic hacking community acting as an infrastructure incarnate, data-as-infrastructure, as a new corporeal flow yet seemingly without body, is underpinned by social bodies and the sociotechnical reconfiguration of all other infrastructural flows.

This intelligence incarnate of the urban, achieved through the application of computational logics to the city's flows, speaks of a new material body that inscribes information onto other bodies. As insightfully pointed in Jennifer Gabrys's work, the entities created by data, sensors, mapping, and calculation are not simply detached objects. They are processes that subsume experience and relations; they get entangled in generative processes and relations, giving birth to a new set of bodies-in-formation. Their generative power has a politics in its own right, establishing what matters flow and what experience matters; transforming the politics that unfold by advancing "particular ways of 'possessing'—and making—worlds" (Gabrys 2016, 253).[1] This is a way of signaling to the entangled embodiments and potential power reconfigurations at stake in the digital transformation of urban flows. In what Gabrys (2016) calls "interoperable streams of data," digital sensors transmute flow into data and vice versa; they create common languages (what Dillon [2003, 124] calls a "capacity to tell signs") and, through this, embody bodies with information. For us, here lies both ontology and ontogenesis within urban computational logics, from datafication to sensing: this is not simply about generating entities and environments (cf. Gabrys 2016), but about transmuting toward calculative sites and bodies that, regardless of difference, operate on the same ontological plane—that of calculability. And here also lie some of the politics of the digital city. A politics that is epistemological (as new forms of knowing are at stake), ontogenetic (in engendering new forms of being), and relational (by instilling calculation as a privileged form of generative interaction).

Sensing, Mapping and Prediction: Expanding the Horizons of Accumulation

As we discovered in Barcelona, digitally *sensing*, as a new technology for governing the urban, transforms the sites of value creation of the city. In effect, it creates new forms of value through engendering digital assets—an accelerated form of commodification of the urban through digital hyperfragmentation. Chapter 4 discussed how sensing transforms potential into action, resulting from the digitization of all things urban. The sensor (and its platform) is the body that translates and mediates between the material domains of the city and their digitization, *embodying* the informational diagrammatic characteristic of the Urban OS. Embodying the coming together of urban flows and data, sensors are critical for the formation of new corporealities. They transform flows into datasets, playing a key role in the Urban OS's ability to dis- and re-assemble urban circulations. In effect, it is a strategy to render calculative intelligibility across urban processes, providing the technomaterial substrate for an urban economy based on data flows. The resulting flows remake the material foundations of value generation in cities, complementing traditional forms of value embedded within land and resources with forms of value that emerge from the flow of incarnated urban information.

Through the urban computational logic of *mapping*, discussed in chapter 5, the Urban OS interacts in complex ways with territory and sovereignty. Our analysis of a project by Google Maps to map favelas in Rio de Janeiro uncovered the coming together of space and the business database—a calculative practice that does not simply represent space but produces a territorial formation that prioritizes economic flow over social or political logics. Here digital mapping, rather than simply representing space, remakes territory through recalculation. In the case of favelas, digital advocates have boasted of the power of digital maps to establish citizenship and providing inclusion, breaking down the wall that separates these unmapped areas from the rest of the city. Our argument challenges this assumption, pointing to the ways in which the problems and aspirations of the entire community are reduced to a series of economic potentialities. Such digitization of territory recasts what a *point of interest* is, emphasizing entrepreneurial sites and narratives as the primary loci of activity of the city. Google's digital map paves the way for digitally mediated exchanges between local and global economic flows. Rather than breaking down the wall, the digital map opens a gap in order to secure calculability. Like a census, the power of digital mapping is exerted through techniques of enumeration, its aim to ensure that all sectors of the city can be incorporated into broader economic circuits. The exercise of this power recreates the political spatiality that characterizes territory: still in constant dialogue with (and depending on) preexisting sovereign powers (from the state, to militias or drug-trafficking networks), digital mapping signals to a relocation of sovereignty in the hands of the informational corporation—a claim that draws not only on the latter's assertion to possess an ability to suspend a condition of exception (e.g., limited rights, exclusion, or lack of citizenship), but also from its practice of counting, enumerating, and directing data flows.

Our fieldwork in Chicago suggested that space and time in datafied forms are the key common denominators in the re-assembly of the computational city. Examining the urban computational logic of *prediction* (via predictive analytics platforms), chapter 6 explained how a translation of time-space into data formats enables interoperability across seemingly disconnected urban domains. This occurs through the recombination of three distinct datasets: spatial coordinates recorded by a GIS system, time intervals associated with urban events, and the city's databases that over decades have recorded urban transactions (i.e., crime, taxation, service provision, citizen complaints, etc.). In the first instance, the recombination of urban transactions (as recorded within traditional municipal databases) is underpinned by spatial coordinates acting as the linking element for all transactions (in other words, acting as a common denominator for disconnected urban processes). The addition of tightly defined time intervals (T1, T2, T3, etc.) allows for calculating the urban across time. Both steps foreground the extent to which urban prediction is ingrained with a fragmented understanding of the city. Urban prediction prioritizes short-term, operational temporalities (where accuracy is more likely to be achieved), not the longer-term horizons much needed for urban planning. Critically, prediction tends to reinforce the socioeconomic conditions of the status quo: rather than being transformative, it is performative, giving rise to the very future that it anticipates (cf. De Goede and Randalls 2009) and in this way reproducing the city and its existing inequalities. As a computational logic that historically evolved from targeting practices, urban prediction justifies the establishment of differential strategies for controlling and governing different areas or neighborhoods of the city—potentially mobilizing a "known," yet nonexistent, future to discriminate against areas with what is deemed as "problematic" profiles.

Circulation and Resistance: Losing the City's Politics to Logistical Efficiency
The Urban OS also seeks to put in place new forms of circulatory control with the aim of maintaining efficient and effective flow under conditions of ecological, political, or social turbulence (cf. Cooper 2010). Chapter 7 examined *circulation* as an urban computational logic and its reframing of the city as a logistical enterprise—by looking at the case of Rio de Janeiro's Operations Center (the *Centro de Operações Rio*, or COR). Here, through digitally enabled control rooms, dashboards, and institutional integration, new understandings of the city are being developed, representing a new mode of urban infrastructure based on the partial and selective rebundling of splintered networks and fragmented urban space. The COR operates through an "un-black boxing" of urban infrastructures, wherein the extension of control room logics to the totality of the city (where the public, via traditional and digital media, is given continuous access to infrastructural operations) points to the fragility of urban infrastructures and the continuous effort involved in their operational accomplishment. It also functions through a collapse in forms of control of the everyday and the emergency, where the city is increasingly imagined as a place that is constantly in a fragile state of imminent emergency. This, alongside the incorporation of the public in infrastructural management via digital tools (e.g., social media, apps, others), further raises public awareness of urban infrastructures. These characteristics point to a specific form of urban governmentality based on the operationalization of infrastructural flows and the development of

novel ways of seeing and engaging with the city. The form of governmentality established by the COR, where the city is managed like a logistical enterprise, does not question established orders. Instead, it seeks to ensure their maintenance without changing organization, ownership, or orientation. In being offered the viewpoint of the control room, the citizen, rather than a political subject, becomes an operational component of the infrastructure.

The final urban computational logic examined in the book is *resistance*, or the possibility and significance of supporting political protest via a mashup of digital urban systems. Looking at the 2014 Hong Kong Umbrella Movement, chapter 8 examines how contemporary forms of urban protest based on spatial occupation mobilize digital systems to garner public support, as well as coordinate logistics, spatial analysis, media coverage, provisions, and infrastructure supply. The analysis showed how, despite the mobilization of a range of digital systems, urban occupation relies primarily on in-person exchanges as well as physical and material networks, rather than digital processes for coordination. Beyond an initial wave of critical support provided by social media for the purpose of public support, crowd gathering, and agglomeration, the long-term occupation of space characteristic of contemporary urban protest relies on traditional urban flows (e.g., energy, potable water) and a temporary infrastructure for the occupation itself (via, e.g., sanitation and logistics). In this context, the power of computation is relatively limited. Hong Kong's Umbrella Movement mobilized an impressive array of digital systems, including purpose-built, real-time digital platforms. However, this emerging and informal Urban OS in support of the protest played a minor role when compared to other forms of nondigital knowledge, flows, and expertise. The material obduracy of urban occupation resisted and challenged the power of the Urban OS: contemporary urban protest based on occupation relies on human bodies on the streets and infrastructural forms that provide life support. This analysis illustrates a more-than-digital circulatory politics in the city, where who defines the priorities of material infrastructural flows and who has the ability to meaningfully reshape them in the metropolitan context (turn on/off, disrupt, filter, etc.) is contested both online and offline, through digital and nondigital means. Resistance through and to the Urban OS is not just based on logistical efficiency but also draws on different rationalities, including the politicization of urban space.

The seven urban computational logics that we have identified in this book produce three interlinked processes. First, they tend toward a rationalization of public services, where the city is modeled after an idealized, efficient, and highly integrated corporate entity. The utopian promise of the Urban OS is the capture of an infrastructural totality in the city in real time, yet to achieve this, computational logics subordinate urban flows to a standardized, calculative form that not only excludes large swathes of urban experience but also enables infrastructures to be subdivided in new ways, creating a newly digital form of splintered urbanism (cf. Graham and Marvin 2001). Second, and leading on from this, computational logics create new penetration points for capital within public infrastructures and services, disaggregating elements within flows and commodifying them in new economic circuits. This can lead to new types of political and economic territorialization, as space is reconfigured via market logics. Third, the Urban OS extends forms of "emergency" management to the city's everyday context, an emerging strategy to secure the city by maintaining economic configurations and preserve the flows of business as usual through infrastructural flows. Underneath a veneer of openness and transparency, this does not fundamentally transform modes of ownership and control of infrastructure; rather, it adds layers of opacity in the shape of a series of underlying, invisible, and uninterrogated assumptions that shape the data.

Depoliticizing the City through Operationalization

Unrestrained, and through the idealization of its own narrow epistemology, the Urban OS lead to *a digital hollowing of the polis*: the absence of politics and the takeover of circulatory management. Our final contribution is to assess the implications of the Urban OS for urban life and the future of urbanism. Are they transformative, developing entirely new ways of living? Or are they much more modest, in primarily enabling the continuation of business as usual? Here we explore further some of the dimensions of the computational logics discussed in previous pages, which, we argue, raise critical limits about the potential for progressive transformation.

The first issue is the rather *exclusive coalition of societal interests* that have constituted the city as a test bed for computational urbanism. Across our case studies, we find that the software and hardware industry, internet and social media companies, national innovation agencies, technology entrepreneurs, and municipal agencies predominate. The tech sector has sought to reconstitute the urban context as a significant new market for software and technical products, and in doing so has sought to reinvent the city as a computer. Even where we have sought out examples of "nonstandard" urban operating systems, with the most emblematic cases discussed by us being those designed by civic hackers in the context of prodemocracy movements in Taiwan and Hong Kong (chapter 8), we have struggled to find a meaningful involvement of communities and stakeholders who are not defined by their relationship with the IT sector or by a desire to mobilize technology toward economic growth. Particularly, we struggled to find substantive involvement from marginalized communities or from those who, in one way or another, inhabit the periphery of either city or society. Of course, there are plenty of exceptions to this, from art collectives engaging digital technologies to reimagine the city and concerned professionals finding ways to use the skills of the civic hacker in support of social causes, to social collectives and data journalism organizations in low-income neighborhoods mobilizing data to visibilize their political voice. But these are outliers, and their absence within the dominant landscape speaks to the direction of travel of the past two decades. Computational urbanism is, then, characterized by a rather exclusive coalition of social interests in which we find only a limited number of voices making the case for different ecological conditions, social equity, and just cities.

Urban computational logics also advance a *techno-managerial focus*. Within this computational city, only urban processes amenable to quantification count; only issues amenable to numeric calculation can become the focus of concern and intervention; and only things amenable to datafication matter within this understanding of the urban context. Yet complex urban challenges—like social injustice, land struggles, racial discrimination, gender inequality, and ecological sustainability—easily fall outside of these criteria and could therefore not be registered by computational logics, nor be a subject of action within it. Alongside *data*, these problems need *narratives* to convey their political substance and wider context. They generally require longer-term forms of intervention than those enabled by a narrow logic of calculation. Given the origins of the Urban OS in computational systems developed to render corporate entities more predictable, manageable, and efficient, it is not surprising that such systems have a relatively narrow focus. Urban operating systems treat the city as a digitally enabled corporate entity and seek to reproduce the same rationalities and priorities. This places a premium on the maintenance of operations, small productivity gains, identifying new economic opportunities, finding underutilized resources, searching for value, and creating new commercial services. While the search for operational efficiencies in urban services and the maintenance of circulation under turbulent conditions are sensible and valuable aims, these are not transformative; instead, they seek to ensure the maintenance of business as usual.

We find the priority given by the Urban OS to forms of calculation that allocate a key role to data and its manipulation as a technique for understanding urban life and material flows deeply problematic. The data-based epistemologies of the Urban OS advance a *limited understanding of the urban and its futures*. They conceptualize the city in a set of standardized ways, while putting in place a series of closed loops that define how decision-makers encounter and access the information they require to achieve a set of narrowly defined goals. This mode of engagement excludes other ways of knowing the city, such as experiential, collective, deliberative, tacit, and even certain types of professional knowledge and expertise. Computational logics thus impose a simplified form of transactional mechanics on the urban context (hierarchical control, automation, prediction, and sensing) as a substitute for human agency. They prioritize a view of the city as always amenable to a kind of tweakable customization; a mode of urban control that continuously aims to dis- and re-assemble the urban context in ever more precise ways. Despite claims of transformation and change, by making the urban into a technical matter, the Urban OS reduces flexibility and curtails transformative and radical possibilities for the future.

Our work has striven to move beyond simple dichotomies that contrast bottom-up and top-down technological configurations of the city. Avoiding common juxtapositions of dominant versus alternative interventions, we have argued that the progressive potential of digital urbanism is likely to emerge only through processes that subject its modes of calculation to scrutiny and question the very epistemological underpinnings of computation. We hope that we have made progress toward this goal in this book. As we have shown, digital systems are already fully enmeshed, entangled, and embedded in the control and mediation of urban life. Their further intensification and acceleration into new forms of Urban OS is inescapable (via, e.g., their extension into artificial intelligence, automation, and robotics).

The key question is not whether digital urbanisms can or should be contested, but to understand their limitations, contradictions, and potentials more clearly, continuously interrogating the rather utopian claims.

We believe that researchers have a key role to play in questioning computational urbanisms. In particular, there are three critical areas in which more work is needed. First, we must unpack the hidden assumptions of computational logics, along with developing an in-depth understanding of the history, rationalities, and systemic qualities underpinning the Urban OS. This will allow us to draw attention to the exclusions, presumptions, and blind spots of these systems. It should also help us build a challenge to the claims that computation constitutes a more efficient and effective form of decision-making, pointing to its short-term temporal horizon, its lack of strategic and transformative long-term ambitions, and its inattentiveness to issues of justice, equity, inclusivity, and ecological degradation. Second, we must question and resist international efforts to accelerate the implementation of computational logics in our cities, challenging continued attempts to both homogenize and reshape urban contexts to better match the presumptions of computational systems. These technological imaginaries, mobilized via interventions such as standard-setting and universal systems of data ontologies, have a power of their own and are shaping how limited urban resources are being prioritized and used. Third, we must insist on the need for highlighting difference and contrast from and to computational logics, bringing in other forms of knowledge and expertise within urban decision-making, celebrating narrative, and recognizing the importance of values and deliberation in informing urban priorities. Politics, in its agonistic forms, needs to be seen as playing an important role in keeping open a more strategic and longer-term set of priorities for the city. Our concern is that a singular mode of decision-making is exclusive and narrow, in terms of both the professional expertise it foregrounds (new urban technocrats) and the forms of knowledge it privileges (datafication and calculation). There is a need to multiply both the social interests and forms of knowledge involved in urban decision-making in order to ensure that the Urban OS is not the singular and exclusive mode of future urban decision-making. Key to this is developing new urban imaginaries, moving beyond the vision of the digitally enabled corporate entity as the analog for the ideal organization of both society and the city.

Notes

2 Operationalization

1. Zwick was presenting at the First Annual Conference on Urban Planning Information Systems and Programs, organized by Edgar Horwood and held at the University of Southern California in 1963. The conference led to the establishment of the Urban and Regional Information Systems Association (URISA). It is hailed by many as one of a few pivotal events marking the birth of GIS (Tomlinson 2012).

2. Within municipal government, ERP systems have been used extensively since the early 2000s to streamline internal operations, linking finance, procurement, payroll, human resources, and e-government in cities such as Des Moines, Pasadena, San Diego, and Cape Town, among others (Beheshti 2006; Raymond, Uwizeyemungu, and Bergeron 2006; Saran 2013; Jeffery et al. 2017).

3. Our way of looking at these illustrations has also been influenced by an acknowledgment of the power of the visual in social science and the extent to which both researcher and informant share a visual culture (Rose 2014). Drawing on concerns around the spatial organization of an image (Rose 2012), visual qualities within the illustrations operate as a point of departure for interpreting the Urban OS. Using a research technique known as graphic elicitation (Crilly, Blackwell, and Clarkson 2006), we treated these paradigmatic framings of the Urban OS as stimuli for a set of research interviews. Methodologically, the analysis of illustrations was complemented with eight interviews with computer scientists and software engineers, working in both the public and corporate sectors. During these interviews, informants provided their own explanations and interpretations of the illustration, which we used to develop analytical interpretations linking the domains of IT, software design, corporate products, and urbanism.

3 Datafication

1. Rob Kitchin speaks of the current data revolution as a discursive regime: "a set of interlocking discourses that justifies and sustains new developments and naturalizes

their use" (Kitchin 2014a, 113). Espoused by a multiplicity of actors who might use the same arguments despite significantly different agendas (Kitchin 2014a), urban data narratives as discursive formations find their unity precisely in their dispersion; their power in their ability to constantly generate new objects and purposes; and their transcendence in the coexistence of heterogeneity (cf. Foucault 1972).

2. For Bruno Latour, the statistical fact constitutes an *immutable mobile*: a reproducible object that can be moved from context to context as a material instrument for the reproduction of capitalism (Latour 1987).

3. In 2017 BRIDJ ceased operations in the United States, after failing to develop a viable business model in the cities where it was operating. Despite the failure of the on-demand transport model advanced, BRIDJ is hailed by technology commentators as a template for future public transport provision (Bliss 2017; Marshall 2017). As of 2019, the company continued operations in Sydney, Australia.

4. Crawford, Gray, and Miltner (2014) point to the need to uncover big data science as a mythological artefact. They take on the claim that, given the large scale of datasets and the unexpected correlations they reveal, big data implies the end of theory (Anderson 2008)—a world of knowledge in which algorithmically driven statistical correlation is enough and there is no need to develop and test hypotheses or develop theory (Graham 2012). In contrast, Crawford, Gray, and Miltner propose that big data *is* theory—that its mythic power plays a role in unifying the concept and adding legibility. Big data, as an emerging theory of knowledge, informs how we encounter political, economic, and cultural worlds. Shaped by neoliberal economic logics, big data is used in ways that speak "to the issues of class, race, gender, sexuality, and geography" (2014, 1665).

5. This is illustrated by the promotional material of Rio de Janeiro's Operations Center (see chapter 7): "[The Rio Operations Center] is the heart, or the brain, of Rio de Janeiro. . . . Today the world operates based on information. Here we are talking about an [information based] system that is public; information is also a public body" (Sávio Franco, 2012 Director of Rio de Janeiro's Center of Operations; quoted from Operação Lei Seca 2012).

6. In 2009, for example, the Obama administration released the Open Government Directive for the United States, a move that was followed in 2013 by Executive Order 13642 (titled *Making Open and Machine Readable the New Default for Government Information*). Data.gov, the US government's repository for open data, has supported the adoption of open data standards at both federal and local levels (White House 2016). In the United Kingdom, the Government Digital Service, part of the UK Cabinet Office, has developed a range of initiatives aimed at supporting local governments in adopting open data principles and technologies. This is part of its *Government as a Platform* policy, mentioned in the text and described as "a new way of building digital services . . . a set of shared components, service designs, platforms,

data and hosting, that every government service can use" (UK Government Digital Service, n.d.).

7. We originally accessed the list compiled by Opendatasoft at https://www .opendatasoft.com/a-comprehensive-list-of-all-open-data-portals-around-the -world/. That link is no longer operational, but has been replaced by https:// opendatainception.io/ and https://data.opendatasoft.com/explore/dataset/open-data -sources%40public/table/?sort=code_en, recording over 3,800 entries.

8. For early internet advocates like Tim O'Reilly, who is credited with developing the idea of open source, "the principles of the 'open source' software movement— shareable, re-usable code as the basis for improved software products—should in turn inform how we think about the design of public institutions" (Barns 2016, 557).

9. The Open Knowledge Foundation (OKF) is a global nonprofit organization that promotes the idea of open knowledge. OKF, founded in 2004 in Cambridge, England, operates in partnership and with support from the World Bank, among several other funders.

10. For a useful list of US and Canadian open data laws and policies, compiled and updated by volunteers through crowdsourcing, see https://docs.google.com/ spreadsheets/d/1ETZuGZBK24J2viZdxmhyIlIKiJuytAu3Bh1ofo_HVBw/edit#gid=0.

11. In his biography Bloomberg tells a story of bold personal advancement and organizational progress through information. In a chapter titled "Computers for Virgins," he describes the links between the mobilization of data and the possibility for transformation: "Two things haven't changed in twenty years or twenty centuries: the need for information; and the users of data, with their bravery, jealousy, adventurousness, and fear of the new. No matter what systems we create in the next decades, these two statements will be the same" (Bloomberg 1997, 131).

12. As of 2011, the Bloomberg Terminal still accounted for 85 percent of the annual revenue of Bloomberg LP (MacSweeney 2011); by 2015, the service counted over three hundred thousand subscribers (McCracken 2015).

13. Founded in 2007, Socrata was acquired by Tyler Technologies in 2017, becoming the Data and Insights division of "the largest software company in the [United States] solely focused on providing technology to the public sector" (Tyler Technologies, n.d.).

14. We recognize that there are marked differences in the political orientation of civic hacking communities across countries. However, our experience interacting with hacking communities in various contexts—in the US, UK, Brazil, Taiwan, Hong Kong, and Spain—indicates that there are strong common themes, practices, and shared beliefs, with little space for translation across different cultural contexts.

15. Roadify collects transit data from over four hundred public agencies and bike-share and carshare businesses, disseminating transport data through a smartphone app and via commercial signage companies.

16. Although there are continued attempts to reinforce the embedding of open data into NYC departments, there are has been relatively little analysis of the use of the data. A notable exception is a 2016 exploratory review of open data that considered seventy-seven uses for a diverse range of products, tools, and analyses (Okamoto 2016). These include "the Business Atlas (maps.nyc.gov/businessatlas), a website created by the New York City government to provide business data to entrepreneurs, and Citygram (www.citygram.nyc), a service developed by volunteers from the non-profit, civic technology organization, Beta NYC, which sends updates to users on selected city service activities and complaints within a specified neighborhood. The NYC Cares mobile app (http://apple.co/28Q7Bhp) was created to help senior citizens find food pantries in the city, while Cloudred have provided an interactive visualization (www.cloudred.com/labprojects/nyctrees) that illustrates the diversity of trees in the city. Finally, Death Map (http://deathmapnyc.com) shows the location of homicides and traffic fatalities during a two-year period" (Okamoto 2016, 4). Sixty-one percent of these applications were developed by individuals with tech backgrounds, indicating that the use of open data requires a high degree of technological skill and knowledge.

17. We use the word *incarnate* as both verb and adjective, drawing on the Latin *incarnare*, to make flesh. To incarnate is to take bodily form and become corporeal. It is worth noting that traditional definitions of the word emphasize the transmutation of spirits or deities into human form, a sense that ironically is not detached from popular fetishizations of the digital-technological as the all-embracing power of our times.

4   Sensing

1. An early example is provided by SOSUS, an oceanic sound surveillance system developed by the US Navy in the early 1950s and arguably an early prototype for today's wireless sensor networks (WSNs; Chong and Kumar 2003). SOSUS, which operated through hydrophones interconnected by wired cables, was originally aimed at identifying Soviet submarines reaching US coasts.

2. Such use of sensors prefigures the technical infrastructures of today's wars, which include drones, real-time visual surveillance, and networked sensor-shooter systems (Gregory 2013; Shaw 2016). In the resulting electronic battlefield, the enemy "existed as an abstract signal generated by remote sensors," supporting "a mode of atmospheric warfare that sought to enclose, police, and pacify hostile forms of life" (Shaw 2016, 689, 695).

3. Urbiotica has designed, piloted, and implemented urban sensors for waste collection, parking, noise, air quality, and other environmental conditions. Founded in 2008 in Barcelona, the company grew rapidly to become an internationally recognized player within the growing market of the Internet of Things. Sensing solutions piloted in their home city led the company to acquire a global presence, with projects in over twenty countries by 2017.

4. Barcelona's City OS was originally planned under the administration of Mayor Xavier Trias (2011–2015), but largely cast aside under the administration of Ada Colau (2015–).

5. Sentilo has been developed via a collaboration between public and private sector partners, including Urbiotica, the Catalan Water Agency, Worldsensing, the Dubai Municipality, and over thirty-five other bodies. While the platform was designed in and by Barcelona, its open-source nature means that the original source code is freely available for others to use, modify, and redistribute. As a result, the system has also been piloted in the cities of Reus, Terrassa, Cambrils, Tarragona, and Dubai.

6. SCADA technologies are used extensively within industrial and financial operations, given their relative high fidelity and low latency. That means that they are particularly well suited for moving large quantities of data in accurate ways, frequently and with little delay—often in close to real time. This makes SCADA technologies relatively expensive systems. The more often a sensor sends information, the less likely it is that its batteries will function for a long period of time. Costly and laborious replacements are therefore required.

7. For example, a city interested in locating sensors in its lamp posts might have over one hundred thousand such fixtures. Given budgetary constraints, it might not be able to fit sensors to all of them within a single procurement cycle. The separation between software of control and urban assets allows for incremental processes of upgrading, allowing the city's operating system to cope with a range of different types and generations of technology.

8. We use the notion of financialization in a broad sense, emphasizing processes of intermediation, value creation through agglomeration, and the capitalization of the future (monetization and the potential for speculation) over the use of financial markets, financial actors, or financial institutions.

9. It is worth noting that Langley and Leyshon (2017) use the notion of platform in a tightly defined sense, focusing on intermediary applications within the IT sector, including social media (e.g., Facebook, Twitter) and sharing economy business (e.g., Uber, Airbnb), but not, for example, aggregator interfaces that provide price-based comparisons (e.g., MoneySuperMarket) or user-generated reviews (e.g., Tripadvisor). Our use of the notion of platform capitalism, while also drawing on the platform's intermediary (brokering) nature, is broader in the sense that it relates to the

sociotechnical arrangements (technologies and practices that provide a base for other applications, processes, or technologies to be developed) for capital accumulation in an emerging digital economy. Such a digital economy transcends the IT sector and cuts across other sectors, such as manufacturing, service provision, and transportation. It is made up of "those businesses that increasingly rely upon information technology, data, and the internet for their business models" (Srnicek 2017, 5).

10. This process of sensing the city, as well as the upcoming spread of urban applications within the Internet of Things, is reminiscent of the early days of the internet. Back then, new value chains were being created through the emergence of digital assets, a process captured by Dodge and Shiode's analysis of the geography of internet real estate (2000). They realized that points of information networked through ICT technologies created new forms of tradable ownership. In a rather humorous and somewhat simplistic way, this is exemplified by the story of Alex Tew (reported by the *Guardian*): Tew, a twenty-one-year-old British student, made a small fortune by selling one million web page screen pixels for one dollar each (Morris 2005).

11. This further advances a condition of splintering urbanism and the commodification of formerly public or universally available goods and/or services (Graham and Marvin 2001)—with the particularity that in the case of the Urban OS, the means through which the system works involve both fragmentation and reintegration (and not solely splintering). The political economic tendency of the Urban OS is aligned with processes of economic splintering. By way of background, Graham and Marvin's *Splintering Urbanism* (2001) looks at how the privatization and liberalization of utilities during the second part of the twentieth century resulted in processes of urban splintering rather than integration. Infrastructure networks were formerly seen by planners, engineers, and architects as a way of integrating urban space, but have been reconfigured as specialized, privatized, and customized. Rather than connectivity being something universal, it is offered on an unequal and piecemeal basis. The resulting trend encouraged the fragmentation of the sociomaterial fabric of the city and exacerbated spatial segregation and social polarization, raising questions about the existence of the city as a whole.

12. We agree with Agnieszka Leszczynski and others on the need to challenge narratives of hybridity and virtualization resulting from an encounter with digital technologies, as these assume that digital spaces and real spaces were at some point epistemologically distinct and separate. In effect, physical spaces (or flows, for that matter) are always already information spaces/flows and vice versa. As put by Leszczynski when discussing spatial media, drawing on Zimmermann (2007), "rather than merging virtual and real spaces, the convergence of web-based media and location serves to actually '[anchor] the digital,' which is otherwise 'viewed as ambling around in a placeless realm, in geographic space' [Zimmermann 2007, 80]. . . . Spatiality, therefore, must be understood as mediated in the sense of being a project of becoming that is never completed" (Leszczynski 2015b, 745).

5 Mapping

1. Such claims are particularly salient in Brazil, a nation that struggled to achieve democracy throughout the second part of the twentieth century following over twenty years of military dictatorship. Despite a notionally inclusive political system, police violence in favelas continues to rise (Arias 2006; D. M. Goldstein 2013), in part due to the criminalization of poverty and the reliance on police to maintain forms of exclusion that have been normalized (Garmany 2014). Favelas are marked by a history of squatting followed by official threats to forcibly relocate those who live there; they are the spatial expression of a "differentiated citizenship" that assigns rights, opportunities, and privileges in unequal ways (Holston 2008). This is also a type of "citizenship that manages social differences by legalizing them in ways that legitimate and reproduce inequality" (Holston 2008, 3; see also Wacquant 2008).

2. Often aided by spatial media or other technological developments, participatory mapping is frequently supported by local organizations and federations of the urban poor. In the hands of such organizations, these calculative ways of knowing urban informality "can help to build a community, define a collective identity, facilitate development priority setting and provide a basis for engagement between communities and government on planning and development" (Patel, Baptist, and d'Cruz 2012, 13). They provide the basis for local planning and upgrade projects and can potentially contribute toward securing tenure and fostering collective discussions around urban issues (Karanja 2010; Livengood and Kunte 2012).

3. In September 2016, AfroReggae filed in California a lawsuit against Google, Inc. and Google Brasil Internet Ltda. for failing to acknowledge AfroReggae as a partner in Rio: Beyond the Map.

4. Often imagined either as a space of crime and poverty or as a site of freedom and creativity, *the favela* (a singular noun that evokes an unfounded spatial homogeneity) is also a historical and political invention (Valladares 2005). For Reyes Novaes (2014), the exclusion of favelas from the map established a "double discourse" that separates ungoverned subalterns and governed middle classes, a perspective that resonates with Holston's (2008) thesis of differentiated citizenship.

5. Breaking through the limitations imposed by a representational reading of favelas (i.e., one that prioritizes invisibility over visibility), Perlman speaks of "the myth of marginality": residents of favelas "are not economically and politically marginal, but are exploited, manipulated, and repressed . . . inexorably integrated into society, albeit in a manner detrimental to their own interests" (Perlman 2005, 18).

6. Alvarez León has examined the role of digital mapping in advancing the economic incorporation of space. He argues that Google Maps is embroiled in processes of commodification, "transforming informational resources into market goods" (Alvarez León 2016, 1). However, his analysis of the digitization of spatial resources focuses mainly on how information leads to new property regimes.

6 Prediction

1. Early commercial uses of predictive analytics focused on managing credit risk by predicting likelihood of payment default through credit scoring, a technology that by the 1980s "had become the primary decision-making tool across the financial services industry" (Finlay 2014, 2). In the insurance industry in particular, predictive analytics found application in all three core insurer functions: in marketing (to analyze purchasing patterns of customers), in underwriting (to filter out applicants), and in claims (to identify fraudulent claims; Nyce 2007). The use of predictive analytics in the identification of fraud also became important in banking, initially as a mechanism to screen against money laundering (Taylor 2011).

2. This typically involves a series of stages, starting with data aggregation and "cleansing," followed by the creation of sample groups (both to create and test models), data mining (to identify "underlying trends, patterns, or relationships" [Nyce 2007, 8]), model development (searching specific relationships between variables), and validation. Although data mining is a key stage of predictive analytics, the two should not be conflated. Data mining is a stage of the analytic process that is critical in the identification of "trends, patterns, or relationships . . . [that] can then be used to develop a predictive model" (Nyce 2007, 1)—that is, generalizations that are applicable to other datasets (Kotu and Deshpande 2014, 3; Hair 2007).

3. PredPol's website boasts "a 20% drop in predicted crimes year over year from January 2013 to January 2014" for Los Angeles (CA); and an "aggregate crime decreased by 8% and 9% in the two areas that first deployed PredPol in July 2013" for Atlanta (GA). In the case of Santa Cruz (CA), the "Police Department saw assaults drop by 9%, burglaries decrease by 11%, and robberies down 27% in its first year using the software" (PredPol n.d., "Proven Crime Reduction Results").

4. Following a period as a fellow in urban science at the University of Chicago, in 2019 Goldstein was appointed director of the Defense Digital Service office of the United States Department of Defense.

5. This includes programmes such as the University of Chicago's MS in Computational Analysis and Public Policy (MS-CAPP), offered jointly with the Harris School of Public Policy and the Department of Computer Science; Northwestern University's Masters in Data Science; City Scholars, an initiative by the University of Illinois at Urbana-Champaign's College of Engineering; and the Data Science for Social Good Summer Fellowship at the University of Chicago.

6. *Black bloc* is a form of protest in which protesters wear black clothing, scarves, sunglasses, and masks as a means of concealing their identity.

7. Within the media, WindyGrid is at times described as a system that enables access to the city's SmartData Platform, and at times as its precursor or first stage. GitHub

(acquired by Microsoft in 2018) provides a clue to the relationship between Windy-Grid and Chicago's SmartData Platform. There the latter is described as consisting of "several principal components," with WindyGrid as the system's user interface. According to Chicago's web-based system for collaborative software development, hosted by GitHub, Chicago's SmartData Platform components are "a user interface which allows users to explore historical data as well as future predictions, analytics services which actually performs the predictions, ontology layer which combines data (namely, matches all business-level data with any records pertaining to businesses), and a data services layer which stores data and makes it available through an API" (City of Chicago, n.d.).

8. According to information recorded on GitHub, the SmartData Platform is being developed "through a consortium of partners, including University of Chicago, Argonne National Laboratories, DePaul University, University of Illinois at Chicago, and Smart Chicago Collaborative" (City of Chicago, n.d.).

9. As such, in comparison to deductive reasoning, predictive analytics claims a more revolutionary relationship with theory. Where traditional deductive analytical research starts with hypothesis testing, predictive analytics proceeds inductively or *abductively* (Berry 2014, 20). It starts from the idea that there are unseen patterns within the data: "data mining and predictive analytics begin by identifying relationships in data . . . hypotheses are then developed and tested as part of model building and validation" (Hair 2007, 306).

10. Furthermore, and as already pointed out in this and other chapters (see chapter 2 in particular), the system effectively excludes everything that cannot be reduced to its standardized, gridded and numeric logic, which also influences the type of urban questions that can be asked.

7 Circulation

1. Empresa Municipal de Informática—IPLANRIO, the municipal company responsible for managing the information and communication technology resources of the city of Rio de Janeiro.

2. By way of context, it is important to mention that, in a city like Rio de Janeiro, large segments of the population continuously experience infrastructures in an almost permanent state of disrepair and improvisation, providing the context for fragmented urban fabrics (cf. Coutard 2008; Graham and Thrift 2007; McFarlane 2010).

3. Providing a broader Latin American context, this is consistent with Eden Medina's (2011) findings in her examination of the links between national politics and computing technology in Chile during the 1970s (the latter, heavily influenced

by Stafford Beer's conceptualization of cybernetics; at the time, President Salvador Allende attempted to manage Chile's economy through a distributed decision support system, known as Project Cybersyn, that included among other components a sophisticated operations room). Medina, discussing the take-up of cybernetics around the world, differentiates between US and UK configurations of cybernetics. In the United States, command and control logics within cybernetics had a significant influence, partly through the work carried out by Norbert Wiener in collaboration with the US military and think tanks such as RAND—foregrounding the idea of domination. In the United Kingdom, more indebted to the work of Beer, control within cybernetics is not a function of domination but a form of self-regulation, "the ability of a system to adapt to internal and external changes and survive" (Medina 2011, 26). The COR illustrates a form of urban computing in which links between military and urban operations are neither direct nor clear. As this chapter illustrates, rather than being influenced by the military, the COR evolves from an organizational, business, and logistics perspective applied to the city.

4. In the history of computing in Brazilian cities, municipal institutes of informatics appear to have a played a central role over and above that of external consultants with links to the military—a point of contrast with the history of computing in cities in the North American context (as examined in chapter 2). See also note 3, this chapter.

5. For an analysis specific to Rio de Janeiro, see Cardoso 2012.

6. In order to guarantee security (in its more traditional sense) for the 2014 World Cup, state and federal governments established another control room, the Integrated Centre for Command and Control (CICC). This integrated a variety of state and federal policing agencies, including the armed forces, civil police, and military police. Although the CICC and the COR exchange information and use similar technological platforms, arguably the CICC operates primarily within the domains of coercion and surveillance, while the COR operates mostly in a governmental fashion.

7. The Complexo da Maré and the Complexo do Alemão are two of Rio de Janeiro's largest favela clusters. Located in the North Zone of the city, they have a combined population of 200,000 and some of the city's lowest social development indicators.

8. *Olhos da Cidade* was short-lived. In 2019, the COR launched a new mobile phone app called COR.RIO.

9. In 2016, with the support of the Rockefeller Foundation and as part of the 100 Resilient Cities program, Rio released its resilience strategy. Rio's COR features extensively here, as well as in the literature of the Rockefeller Foundation's 100 Resilient Cities program (Rockefeller Foundation, n.d.). The municipality has designated the COR as the primary site from which the city's resilience strategy is to be designed and implemented, with the director of the COR acting also as the city's director of resilience.

10. For Cooper, there are marked similarities and linkages between how contemporary financial markets and environmental crises are dealt with. In both cases, and often working through each other, the primary aim is to maintain "the topological cohesion of a world in and through the most extreme periods of turbulence"—something that has pervasively come to be known as *resilience*. As we enter a world in which turbulence cannot be avoided, "the precise when and where of turbulence is indifferent. What matters is whether the accidental event of turbulence can be harnessed to . . . strategic ends" (Cooper 2010, 183, 184).

8   Resistance?

1. It is worth noting that this is precisely the conceptualization that Hughes sought to challenge in her analysis of resistance, given the *"predetermination of form* that particular actions or actors must assume to constitute resistance" (2019, 1, original emphasis). However, for the purpose of our analysis, what is at stake is precisely the constitution of such form, and therefore we decided to use the conventional definition of resistance over the more "emergent" configuration put forward by Hughes.

2. For a critical account of the dominance of social media in the mobilization of protesters, see Chu (2018).

3. By bypassing the mobile cellular network, Firechat would also allow protesters to communicate if the mobile network were to be taken down by the authorities precisely for the purpose of curtailing connectivity. However, in the Umbrella Movement, the popularity of Firechat was short-lived. At the time of the protests, it did not have the capacity to provide private messages; instead, it operated through open chatrooms that anyone could create and where anyone could participate (R. Chao 2014; Li 2015). Chatrooms (and users) proliferated during the protest, often flooding feeds with spam and irrelevant messages. This led to a lack of focus in communications, making it impossible to distinguish what was real from what was fake.

4. The game awards points to players as they defend themselves against the police, angry pro-China locals, and the city's chief executive, Leung Chun-ying.

5. Hackpad closed in 2018 after being acquired by Dropbox.

6. In June 2019, at the start of a new wave of prodemocracy protests in Hong Kong, the UK newspaper the *Guardian* was reporting that technology that in the past helped protesters was now being used against them, as social media and messaging apps became a key tool of the Chinese state for monitoring and surveillance purposes: "Wary of being tracked and targeted like activists inside China, protesters are keeping a low profile online" (Kuo 2019).

9   Conclusion

1. In Gabrys's view, computational processes in the city, such as sensing, generate new infrastructural agents, whether through measurement, automation, or contingency. These infrastructural agents are not simply the coming together of code, software, and the materiality of the city, but "transductive articulations of urban environments, technologies and inhabitants" (Gabrys 2016, 254). Measurement, in particular, becomes infrastructural—both a condition and a resource for new urban processes. In the Urban OS and the digital infrastructures that it relies upon, using the language of Gabrys, a "becoming with others" occurs through a "becoming calculable."

References

ABC News. 2014. "Hong Kong protests: High Court Orders Main Protest Site in Admiralty to Be Cleared." ABC News, December 8, 2014. https://www.abc.net.au/news/2014-12-09/hong-kong-court-orders-protest-sites-to-be-cleared/5954656.

AfroReggae. 2014. "8ao80—Vídeo Educativo VI." YouTube, May 1, 2014. https://www.youtube.com/watch?v=N5P5ISEDpVg.

Agamben, Giorgio. 2005. *State of Exception.* Chicago: University of Chicago Press.

Agamben, Giorgio. 2009. *"What Is an Apparatus?" and Other Essays.* Redwood, CA: Stanford University Press.

Ajuntament de Barcelona. 2015. "Barcelona 5.0 Smart City [PPT presentation by Julia Lopez]." Seminario Smart Cities en la práctica (VII), Madrid, April 22.

Ajuntament de Barcelona. n.d. "Sentilo BCN | Plataforma de Sensors i Actuadors de Barcelona." Accessed March 21, 2019. http://sentilo.bcn.cat/.

Alvarez León, Luis F. 2016. "Property Regimes and the Commodification of Geographic Information: An Examination of Google Street View." *Big Data and Society* 3 (2): 1–13.

Amoore, Louise. 2011. "Data Derivatives: On the Emergence of a Security Risk Calculus for Our Times." *Theory, Culture & Society* 28 (6): 24–43.

Amoore, Louise. 2013. *The Politics of Possibility: Risk and Security beyond Probability.* Durham, NC: Duke University Press.

Amoore, Louise. 2018. "Cloud Geographies: Computing, Data, Sovereignty." *Progress in Human Geography* 42 (1): 4–24.

Amoore, Louise, and Rita Raley. 2017. "Securing with Algorithms: Knowledge, Decision, Sovereignty." *Security Dialogue* 48 (1): 3–10.

Amstutz, Arnold E. 1968. "City Management—A Problem in Systems Analysis." Working paper. MIT Sloan School of Management, Cambridge, MA.

Anderson, Ben, and Rachel Gordon. 2017. "Government and (Non) Event: The Promise of Control." *Social and Cultural Geography* 18 (2): 158–177.

Anderson, Ben, and Colin McFarlane. 2011. "Assemblage and Geography." *Area* 43 (2): 124–127.

Anderson, Chris. 2008. "The End of Theory: The Data Deluge Makes the Scientific Method Obsolete." *Wired.* Accessed August 3, 2018. https://www.wired.com/2008/06/pb-theory/.

Appel, Sheila U., Derek Botti, James Jamison, Leslie Plant, Jing Y. Shyr, and Lav R. Varshney. 2014. "Predictive Analytics Can Facilitate Proactive Property Vacancy Policies for Cities." *Technological Forecasting and Social Change* 89:161–173.

Aradau, Claudia, and Tobias Blanke. 2010. "Governing Circulation: A Critique of the Biopolitics of Security." In *Security and Global Governmentality*, edited by Miguel de Larrinaga and Marc G. Doucet, 44–58. New York: Routledge.

Aradau, Claudia, and Tobias Blanke. 2017. "Politics of Prediction: Security and the Time/Space of Governmentality in the Age of Big Data." *European Journal of Social Theory* 20 (3): 373–391.

Arias, Enrique Desmond. 2006. *Drugs and Democracy in Rio de Janeiro: Trafficking, Social Networks, and Public Security.* Chapel Hill: University of North Carolina Press.

Ash, James, Rob Kitchin, and Agnieszka Leszczynski. 2018. "Digital Turn, Digital Geographies?" *Progress in Human Geography* 42 (1): 25–43.

Atomic Heritage Foundation. 2014. "Computing and the Manhattan Project." Accessed October 8, 2018. https://www.atomicheritage.org/history/computing-and-manhattan-project.

Austen, Kat. 2015. "Environmental Science: Pollution Patrol." *Nature* 517 (7533): 136–138.

Barber, Elizabeth. 2014a. "At Home in Hong Kong's Surprisingly Comfortable Protest Camps." *Time*, November 12, 2014. http://time.com/3581690/life-in-hong-kong-occupy-protest-camps/.

Barber, Elizabeth. 2014b. "The Main Hong Kong Protest Site Is a Perfect Anarchist Collective." *Time*, October 20, 2014. http://time.com/3523217/occupy-central-hong-kong-harcourt-road-admiralty-democracy-anarchism-anarchist-collective-china-protest/.

Barns, Sarah. 2016. "Mine Your Data: Open Data, Digital Strategies and Entrepreneurial Governance by Code." *Urban Geography* 37 (4): 554–571.

Batty, Michael. 1971. "Modelling Cities as Dynamic Systems." *Nature* 231:425–428.

Batty, Michael. 2013. *The New Science of Cities.* Cambridge, MA: MIT Press.

Batty, Michael. 2017. "Editorial: The Future Journal." *Environment and Planning B: Urban Analytics and City Science* 44 (1): 6–9.

Bauer, A. J., and Michael Ralph. n.d. "The Question of Infrastructure: An Interview with Michael Ralph." Is This What Democracy Looks Like? Accessed March 21, 2019. https://what-democracy-looks-like.org/the-question-of-infrastructure-an-interview -with-michael-ralph/.

Beheshti, Hooshang M. 2006. "What Managers Should Know about ERP/ERP II." *Management Research News* 29 (4): 184–193.

Bennett, Jane. 2010. *Vibrant Matter: A Political Ecology of Things*. Durham, NC: Duke University Press.

Bennett, W. Lance. 2003. "Communicating Global Activism: Strengths and Vulnerabilities of Networked Politics." *Information, Communication & Society* 6 (2): 143–168.

Berry, David M. 2014. *Critical Theory and the Digital*. London: Bloomsbury.

Bettencourt, Luís M. A., José Lobo, Dirk Helbing, Christian Kühnert, and Geoffrey B. West. 2007. "Growth, Innovation, Scaling, and the Pace of Life in Cities." *Proceedings of the National Academy of Sciences* 104 (17): 7301–7306.

BigApps. n.d. "About." Accessed August 23, 2018. http://www.bigapps.nyc/about/.

Bimber, Bruce, Andrew J. Flanagin, and Cynthia Stohl. 2005. "Reconceptualizing Collective Action in the Contemporary Media Environment." *Communication Theory* 15 (4): 365–388.

Bliss, Laura. 2017. "Bridj Is Dead, But Microtransit Isn't." *CityLab*. Bloomberg L.P. Accessed March 20, 2020. https://www.citylab.com/transportation/2017/05/bridj-is -dead-but-microtransit-isnt/525156/.

Bloomberg, Michael. 2001. *Bloomberg by Bloomberg*. New York: Wiley.

Bloomberg, Michael. 2014. "Foreword." In *The Responsive City: Engaging Communities through Data-Smart Governance*, edited by Stephen Goldsmith and Susan Crawford, v–vi. San Francisco, CA: John Wiley & Sons.

Bolter, J. David, and Richard Grusin. 2000. *Remediation: Understanding New Media*. Cambridge, MA: MIT Press.

Bond-Graham, Darwin, and Ali Winston. 2013. "All Tomorrow's Crimes: The Future of Policing Looks a Lot Like Good Branding." *SFWeekly*, October 30, 2013. https:// archives.sfweekly.com/sanfrancisco/all-tomorrows-crimes-the-future-of-policing -looks-a-lot-like-good-branding/Content?oid=2827968&showFullText=true.

Bonomi, Flavio, Rodolfo Milito, Jiang Zhu, and Sateesh Addepalli. 2012. "Fog Computing and Its Role in the Internet of Things." *MCC '12: Proceedings of the First*

Edition of the MCC Workshop on Mobile Cloud Computing, 13–16. https://doi.org/ 10.1145/2342509.2342513.

Bowker, Geoffrey C., and Susan Leigh Star. 2000. *Sorting Things Out: Classification and Its Consequences*. Cambridge, MA: MIT Press.

Boyer, M. Christine. 1992. "The Imaginary Real World of Cybercities." *Assemblage* 18:115–127.

Boyne, Roy. 2000. "Post-panopticism." *Economy and Society* 29 (2): 285–307.

Brasil 247. 2014. "Wikimapa e a identidade do morador de favela." Accessed July 7, 2017. https://www.brasil247.com/pt/247/favela247/149808/Wikimapa-e-a-identidade -do-morador-de-favela.htm.

Bratton, Benjamin H. 2016. *The Stack: On Software and Sovereignty*. Cambridge, MA: MIT Press.

Braun, Bruce P. 2014. "A New Urban Dispositif? Governing Life in an Age of Climate Change." *Environment and Planning D: Society and Space* 32:49–64.

Brenner, Neil, and Stuart Elden. 2009. "Henri Lefebvre on State, Space, Territory." *International Political Sociology* 3 (4): 353–377.

BRIDJ. n.d. "Autonomous Infrastructure for Cities." Accessed March 8, 2017. http:// www.bridj.com/welcome#how.

Brillembourg, Alfredo, and Hubert Klumpner. 2005. "Imagine the New City." In *Informal City: Caracas Case*, edited by A. Brillembourg, K. Feireiss, and H. Klumpner, 248–259. Munich: Prestel.

Bucher, Taina. 2013. "Objects of Intense Feeling: The Case of the Twitter API." *Computational Culture*, November 16, 2013. http://computationalculture.net/chapter/ objects-of-intense-feeling-the-case-of-the-twitter-api.

Callon, Michel. 1986. "Some Elements of a Sociology of Translation: Domestication of the Scallops and the Fishermen of St Brieuc Bay." In *Power, Action and Belief: A New Sociology of Knowledge*, edited by John Law, 196–233. London: Routledge & Kegan Paul.

Callon, Michel. 1987. "Society in the Making: The Study of Technology as a Tool for Sociological analysis." In *The Social Construction of Technological Systems: New Directions in the Sociology and History of Technology*, edited by Wiebe E. Bijker, Thomas P. Hughes, and Trevor Pinch, 83–103. Cambridge, MA: MIT Press.

Candelieri, Antonio, and Francesco Archetti. 2014. "Smart Water in Urban Distribution Networks: Limited Financial Capacity and Big Data Analytics." *WIT Transactions on the Built Environment* 139:63–73.

Caragliu, Andrea, Chiara Del Bo, and Peter Nijkamp. 2011. "Smart Cities in Europe." *Journal of Urban Technology* 18 (2): 65–82.

Cardoso, Bruno de Vasconcelos. 2012. "The Paradox of Caught-in-the-Act Surveillance Scenes: Dilemmas of Police Video Surveillance in Rio de Janeiro." *Surveillance & Society* 10 (1): 51–64.

Cardoso, Bruno de Vasconcelos. 2013. "Megaeventos esportivos e modernização tecnológica: Planos e discursos sobre o legado em segurança pública." *Horizontes Antropológicos* 19 (40): 119–148.

Cardullo, Paolo, Cesare Di Feliciantonio, and Rob Kitchin. 2019. *The Right to the Smart City*. Bingley, UK: Emerald Publishing.

Carr, Sara Jensen, and Allison Lassiter. 2017. "Big Data, Small Apps: Premises and Products of the Civic Hackathon." In *Seeing Cities through Big Data: Research, Methods and Applications in Urban Informatics*, edited by Piyushimita Vonu Thakuriah, Nebiyou Tilahun and Moira Zellner, 543–559. Cham: Springer.

Chan, Samuel, Phila Siu, Emily Tsang, Elizabeth Cheung, Alan Yu, and Danny Lee. 2014. "Occupy Central Camp in Admiralty Goes Down Quietly as Police Move In." *South China Morning Post*, December 12, 2014. https://www.scmp.com/news/hong-kong/article/1661311/occupy-central-camp-admiralty-goes-down-quietly-police-move.

Chao, Rebecca. 2014. "Firechat Wasn't Meant for Protests. Here's How It Worked (or Didn't) at Occupy Central." TechPresident, October 10, 2014. http://techpresident.com/news/25304/firechat-wasn%E2%80%99t-meant-protests-here%E2%80%99s-how-it-worked-or-didn%E2%80%99t-occupy-central.

Chao, Vincent Y. 2014. "How Technology Revolutionized Taiwan's Sunflower Movement." *Diplomat*, April 15, 2014. https://thediplomat.com/2014/04/how-technology-revolutionized-taiwans-sunflower-movement/?allpages=yes.

Cheney-Lippold, John. 2011. "A New Algorithmic Identity: Soft Biopolitics and the Modulation of Control." *Theory, Culture & Society* 28 (6): 164–181.

Chicago Architecture Center. 2014. "RATS! Predicting the Future with Chicago's Smartdata Platform." YouTube, August 6, 2014. https://www.youtube.com/watch?v=XO-l3egYvA4.

Chong, Chee-Yee, and Srikanta P. Kumar. 2003. "Sensor Networks: Evolution, Opportunities, and Challenges." *Proceedings of the IEEE* 91 (8): 1247–1256.

Chu, Donna S. C. 2018. "Media Use and Protest Mobilization: A Case Study of Umbrella Movement within Hong Kong Schools." *Social Media + Society*, January–March 2018, 1–11. https://journals.sagepub.com/doi/pdf/10.1177/2056305118763350.

Chui, Timothy. 2014. "Young Students Seen Most in Major Occupied Location." *China Daily Asia*, October 1, 2014. https://www.chinadailyasia.com/hknews/2014-10/01/content_15173091.html.

Chun-ho, YU. 2017. "Digital Inclusion in Hong Kong and the United Kingdom." Information Services Essentials. Legislative Council of the Hong Kong Special Administrative Region of the People's Republic of China. January 23, 2017. https://www.legco.gov.hk/research-publications/english/essentials-1617ise08-digital-inclusion-in-hong-kong-and-the-united-kingdom.htm.

Cisco. 2012. *Smart City Framework: A Systematic Process for Enabling Smart+Connected Communities.* By Gordon Falconer and Shane Mitchell. Cisco Internet Business Solutions Group (IBSG). Accessed March 21, 2019. http://www.cisco.com/web/about/ac79/docs/ps/motm/Smart-City-Framework.pdf.

Cisco/Guardian Labs. n.d. "Cities Get Smart: The Digital Future of the Public Sector." *Guardian.* Accessed February 23, 2019. https://www.theguardian.com/connecting-the-future/ng-interactive/2015/jul/01/cisco-internet-smart-cities-sensors-traffic-apps.

CITI-SENSE. n.d. "Project Overview." Accessed March 21, 2019. http://www.citi-sense.eu/Project.aspx.

City of Chicago. 2013. "Chicago Named as One of Five Winners in Bloomberg Philanthropies' Mayors Challenge." City of Chicago, Office of the Mayor. Press release. March 13, 2013. http://www.cityofchicago.org/city/en/depts/mayor/press_room/press_releases/2013/march_2013/chicago_named_asoneoffivewinnersinbloomberg philanthropiesmayorsc.html.

City of Chicago. 2015. "OpenGrid." Accessed March 21, 2019. http://opengrid.io/.

City of Chicago. 2017. "GitHub—Chicago/Smart-Data-Platform." Last modified May 3, 2017. https://github.com/Chicago/smart-data-platform.

City of Chicago. n.d. "Smart-Data-Platform by Chicago." Accessed November 20, 2018. https://chicago.github.io/smart-data-platform/.

City of Chicago. 2018. "2019 Budget Overview." Accessed November 20, 2018. https://www.chicago.gov/content/dam/city/depts/obm/supp_info/2019Budget/2019BudgetOverview.pdf.

City OS/Ajuntament de Barcelona. n.d. "City OS." Accessed April 1, 2015. http://cityos.io.

Clarke, George Leonard. 1954. *Elements of Ecology.* New York: John Wiley.

Cloot, P. L. 1965. "What Is the Use of Operating Systems?" *The Computer Journal* 7 (4): 249–254.

Coaffee, Jon. 2013. "Towards Next-Generation Urban Resilience in Planning Practice: From Securitization to Integrated Place Making." *Planning Practice & Research* 28 (3): 323–339.

Coaffee, Jon. 2015. "The Uneven Geographies of the Olympic Carceral: From Exceptionalism to Normalisation." *The Geographical Journal* 181 (3): 199–211.

Coaffee, Jon, David Murakami Wood, and Peter Rogers. 2009. *The Everyday Resilience of the City: How Cities Respond to Terrorism and Disaster*. Vol. 10. New York: Palgrave Macmillan.

Coca, Nithin. 2016. "Blooming Digital Democracy in Taiwan's Sunflower Movement." MobLab, January 25, 2016. https://mobilisationlab.org/blooming-digital-democracy-taiwan-sunflower-movement/.

Collier, Stephen J., and Andrew Lakoff. 2015. "Vital Systems Security: Reflexive Biopolitics and the Government of Emergency." *Theory, Culture & Society* 32 (2): 19–51.

Conover, Michael D., Emilio Ferrara, Filippo Menczer, and Alessandro Flammini. 2013. "The Digital Evolution of Occupy Wall Street." *PLOS ONE* 8 (5): e64679. https://doi.org/10.1371/journal.pone.0064679.

Cooper, Melinda. 2010. "Turbulent Worlds." *Theory, Culture & Society* 27 (2–3): 167–190.

Corsín Jiménez, Alberto. 2014. "The Right to Infrastructure: A Prototype for Open Source Urbanism." *Environment and Planning D: Society and Space* 32 (2): 342–362.

Cosgrove, Denis. 2003. *Apollo's Eye: A Cartographic Genealogy of the Earth in the Western Imagination*. Baltimore, MD: Johns Hopkins University Press.

Coutard, Olivier. 2008. "Placing Splintering Urbanism: Introduction." *Geoforum* 39 (6): 1815–1820.

Cowen, Deborah. 2014. *The Deadly Life of Logistics: Mapping Violence in Global Trade*. Minneapolis: University of Minnesota Press.

Crampton, Jeremy. 2017. "Digital Mapping." In *Understanding Spatial Media*, edited by R. Kitchin, T. Lauriault, and M. Wilson, 35–43. London: SAGE.

Crampton, Jeremy. 2011. "Cartographic Calculations of Territory." *Progress in Human Geography* 35 (1): 92–103.

Crampton, Jeremy, and Stuart Elden. 2006. "Space, Politics, Calculation: An Introduction." *Social & Cultural Geography* 7 (5): 681–685.

Crang, Mike. 2010. "Cyberspace as the New Public Domain." In *Urban Diversity: Space, Culture and Inclusive Pluralism in Cities Worldwide*, edited by Caroline Wanjiku Kihato, Mejgan Massoumi, Blair A. Ruble, Pep Subirós, and Allison M. Garland, 99–122. Baltimore: Johns Hopkins University Press.

Crang, Mike, and Stephen Graham. 2007. "Sentient Cities: Ambient Intelligence and the Politics of Urban Space." *Information, Communication & Society* 10 (6): 789–817.

Crawford, Kate. 2014. "The Anxieties of Big Data." *The New Inquiry*, May 30, 2014. https://thenewinquiry.com/the-anxieties-of-big-data/.

Crawford, Kate, Mary L. Gray, and Kate Miltner. 2014. "Critiquing Big Data: Politics, Ethics, Epistemology." *International Journal of Communication* 8:10.

Crilly, Nathan, Alan F. Blackwell, and P. John Clarkson. 2006. "Graphic Elicitation: Using Research Diagrams as Interview Stimuli." *Qualitative Research* 6 (3): 341–366.

Dalton, Craig, and Jim Thatcher. 2014. "What Does a Critical Data Studies Look Like, and Why Do We Care? Seven Points for a Critical Approach to 'Big Data.'" *Society & Space* 29. Accessed May 12, 2014. https://www.societyandspace.org/articles/what-does-a-critical-data-studies-look-like-and-why-do-we-care.

Dastjerdi, Amir Vahid, and Rajkumar Buyya. 2016. "Fog Computing: Helping the Internet of Things Realize Its Potential." *Computer* 49 (8): 112–116.

Datta, Ayona. 2018. "The Digital Turn in Postcolonial Urbanism: Smart Citizenship in the Making of India's 100 Smart Cities." *Transactions of the Institute of British Geographers* 43 (3): 405–419.

Datta, Ayona. 2019. "Postcolonial Urban Futures: Imagining and Governing India's Smart Urban Age." *Environment and Planning D: Society and Space* 37 (3): 393–410.

Datta, Ayona, and Padmini Murray. 2018. "Gendering the Smart City: A Subaltern Curation Network on Gender Based Violence (GBV) in India." Grant proposal. UKRI—Arts and Humanities Research Council (Grant Number AH/R003866/1). Accessed October 1, 2019. https://gtr.ukri.org/project/75DDB3B1-B5FA-4716-8025-9AEC5555A0CB.

Datta, Ayona, and Nancy Odendaal. 2019. "Smart Cities and the Banality of Power." *Environment and Planning D: Society and Space* 37 (3): 387–392.

Davenport, Thomas H. 1998. "Putting the Enterprise into the Enterprise System." *Harvard Business Review* 76 (4): 121–131.

Davies, Sally. 2014. "Glasgow Aims to Be First 'Smart City.'" *Financial Times*, June 3, 2014. https://www.ft.com/content/d119ac06-e57e-11e3-a7f5-00144feabdc0.

Daybreak Editor. 2017. "g0v—During the Sunflower Movement, g0v Coordinated Much Information-Sharing and Crowdsourcing on the Internet." Daybreak Project, June 14, 2017. https://daybreak.newbloommag.net/2017/06/14/g0v/.

De Goede, Marieke, and Samuel Randalls. 2009. "Precaution, Preemption: Arts and Technologies of the Actionable Future." *Environment and Planning D: Society and Space* 27 (5): 859–878.

De Landa, Manuel. 2000. "Deleuze, Diagrams, and the Genesis of Form." *Amerikastudien/American Studies* 45 (1): 33–41.

de Lange, Michiel, Nanna Verhoeff, Martijn de Waal, Marcus Foth, and Martin Brynskov. 2015. "Digital Cities 9 Workshop—Hackable Cities: From Subversive City Making to Systemic Change." *C&T '15: Proceedings of the 7th International Conference on Communities and Technologies*, June 2015, 165–167. https://doi.org/10.1145/2768545.2768564.

de Waal, Martijn. 2011. "The Ideas and Ideals in Urban Media." In *From Social Butterfly to Engaged Citizen: Urban Informatics, Social Media, Ubiquitous Computing, and Mobile Technology to Support Citizen Engagement*, edited by Marcus Foth, Laura Forlano, and Christine Satchell, 5–20. Cambridge, MA: MIT Press.

Dean, Mitchell M. 2010. *Governmentality: Power and Rule in Modern Society*. London: Sage.

Deitchman, Seymour J. 2008. "The 'Electronic Battlefield' in the Vietnam War." *Journal of Military History* 72 (3): 869–887.

Deleuze, Gilles. 1987. *A Thousand Plateaus: Capitalism and Schizophrenia*. Minneapolis: University of Minnesota Press.

Deleuze, Gilles. 1992. "Postscript on the Societies of Control." *October* 59:3–7.

Deleuze, Gilles. 2006. *Foucault*. London: Continuum.

Deleuze, Gilles, and Félix Guattari. 2004. *A Thousand Plateaus: Capitalism and Schizophrenia*. London: Continuum.

Dickson, Paul. 2012. "The Electronic Battlefield." Takoma Park, MD: FoxAcre Press.

Dillon, Michael. 2003. "Intelligence Incarnate: Martial Corporeality in the Digital Age." *Body & Society* 9 (4): 123–147.

Dillon, Michael. 2015. *Biopolitics of Security: A Political Analytic of Finitude*. London: Routledge.

Dingle, Peter. 2014. "Behind the Technology of Hong Kong's #UmbrellaRevolution." ClickZ, October 1, 2014. https://www.clickz.com/behind-the-technology-of-hong-kongs-umbrellarevolution/29423/.

Dodge, Martin, and Rob Kitchin. 2013. "Crowdsourced Cartography: Mapping Experience and Knowledge." *Environment and Planning A* 45 (1): 19–36.

Dodge, Martin, Rob Kitchin, and Matthew Zook. 2009. "How Does Software Make Space? Exploring Some Geographical Dimensions of Pervasive Computing and Software Studies." *Environment and Planning A* 41 (6): 1283–1293.

Dodge, Martin, and Narushige Shiode. 2000. "Where on Earth Is the Internet? An Empirical Investigation of the Geography of Internet Real Estate." In *Cities in the Telecommunications Age: The Fracturing of Geographies*, edited by J. Wheeler, Y. Aoyama, and B. Warf, 42–53. New York: Routledge.

Donovan, Kevin P. 2012. "Seeing Like a Slum: Towards Open, Deliberative Development." *Georgetown Journal of International Affairs* 13:97–104.

Easterling, Keller. 2014. *Extrastatecraft: The Power of Infrastructure Space*. London: Verso.

Economist. 2016. *Hong Kong*. *Economist* Intelligence Unit and TELSTRA. Accessed July 11, 2018. http://connectedfuture.economist.com/connecting-capabilities/wp -content/uploads/2016/11/Connecting-Capabilities_HONGKONG_v6.pdf.

Edwards, Paul N. 1996. *The Closed World: Computers and the Politics of Discourse in Cold War America*. Cambridge, MA: MIT Press.

Elden, Stuart. 2010. "Land, Terrain, Territory." *Progress in Human Geography* 34 (6): 799–817.

Elden, Stuart. 2013a. *The Birth of Territory*. Chicago: University of Chicago Press.

Elden, Stuart. 2013b. "Secure the Volume: Vertical Geopolitics and the Depth of Power." *Political Geography* 34:35–51.

Elwood, Sarah, Michael F. Goodchild, and Daniel Z. Sui. 2012. "Researching Volunteered Geographic Information: Spatial Data, Geographic Research, and New Social Practice." *Annals of the Association of American Geographers* 102 (3): 571–590.

Elwood, Sarah, and Agnieszka Leszczynski. 2013. "New Spatial Media, New Knowledge Politics." *Transactions of the Institute of British Geographers* 38 (4): 544–559.

Elwood, Sarah, and Agnieszka Leszczynski. 2018. "Feminist Digital Geographies." *Gender, Place & Culture* 25 (5): 629–644.

Etling, Bruce, Robert Faris, and John Palfrey. 2010. "Political Change in the Digital Age: The Fragility and Promise of Online Organizing." *SAIS Review of International Affairs* 30 (2): 37–49.

Evans, James R., and Carl H. Lindner. 2012. "Business Analytics: The Next Frontier for Decision Sciences." *Decision Line* 43 (2): 4–6.

Fabricius, Daniela. 2008. "Resisting Representation: The Informal Geographies of Rio de Janeiro." *Harvard Design Magazine* 28 (Spring/Summer): 4–17.

Farish, Matthew. 2010. *The Contours of America's Cold War*. Minneapolis: University of Minnesota Press.

Farman, Jason. 2010. "Mapping the Digital Empire: Google Earth and the Process of Postmodern Cartography." *New Media & Society* 12 (6): 869–888.

Fenton, Natalie. 2008. "Mediating Hope: New Media, Politics and Resistance." *International Journal of Cultural Studies* 11 (2): 230–248.

Fenton, Natalie. 2016. *Digital, Political, Radical*. Cambridge: John Wiley & Sons.

Ferguson, Andrew Guthrie. 2017. "Policing Predictive Policing." *Washington University Law Review* 94 (5): 1109–1190.

Fields, Desiree. 2019. "Automated Landlord: Digital Technologies and Post-crisis Financial Accumulation." Forthcoming in *Environment and Planning A: Economy and Space*. https://doi.org/10.1177/0308518X19846514.

Filipponi, Luca, Andrea Vitaletti, Giada Landi, Vincenzo Memeo, Giorgio Laura, and Paolo Pucci. 2010. "Smart City: An Event Driven Architecture for Monitoring Public Spaces with Heterogeneous Sensors." Paper presented at the Fourth International Conference on Sensor Technologies and Applications, Venice, Italy, July 18–25, 2010.

Finlay, Steven. 2014. *Predictive Analytics, Data Mining and Big Data: Myths, Misconceptions and Methods*. Basingstoke: Palgrave Macmillan.

Fitzpatrick, Jen. 2016. "Horizon—Jen Fitzpatrick—Going Beyond the Map. Google Cloud Platform." YouTube, October 7, 2016. https://www.youtube.com/watch?v=bPo_fLznqZ0.

Flock, Elizabeth. 2011. "Byte Cop." *University of Chicago Magazine*, July–August. Accessed March 21, 2019. http://magazine.uchicago.edu/1102/arts_sciences/byte-cop.shtml.

Forlano, Laura. 2009. "WiFi Geographies: When Code Meets Place." *Information Society* 25 (5): 344–352.

Forrester, Jay W. 1961. *Industrial Dynamics*. Waltham, MA: Pegasus Communications.

Forrester, Jay W. 1969. *Urban Dynamics*. Cambridge, MA: MIT Press.

Forrester, Jay W. 1975. *Collected Papers*. Cambridge, MA: Wright-Allen.

Foucault, Michel. 1970. *The Order of Things: An Archeology of the Human Sciences*. London: Tavistock Publications.

Foucault, Michel. 1972. *The Archaeology of Knowledge*. New York: Pantheon Books.

Foucault, Michel. 1995. *Discipline and Punish*. New York: Vintage.

Foucault, Michel. 2009. *Security, Territory, Population: Lectures at the College de France 1977–1978*. New York: Palgrave Macmillian.

Freeman, James. 2014. "Raising the Flag over Rio de Janeiro's Favelas: Citizenship and Social Control in the Olympic City." *Journal of Latin American Geography* 13 (1): 7–38.

Frey, Christopher. 2014. "World Cup 2014: Inside Rio's Bond-Villain Mission Control." *Guardian*, May 23, 2014. http://www.theguardian.com/cities/2014/may/23/world-cup-inside-rio-bond-villain-mission-control.

Fuchs, Christian. 2014. *OccupyMedia! The Occupy Movement and Social Media in Crisis Capitalism*. Winchester: Zero Books.

Fussey, Pete. 2015. "Command, Control and Contestation: Negotiating Security at the London 2012 Olympics." *Geographical Journal* 181 (3): 212–223.

Fussey, Pete, and Francisco Klauser. 2015. "Securitisation and the Mega-event: An Editorial Introduction." *Geographical Journal* 181 (3): 194–198.

Gabrys, Jennifer. 2014. "Programming Environments: Environmentality and Citizen Sensing in the Smart City." *Environment and Planning D: Society and Space* 32 (1): 30–48.

Gabrys, Jennifer. 2016. *Program Earth: Environmental Sensing Technology and the Making of a Computational Planet*. Minneapolis: University of Minnesota Press.

Gaby, Sarah, and Neal Caren. 2012. "Occupy Online: How Cute Old Men and Malcolm X Recruited 400,000 US Users to OWS on Facebook." *Social Movement Studies* 11 (3–4): 367–374.

Gaffney, Christopher. 2010. "Mega-events and Socio-spatial Dynamics in Rio de Janeiro, 1919–2016." *Journal of Latin American Geography* 9 (1): 7–29.

Galloway, Anne. 2004. "Intimations of Everyday Life: Ubiquitous Computing and the city." *Cultural Studies* 18 (2–3): 384–408.

Garmany, Jeff. 2014. "Space for the State? Police, Violence, and Urban Poverty in Brazil." *Annals of the Association of American Geographers* 104 (6): 1239–1255.

Garnier, Manon. 2014. "Chicago Advocates Open Source Predictive Analytics for City Management." L'Atelier Bnp Paribas. Accessed November 20, 2018. https://atelier.bnpparibas/en/smart-city/article/chicago-advocates-open-source-predictive-analytics-city-management.

Gates, Bill. 1995. *The Road Ahead*. London: Hodder and Stoughton.

Gaur, Aditya, Bryan Scotney, Gerard Parr, and Sally McClean. 2015. "Smart City Architecture and Its Applications Based on IoT." *Procedia Computer Science* 52:1089–1094.

Gillespie, Tarleton. 2014. "The Relevance of Algorithms." In *Media Technologies: Essays on Communication, Materiality, and Society*, edited by Tarleton Gillespie, Pablo J. Boczkowski, and Kirsten A. Foot, 167–193. Cambridge, MA: MIT Press.

GitHub. 2016. "Hackfoldr." Last modified July 1, 2016. https://github.com/hackfoldr/hackfoldr.

Gladwell, Malcolm. 2010. "Small Change: Why the Revolution Will Not Be Tweeted." *New Yorker*, September 27, 2010. https://www.newyorker.com/magazine/2010/10/04/small-change-malcolm-gladwell.

Goldsmith, Stephen, and Susan Crawford. 2014. *The Responsive City: Engaging Communities through Data-Smart Governance.* San Francisco: John Wiley & Sons.

Goldstein, Brett. 2013. "Preface." In *Beyond Transparency: Open Data and the Future of Civic Innovation,* edited by Brett Goldstein and Lauren Dyson, ix–xi. San Francisco: Code for America Press.

Goldstein, Brett. 2015. "How to Use Data as a Driver for Urban Transformation." In *Towards Data-Driven Cities?*, 5–10. Paris: La Fabrique de la Cité.

Goldstein, Donna M. 2013. *Laughter Out of Place: Race, Class, Violence, and Sexuality in a Rio Shantytown.* Berkeley: University of California Press.

Golumbia, David. 2009. *The Cultural Logic of Computation.* Cambridge, MA: Harvard University Press.

Goodchild, Michael F. 2007. "Citizens as Sensors: The World of Volunteered Geography." *GeoJournal* 69 (4): 211–221.

Google. n.d. "Rio: Beyond the Map." Interactive web documentary. Accessed February 4, 2017. https://beyondthemap.withgoogle.com/en-us/beyond-the-map.

Google/AfroReggae. 2014. "Tá no Mapa!" Video, dir. Flavio Barone. Rio de Janeiro: J. Walter Thompson Brasil. https://www.youtube.com/watch?v=1CI6KEYTGB4.

Google Developers. n.d. "Awareness and Location APIs." Accessed February 20, 2017. https://developers.google.com/awareness-location/.

Gordon, Rachel. 2012. "Ordering Networks: Motorways and the Work of Managing Disruption." PhD thesis, Durham University.

Gordon, Rachel, Ben Anderson, Michael Crang, and Simon Marvin. 2014. "Controlling Networks: Modes of Governing Infrastructural Assemblages." Working paper, Durham University.

Gouverneur, David, and Oscar Grauer. 2008. "Urban Connectors: Fostering a Nonhierarchical Integration of Formal and Informal Settlements." *Harvard Design Magazine* 28 (Spring/Summer): 24–30.

Government Innovators Network. n.d. "Citizen and Law Enforcement Analysis and Reporting (CLEAR)." Accessed October 9, 2018. https://www.innovations.harvard.edu/citizen-and-law-enforcement-analysis-and-reporting-clear.

GovHK. 2016. *Telecommunications.* The Government of the Hong Kong Special Administrative Region. (Hong Kong). Accessed March 21, 2019. https://www.gov.hk/en/about/abouthk/factsheets/docs/telecommunications.pdf.

Graham, Mark. 2012. "Big Data and the End of Theory?" *Guardian*, March 9, 2012. https://www.theguardian.com/news/datablog/2012/mar/09/big-data-theory.

Graham, Stephen. 1998. "Spaces of Surveillant Simulation: New Technologies, Digital Representations, and Material Geographies." *Environment and Planning D* 16 (4): 483–504.

Graham, Stephen. 2004a. "Introduction." In *The Cybercities Reader*, edited by Steve Graham, 1–29. London: Routledge.

Graham, Stephen. 2004b. "Postmortem City: Towards an Urban Geopolitics." *City* 8 (2): 165–196.

Graham, Stephen. 2005. "Software-Sorted Geographies." *Progress in Human Geography* 29 (5): 562–580.

Graham, Stephen. 2010. "When Infrastructures Fail." In *Disrupted Cities*, edited by S. Graham, 1–26. London: Routledge.

Graham, Stephen. 2011. *Cities under Siege: The New Military Urbanism*. London: Verso.

Graham, Stephen. 2016. *Vertical: The City from Satellites to Bunkers*. London: Verso Books.

Graham, Stephen, and Simon Marvin. 1996. *Telecommunications and the City: Electronic Spaces, Urban Places*. London: Routledge.

Graham, Stephen, and Simon Marvin. 2001. *Splintering Urbanism: Networked Infrastructures, Technological Mobilities and the Urban Condition*. London: Routledge.

Graham, Stephen, and Nigel Thrift. 2007. "Out of Order: Understanding Repair and Maintenance." *Theory Culture and Society* 24 (3): 1–25.

Graham, Stephen, and David Wood. 2003. "Digitizing Surveillance: Categorization, Space, Inequality." *Critical Social Policy* 23 (2): 227–248.

Grand View Research. 2020. "Smart Cities Market Size Worth $463.9 Billion By 2027 | CAGR: 24.7%." Grand View Research. Accessed March 23, 2020. https://www.grandviewresearch.com/press-release/global-smart-cities-market.

Grasty, Tom. 2017. "How a Simple Messaging App Toppled the Great 'Firewall' of China." *Huffington Post*, last updated December 6, 2017. https://www.huffingtonpost.com/tom-grasty/how-a-simple-messaging-ap_b_6023646.html?guccounter=2.

Greenfield, Adam. 2006. *Everyware: The Dawning Age of Ubiquitous Computing*. Berkeley, CA: Pearson Education.

Greenfield, Adam. 2013. *Against the Smart City (Part 1 of The City Is Here for You to Use)*. New York: Do Projects.

Gregg, Melissa. 2015. "Hack for Good: Speculative Labour, App Development and the Burden of Austerity." *Fibreculture Journal* 25:183–201.

Gregory, Derek. 2013. "Lines of Descent." In *From above: War, Violence and Verticality*, edited by Peter Adey, Mark Whitehead, and Alison Williams, 41–69. London: Hurst.

Grusin, Richard. 2010. *Premediation: Affect and Mediality in America after 9/11*. New York: Palgrave Macmillan.

Gualtieri, Mike, Stephen Powers, and Vivian Brown. 2013. *The Forrester Wave™: Big Data Predictive Analytics Solutions, Q1 2013*. Cambridge, MA: Forrester Research Inc. http://g1.computerworld.pl/cw/pdf/bigdata/Forrester_Predictive_Analytics_Solutions.pdf.

Gubbi, Jayavardhana, Rajkumar Buyya, Slaven Marusic, and Marimuthu Palaniswami. 2013. "Internet of Things (IoT): A Vision, Architectural Elements, and Future Directions." *Future Generation Computer Systems* 29 (7): 1645–1660.

Gurumurthy, Anita, Nandini Chami, and Sanjana Thomas. 2016. "Unpacking Digital India: A Feminist Commentary on Policy Agendas in the Digital Moment." *Journal of Information Policy* 6 (1): 371–402.

Haas, Peter J., Paul P. Maglio, Patricia G. Selinger, and Wang Chiew Tan. 2011. "Data Is Dead . . . without What-If Models." *Proceedings of the VLDB Endowment* 4 (12): 1486–1489.

Hacking, Ian. 1990. *The Taming of Chance*. Cambridge: Cambridge University Press.

Hagen, Erica. 2011. "Mapping Change: Community Information Empowerment in Kibera (Innovations Case Narrative: Map Kibera)." *Innovations: Technology, Governance, Globalization* 6 (1): 69–94.

Haigh, Thomas, Mark Priestley, and Crispin Rope. 2016. *ENIAC in Action: Making and Remaking the Modern Computer*. Cambridge, MA: MIT Press.

Hair, Joe F., Jr. 2007. "Knowledge Creation in Marketing: The Role of Predictive Analytics." *European Business Review* 19 (4): 303–315.

Haklay, Mordechai. 2010. "How Good Is Volunteered Geographical Information? A Comparative Study of OpenStreetMap and Ordnance Survey Datasets." *Environment and Planning B: Planning and Design* 37 (4): 682–703.

Halpern, Orit. 2014. *Beautiful Data: A History of Vision and Reason since 1945*. Durham, NC: Duke University Press.

Halpern, Orit, Jesse LeCavalier, Nerea Calvillo, and Wolfgang Pietsch. 2013. "Test-Bed Urbanism." *Public Culture* 25 (2): 272–306.

Hannah, Matthew G. 2001. "Sampling and the Politics of Representation in US Census 2000." *Environment and Planning D: Society and Space* 19 (5): 515–534.

Hansen, Thomas Blom, and Finn Stepputat. 2006. "Sovereignty Revisited." *Annual Review of Anthropology* 35:295–315.

Haraway, Donna. 1985. "A Manifesto for Cyborgs: Science, Technology, and Socialist Feminism for the 1980s." *Socialist Review* 15 (2): 65–107.

Hardt, Michael, and Antonio Negri. 2000. *Empire.* Cambridge, MA: Harvard University Press.

Harley, John Brian. 1988. "Maps, Knowledge and Power." In *The Iconography of Landscape: Essays in the Symbolic Representation Design and Use of Past Environments,* edited by Stephen J. Daniels and Denis Cosgrove, 277–312. Cambridge: Cambridge University Press.

Harris, Britton. 1966. "The Uses of Theory in the Simulation of Urban Phenomena." *Journal of the American Institute of Planners* 32 (5): 258–273.

Heidegger, Martin. 1966. *Discourse on Thinking.* New York: Harper and Row.

Hernández-Muñoz, José M., Jesús Bernat Vercher, Luis Muñoz, José A. Galache, Mirko Presser, Luis A. Hernández Gómez, and Jan Pettersson. 2011. "Smart Cities at the Forefront of the Future Internet." In *The Future Internet,* edited by John Domingue, Alex Galis, Anastasius Gavras, Theodore Zahariadis, Dave Lambert, Frances Cleary, Petros Daras, et al., 447–462. Heidelberg: Springer.

Hidalgo, Noel. 2015. "Civic Hacknight at Civic Hall." Meetup. August 12, 2015. https://www.meetup.com/betanyc/events/223205836/.

High Court of the Hong Kong Special Administrative Region. 2014. *HCA 2222 & 2223 of 2014.* High Court of the Hong Kong Special Administrative Region. (Hong Kong). Accessed January 29, 2019. https://legalref.judiciary.hk/lrs/common/ju/ju_frame.jsp?DIS=96020&currpage=T.

Hinchliffe, Steve. 1996. "Technology, Power, and Space—The Means and Ends of Geographies of Technology." *Environment and Planning D* 14:659–682.

Hinds, Kate. 2014. "NYC Opens Traffic Crash Data—Finally." WNYC, May 7, 2014. https://www.wnyc.org/story/nyc-opens-traffic-crash-data-finally/.

Hirst, Tony. 2008. "The Tesco Data Business (Notes on 'Scoring Points')." *OUseful. Info, the blog,* November 6, 2008. https://blog.ouseful.info/2008/11/06/the-tesco-data-business-notes-on-scoring-points/.

Hitachi. 2013. *Hitachi's Vision for Smart Cities.* White Paper, Ver. 2, 2013.9. Tokyo: Hitachi, Ltd., Social Innovation Business Project Division/Smart City Project Division.

Hodson, Mike, and Simon Marvin. 2009. "'Urban Ecological Security': A New Urban Paradigm?" *International Journal of Urban and Regional Research* 33 (1): 193–216.

Hollands, Robert G. 2008. "Will the Real Smart City Please Stand Up? Intelligent, Progressive or Entrepreneurial?" *City* 12 (3): 303–320.

Holston, James. 1989. *The Modernist City: An Anthropological Critique of Brasilia.* Chicago: University of Chicago Press.

Holston, James. 2008. *Insurgent Citizenship: Disjunctions of Democracy and Modernity in Brazil.* Princeton: Princeton University Press.

Hookway, Branden. 2014. *Interface.* Cambridge, MA: MIT Press.

Howard, Alex. 2015. "Chicago's First CDO on Getting Early Wins, Informing Policy, and Developing Your Own View." TechRepublic, April 13, 2015. https://www .techrepublic.com/article/chicagos-first-cdo-on-getting-early-wins-informing-policy -and-developing-your-own-view/.

Howard, Philip N., Aiden Duffy, Deen Freelon, Muzammil M. Hussain, Will Mari, and Marwa Maziad. 2011. "Opening Closed Regimes: What Was the Role of Social Media during the Arab Spring?" Project on Information Technology and Political Islam, Working Paper 2011.1. Accessed March 21, 2019. https://deepblue.lib.umich .edu/bitstream/handle/2027.42/117568/2011_Howard-Duffy-Freelon-Hussain-Mari -Mazaid_PITPI.pdf?sequence=1&isAllowed=y.

Howard, Philip N., and Muzammil M. Hussain. 2011. "The Role of Digital Media." *Journal of Democracy* 22 (3): 35–48.

Hughes, Sarah M. 2019. "On Resistance in Human Geography." *Progress in Human Geography*, October 9, 2019. https://doi.org/10.1177/0309132519879490.

Hughes, Thomas Parke. 1983. *Networks of Power: Electrification in Western Society, 1880–1930.* Baltimore: Johns Hopkins University Press.

IBM. 2009. "Case Study—The City of Albuquerque: From Heterogeneous Data Sources to Public Service Visionary." Accessed November 11, 2016. ftp://ftp.software .ibm.com/software/data/sw-library/cognos/uk/pdfs/brochures/2009UK_cc _Albuquerque.pdf.

IBM. 2012. *IBM Intelligent Operations Center for Smarter Cities Administration Guide.* IBM Redbooks. Raleigh, NC: IBM Corporation, International Technical Support Organization. http://www.redbooks.ibm.com/redbooks/pdfs/sg248061.pdf.

Ikeya, Nozomi. 2003. "Practical Management of Mobility: The Case of the Emergency Medical System." *Environment and Planning A* 35 (9): 1547–1564.

Instituto Data Popular/JWT. 2015. "Project 'Tá no Mapa.' Evaluation and Impact of Tá No Mapa Program (PowerPoint presentation)." Unpublished report. Rio de Janeiro: J. Walter Thompson.

Instituto Pereira Passos. 2014. "Mapeamento Participativo do Rio de Janeiro em Manguinhos." YouTube, August 26, 2014. www.youtube.com/watch?v=YvIwZrOdP08.

Jacobs, F. Robert. 2007. "Enterprise Resource Planning (ERP)—A Brief History." *Journal of Operations Management* 25 (2): 357–363.

Jacomet, Noe, Wu Min Hsuan, and Chia-liang Kao. 2017. "How the g0v Movement Is Forking the Taiwanese Government." *Open Source Politics* (blog), April 13, 2017. https://medium.com/open-source-politics/how-the-g0v-movement-is-forking-the -taiwanese-government-74b7cce0e92b.

Jefferson, Brian Jordan. 2018. "Predictable Policing: Predictive Crime Mapping and Geographies of Policing and Race." *Annals of the American Association of Geographers* 108 (1): 1–16.

Jeffery, Mark, Nancy Kulick, Tim Riitters, Scott Abbott, Douglas Papp, Tiffany Schad, Jed Wallace, and Jeff Wiemann. 2017. "instituto The San Diego City Schools: Enterprise Resource Planning Return on Investment." Kellogg School of Management Cases. Chicago: The Kellogg School of Management at Northwestern University. https://doi.org/10.1108/case.kellogg.2016.000363.

Jin, Jiong, Jayavardhana Gubbi, Slaven Marusic, and Marimuthu Palaniswami. 2014. "An Information Framework for Creating a Smart City through Internet of Things." *IEEE Internet of Things Journal* 1 (2): 112–121.

Joyce, Patrick D. 2003. *The Rule of Freedom: Liberalism and the Modern City*. London: Verso.

Juris, Jeffrey S. 2005. "The New Digital Media and Activist Networking within Anti–corporate Globalization Movements." *Annals of the American Academy of Political Social Science* 597 (1): 189–208.

Juris, Jeffrey S. 2012. "Reflections on #Occupy Everywhere: Social Media, Public Space, and Emerging Logics of Aggregation." *American Ethnologist* 39 (2): 259–279.

Kallinikos, Jannis. 2004. "Deconstructing Information Packages: Organizational and Behavioural Implications of ERP Systems." *Information Technology & People* 17 (1): 8–30.

Kallinikos, Jannis. 2007. *The Consequences of Information: Institutional Implications of Technological Change*. Cheltenham: Edward Elgar Publishing.

Kallinikos, Jannis. 2011. *Governing through Technology: Information Artefacts and Social Practice*. Basingstoke: Palgrave Macmillan.

Karanja, Irene. 2010. "An Enumeration and Mapping of Informal Settlements in Kisumu, Kenya, Implemented by Their Inhabitants." *Environment and Urbanization* 22 (1): 217–239.

Khan, Rafiullah, Sarmad Ullah Khan, Rifaqat Zaheer, and Shahid Khan. 2012. "Future Internet: The Internet of Things Architecture, Possible Applications and

Key Challenges." 2012 Tenth International Conference on Frontiers of Information Technology, Islamabad, India, December 17–19.

King, Riley. n.d. "The Inside Story of Digital Technology in Hong Kong." HAYS. Accessed July 11, 2018. https://www.hays.com.hk/theinsidestory/HAYS_1898841.

Kingsbury, Paul, and John Paul Jones. 2009. "Walter Benjamin's Dionysian Adventures on Google Earth." *Geoforum* 40 (4): 502–513.

Kitchin, Rob. 2014a. *The Data Revolution: Big Data, Open Data, Data Infrastructures and Their Consequences*. London: Sage.

Kitchin, Rob. 2014b. "The Real-Time City? Big Data and Smart Urbanism." *GeoJournal* 79 (1): 1–14.

Kitchin, Rob. 2016. "The Ethics of Smart Cities and Urban Science." *Philosophical Transactions of the Royal Society A* 374 (2083): 20160115.

Kitchin, Rob, and Martin Dodge. 2011. *Code/Space: Software and Everyday Life*. Cambridge, MA: MIT Press.

Kitchin, Rob, Tracey P. Lauriault, and Gavin McArdle. 2015. "Knowing and Governing Cities through Urban Indicators, City Benchmarking, and Real-Time Dashboards." *Regional Studies, Regional Science* 2 (1): 6–28.

Kitchin, Rob, Tracey P. Lauriault, and Gavin McArdle. 2016. "Smart Cities and the Politics of Urban Data." In *Smart Urbanism: Utopian Vision or False Dawn*, edited by Simon Marvin, Andrés Luque-Ayala, and Colin McFarlane, 16–33. London: Routledge.

Kitchin, Rob, Tracey P. Lauriault, and Gavin McArdle. 2018. "Data and the City." In *Data and the City*, edited by Rob Kitchin, Tracey P. Lauriault and Gavin McArdle, 1–14. Abingdon: Routledge.

Klauser, Francisco. 2013. "Spatialities of Security and Surveillance: Managing Spaces, Separations and Circulations at Sport Mega Events." *Geoforum* 49:289–298.

Klauser, Francisco. 2015. "Interacting Forms of Expertise and Authority in Mega-event Security: The Example of the 2010 Vancouver Olympic Games." *The Geographical Journal* 181 (3): 224–234.

Klauser, Francisco, Till Paasche, and Ola Söderström. 2014. "Michel Foucault and the Smart City: Power Dynamics Inherent in Contemporary Governing through Code." *Environment and Planning D: Society and Space* 32 (5): 869–885.

Klauser, Francisco, and Anders Albrechtslund. 2014. "From Self-tracking to Smart Urban Infrastructures: Towards an Interdisciplinary Research Agenda on Big Data." *Surveillance & Society* 12 (2): 273–286.

Kleiman, Mauro. 2001. "Rede viária e estruturacão intra urbana a prioridade dos investimentos na rede viária e seu papel na configuração das cidades: O Rio de Janeiro sobre rodas." In *Anais do IX Encontro Nacional de ANPUR*, 1596–1608. Rio de Janeiro: Associação Nacional de Pós-graduação e Pesquisa em Planejamento Urbano e Regional.

Knoespel, Kenneth J. 2001. "Diagrams as Piloting Devices in the Philosophy of Gilles Deleuze." *Théorie—Littérature—Enseignement* 19:145–165.

Komninos, Nicos. 2002. *Intelligent Cities: Innovation, Knowledge Systems, and Digital Spaces*. London: Taylor & Francis.

Kotu, Vijay, and Bala Deshpande. 2014. *Predictive Analytics and Data Mining: Concepts and Practice with Rapidminer*. Amsterdam: Elsevier/Morgan Kaufmann.

Kreps, Daniel. 2014. "Peter Gabriel, Pussy Riot Show Support for Hong Kong Protestors." *Rolling Stone*, November 29, 2014. https://www.rollingstone.com/music/music-news/peter-gabriel-pussy-riot-show-support-for-hong-kong-protestors-42886/.

Krivý, Maroš. 2018. "Towards a Critique of Cybernetic Urbanism: The Smart City and the Society of Control." *Planning Theory* 17 (1): 8–30.

Kuo, Lily. 2019. "Hong Kong's Digital Battle: Tech that Helped Protesters Now Used against Them." *Guardian*, June 14, 2019. https://www.theguardian.com/world/2019/jun/14/hong-kongs-digital-battle-technology-that-helped-protesters-now-used-against-them.

Lague, David, James Pomfret, and Greg Torode. 2014. "Special Report: In 'Umbrella Revolution,' China Confronts Limits of Its Power." Reuters, October 1, 2014. https://www.reuters.com/article/us-hongkong-china-specialreport-idUSKCN0HQ4ZA20141001.

Langley, Paul, and Andrew Leyshon. 2017. "Platform Capitalism: The Intermediation and Capitalisation of Digital Economic Circulation." *Finance and Society* 3 (1): 11–31.

Lanzeni, Débora. 2016. "Smart Global Futures: Designing Affordable Materialities for a Better Life." In *Digital Materialities: Design and Anthropology*, edited by Sarah Pink, Elisenda Ardèvol, and Dèbora Lanzeni, 45–59. London: Bloomsbury.

Latour, Bruno. 1987. *Science in Action: How to Follow Scientists and Engineers through Society*. Cambridge, MA: Harvard University Press.

Lee, Francis L. F. 2015. "Media Communication and the Umbrella Movement: Introduction to the Special Issue." *Chinese Journal of Communication* 8 (4): 333–337.

Lee, Francis L. F., and Joseph Man Chan. 2016. "Digital Media Activities and Mode of Participation in a Protest Campaign: A Study of the Umbrella Movement." *Information, Communication & Society* 19 (1): 4–22.

Lee, Francis L. F., Hsuan-Ting Chen, and Michael Chan. 2017. "Social Media Use and University Students' Participation in a Large-Scale Protest Campaign: The Case of Hong Kong's Umbrella Movement." *Telematics and Informatics* 34 (2): 457–469.

Lee, Paul S. N., Clement Y. K. So, and Louis Leung. 2015. "Social Media and Umbrella Movement: Insurgent Public Sphere in Formation." *Chinese Journal of Communication* 8 (4): 356–375.

Leszczynski, Agnieszka. 2015a. "Spatial Big Data and Anxieties of Control." *Environment Planning D: Society Space* 33 (6): 965–984.

Leszczynski, Agnieszka. 2015b. "Spatial Media/tion." *Progress in Human Geography* 39 (6): 729–751.

Leszczynski, Agnieszka. 2016. "Speculative Futures: Cities, Data, and Governance beyond Smart Urbanism." *Environment and Planning A* 48 (9): 1691–1708.

Leyshon, Andrew, and Nigel Thrift. 2007. "The Capitalization of Almost Everything: The Future of Finance and Capitalism." *Theory, Culture & Society* 24 (7–8): 97–115.

Li, Jason. 2015. "The Reality behind Hong Kong's FireChat." *Asian Entrepreneur*, February 27, 2015. https://www.asianentrepreneur.org/the-reality-behind-hong-kongs -firechat/.

Li, Shancang, Li Da Xu, and Shanshan Zhao. 2015. "The Internet of Things: A Survey." *Information Systems Frontiers* 17 (2): 243–259.

Li, Tania Murray. 2007. "Practices of Assemblage and Community Forest Management." *Economy and Society* 36 (2): 263–293.

Light, Jennifer S. 2002. "Urban Security from Warfare to Welfare." *International Journal of Urban and Regional Research* 26 (3): 607–613.

Light, Jennifer S. 2003. *From Warfare to Welfare: Defense Intellectuals and Urban Problems in Cold War America*. Baltimore, MD: Johns Hopkins University Press.

Lih, Andrew. 2014. "In Hong Kong's Protests, Technology Is a Battlefield." *Quartz*, October 2, 2014. https://qz.com/274973/in-hong-kongs-protests-technology-is-a -battlefield/.

Livengood, Avery, and Keya Kunte. 2012. "Enabling Participatory Planning with GIS: A Case Study of Settlement Mapping in Cuttack, India." *Environment and Urbanization* 24 (1): 77–97.

Living PlanIT. n.d. "PlanIT UOS." Accessed February 11, 2019. http://www.living-planit .com.

Longo, Francesco, Dario Bruneo, Salvatore Distefano, Giovanni Merlino, and Antonio Puliafito. 2017. "Stack4Things: A Sensing-and-Actuation-as-a-Service Framework for IoT and Cloud Integration." *Annales des Télécommunications* 72 (1–2): 53–70.

Lundberg, Jonas, and Mikael Asplund. 2011. "Communication Problems in Crisis Response." Paper presented at the Eighth International ISCRAM Conference, Lisbon, Portugal, May 8–11, 2011.

Luque-Ayala, Andrés, and Simon Marvin. 2015. "Developing a Critical Understanding of Smart Urbanism?" *Urban Studies* 52 (12): 2105–2116.

Luque-Ayala, Andrés, Colin McFarlane, and Simon Marvin. 2016. "Introduction." In *Smart Urbanism: Utopian Vision or False Dawn?*, edited by Simon Marvin, Andrés Luque-Ayala, and Colin McFarlane, 1–15. London: Routledge.

Lynch, Casey R. 2019. "Contesting Digital Futures: Urban Politics, Alternative Economies, and the Movement for Technological Sovereignty in Barcelona." *Antipode*, March 12, 2019. https://doi.org/10.1111/anti.12522.

Mabert, Vincent A. 2007. "The Early Road to Material Requirements Planning." *Journal of Operations Management* 25 (2): 346–356.

Machado, Andre. 2013. "Waze já tem 6 milhões de usuários no Brasil, que é o 2º mercado do app." *O Globo*, December 13, 2013. https://oglobo.globo.com/economia/tecnologia/waze-ja-tem-6-milhoes-de-usuarios-no-brasil-que-o-2-mercado-do-app-11063642#ixzz3I9ohU2Du.

Machen, Ruth. 2018. "Towards a Critical Politics of Translation: (Re)producing Hegemonic Climate Governance." *Environment and Planning E: Nature and Space* 1 (4): 494–515.

MacSweeney, Greg. 2011. "Inside the Bloomberg Machine." *InformationWeek*, March 22, 2011. http://www.wallstreetandtech.com/trading-technology/inside-the-bloomberg-machine/d/d-id/1264634.html.

Magnusson, Warren. 2011. *Politics of Urbanism: Seeing Like a City*. New York: Routledge.

Mahoney, Joel. 2013. "Open Data and Open Discourse at Boston Public Schools." In *Beyond Transparency: Open Data and the Future of Civic Innovation*, edited by Brett Goldstein and Lauren Dyson, 3–12. San Francisco: Code for America Press.

Maltz, Michael D., Andrew C. Gordon, and Warren Friedman. 2000. *Mapping Crime in Its Community Setting: Event Geography Analysis*. New York: Springer.

Marshall, Aarian. 2017. "How a Failed Experiment Could Still Be the Future of Public Transit." *Wired*. Accessed March 20, 2020. https://www.wired.com/2017/03/failed-experiment-still-future-public-transit/.

Martin, Reinhold. 2011. "Occupy: What Architecture Can Do." *Places Journal*, November. Accessed January 23, 2019. https://placesjournal.org/article/occupy-what-architecture-can-do/.

Marvin, Simon, Andrés Luque-Ayala, and Colin McFarlane, eds. 2016. *Smart Urbanism: Utopian Vision or False Dawn?* Abingdon: Routledge.

Mattern, Shannon. 2013. "Methodolatry and the Art of Measure." *Places Journal*, November. Accessed August 2, 2018. https://doi.org/https://doi.org/10.22269/131105.

Mattern, Shannon. 2015. "Mission Control: A History of the Urban Dashboard." *Places Journal*, March. Accessed July 15, 2015. https://placesjournal.org/article/mission-control-a-history-of-the-urban-dashboard/.

Mayor of London. 2014. "London Infrastructure Plan 2050: A Consultation." London: Mayor of London.

McCann, Eugene, and Kevin Ward, eds. 2011. *Mobile Urbanism: Cities and Policymaking in the Global Age*. Minneapolis: University of Minnesota Press.

McCracken, Harry. 2015. "How the Bloomberg Terminal Made History—And Stays Ever Relevant." *Fast Company*, October 6, 2015. https://www.fastcompany.com/3051883/the-bloomberg-terminal.

McFarlane, Colin. 2010. "Infrastructure, Interruption, and Inequality: Urban Life in the Global South." In *Disrupted Cities: When Infrastructure Fails*, edited by Stephen Graham, 131–144. New York: Routledge.

McFarlane, Colin. 2011. *Learning the City: Knowledge and Translocal Assemblage*. Oxford: Wiley-Blackwell.

McFarlane, Colin, and Jonathan Rutherford. 2008. "Political Infrastructures: Governing and Experiencing the Fabric of the City." *International Journal of Urban and Regional Research* 32 (2): 363–374.

McFarlane, Colin, and Ola Söderström. 2017. "On Alternative Smart Cities: From a Technology-Intensive to a Knowledge-Intensive Smart Urbanism." *City* 21 (3–4): 312–328.

McLuhan, Marshall. 1964. *Understanding Media: The Extensions of Man*. New York: McGraw-Hill.

Medina, Eden. 2011. *Cybernetic Revolutionaries: Technology and Politics in Allende's Chile*. Cambridge, MA: MIT Press.

Meier, Richard L. 1962. *A Communications Theory of Urban Growth*. Cambridge, MA: MIT Press.

Meier, Richard L., and Ricbard D. Duke. 1966. "Gaming Simulation for Urban Planning." *Journal of the American Institute of Planners* 32 (1): 3–17.

Meyer, Robinson. 2014. "What Firechat's Success in Hong Kong Means for a Global Internet." *Atlantic*, October 6, 2014. https://www.theatlantic.com/technology/archive/2014/10/firechat-the-hong-kong-protest-tool-aims-to-connect-the-next-billion/381113/.

Mezzadra, Sandro, and Brett Neilson. 2017. "On the Multiple Frontiers of Extraction: Excavating Contemporary Capitalism." *Cultural Studies* 31 (2–3): 185–204.

Microsoft. 2011. "Predictive Analytics for Traffic." Accessed November 1, 2019. https://www.microsoft.com/en-us/research/project/predictive-analytics-for-traffic/.

Microsoft. 2013. *Microsoft CityNext Technical Reference Model Overview* (Version 1.0, October 2013). Redmond, WA: Microsoft Corporation. Accessed September 4, 2014. http://download.microsoft.com/download/8/C/D/8CD464C6-44BA-45E9-B104 -32014E99A51F/Microsoft%20CityNext%20Technical%20Reference%20Model%20 Overview.pdf.

Microsoft. 2014. "Bing's Collaborative Na Área Project Helps Visitors Discover More of Brazil's Favelas—And Gives Locals a Digital Boost." *Microsoft, the AI Blog*, June 11, 2014. https://blogs.microsoft.com/ai/bings-collaborative-na-rea-project-helps -visitors-discover-more-of-brazils-favelas-and-gives-locals-a-digital-boost-2/.

Miller, Michelle. 2014. "Smart Trash Cans Improve Waste Management. Product Life-cycle Report." *PTC*, August 8, 2014. Accessed August 1, 2018. http://blogs.ptc.com/ 2014/08/08/smart-trash-cans-improve-waste-management/.

Miller, Peter, and Nikolas Rose. 2008. *Governing the Present*. Cambridge: Polity.

Min, Wanli, Laura Wynter, and Yasuo Amemiya. 2007. "Road Traffic Prediction with Spatio-temporal Correlations." IBM Research Report, June 5, 2007. https://domino .watson.ibm.com/library/cyberdig.nsf/papers/80B6905971EDA9E5852572F900560F2F/ $File/rc24275.pdf.

Mitchell, William J. 2004. *Me++: The Cyborg Self and the Networked City*. Cambridge, MA: MIT Press.

Mitton, Nathalie, Symeon Papavassiliou, Antonio Puliafito, and Kishor S. Trivedi. 2012. "Combining Cloud and Sensors in a Smart City Environment." *EURASIP Journal on Wireless Communications and Networking* 247:1–10.

Molnár, Virág. 2014. "Reframing Public Space through Digital Mobilization: Flash Mobs and Contemporary Urban Youth Culture." *Space and Culture* 17 (1): 43–58.

Monahan, Torin. 2007. "'War Rooms' of the Street: Surveillance Practices in Transportation Control Centers." *Communication Review* 10 (4): 367–389.

Monahan, Torin, and Jennifer T. Mokos. 2013. "Crowdsourcing Urban Surveillance: The Development of Homeland Security Markets for Environmental Sensor Networks." *Geoforum* 49:279–288.

Morozov, Evgeny. 2009. "Iran: Downside to the 'Twitter Revolution.'" *Dissent* 56 (4): 10–14.

Morozov, Evgeny. 2011. *The Net Delusion: How Not to Liberate the World*. London: Penguin UK.

Morozov, Evgeny. 2014. *To Save Everything, Click Here: The Folly of Technological Solutionism*. New York: PublicAffairs.

Morris, Steven. 2005. "Million-Dollar Student Hits the Big Time with a Simple Idea." *Guardian*, December 27, 2005. https://www.theguardian.com/technology/2005/dec/27/news.students.

Mosco, Vincent. 1989. *The Pay-Per Society: Computers and Communication in the Information Age*. Toronto: Garamond Press.

Moskvitch, Katia. 2011. "Smart Cities Get Their Own Operating System." BBC News, September 30, 2011. https://www.bbc.co.uk/news/technology-15109403.

National Research Council. 1995. *Expanding the Vision of Sensor Materials*. Washington, DC: National Academies Press.

Negroponte, Nicholas. 1995. *Being Digital*. London: Hodder and Stoughton.

New York City. 2013. *Chief Information & Innovation Officer Progress Report*. Accessed March 21, 2019. https://www1.nyc.gov/assets/doitt/downloads/pdf/CIIO_Report_12_16_13_FINAL.pdf.

New York City Council. 2012. Local Law 11 of 2012 (previously Introduction 0029A-2010). New York: New York City Council. https://www1.nyc.gov/site/doitt/initiatives/open-data-law.page.

Nielsen, Rasmus Kleis. 2013. "Mundane Internet Tools, the Risk of Exclusion, and Reflexive Movements—Occupy Wall Street and Political Uses of Digital Networked Technologies." *Sociological Quarterly* 54 (2): 173–177.

Nitzan, Jonathan, and Shimshon Bichler. 2009. *Capital as Power: A Study of Order and Disorder*. London: Routledge.

Norris, Clive, and Michael McCahill. 2006. "CCTV: Beyond Penal Modernism?" *British Journal of Criminology* 46 (1): 97–118.

NYC Open Data. 2017. "Overview." Accessed August 16, 2018. https://opendata.cityofnewyork.us/overview/.

Nyce, Charles. 2007. "Predictive Analytics White Paper." Malvern, PA: American Institute for CPCU/Insurance Institute of America. https://www.the-digital-insurer.com/wp-content/uploads/2013/12/78-Predictive-Modeling-White-Paper.pdf.

Nye, David E. 1999. *Consuming Power: A Social History of American Energies*. Cambridge, MA: MIT Press.

O'Flaherty, Kate. 2018. "Taiwan's Revolutionary Hackers Are Forking the Government." *WIRED*, May 4, 2018. https://www.wired.co.uk/article/taiwan-sunflower-revolution-audrey-tang-g0v.

O'Grady, Nathaniel. 2013. "Adopting the Position of Error: Space and Speculation in the Exploratory Significance of Milieu Formulations." *Environment and Planning D: Society and Space* 31 (2): 245–258.

O'Neil, Daniel X. 2011. "Incomplete Take on the History of Open Data in Chicago." Derivative Works, September 21, 2011. http://www.derivativeworks.com/2011/09/incomplete-take-on-the-history-of-open-data-in-chicago.html.

Odum, Howard T. 1960. "Ecological Potential and Analogue Circuits for the Ecosystem." *American Scientist* 48:1–8.

OECD. n.d. "Open Government." OECD. Accessed February 17, 2019. http://www.oecd.org/gov/open-government.htm.

OECD. n.d. "Open Government Data." OECD. Accessed February 17, 2019. http://www.oecd.org/gov/digital-government/open-government-data.htm.

Okamoto, Karen. 2016. "What Is Being Done with Open Government Data? An Exploratory Analysis of Public Uses of New York City Open Data." *Webology* 13 (1), June 2016. http://www.webology.org/2016/v13n1/a142.pdf.

Open Knowledge Foundation. n.d. "Glossary." Open Data Handbook. Open Knowledge Foundation. Accessed February 17, 2019. http://opendatahandbook.org/glossary/en/terms/open-movement/.

Open Knowledge Foundation. n.d. "What Is Open Data?" Open Data Handbook. Open Knowledge Foundation. Accessed August 8, 2018. http://opendatahandbook.org/guide/en/what-is-open-data/.

Operação Lei Seca. 2012. "Conheça o Centro de Operações da Prefeitura do Rio de Janeiro. Governo do Estado do Rio de Janeiro." YouTube, August 7, 2012. https://www.youtube.com/watch?v=5Hwh2n6TKZs.

Osborne, Thomas, and Nikolas Rose. 1999. "Governing Cities: Notes on the Spatialisation of Virtue." *Environment and Planning D: Society and Space* 17 (6): 737–760.

Osborne, Thomas, and Nikolas Rose. 2004. "Spatial Phenomenotechnics: Making Space with Charles Booth and Patrick Geddes." *Environment and Planning D: Society and Space* 22 (2): 209–228.

Otter, Chris. 2007. "Making Liberal Objects: British Techno-social Relations 1800–1900." *Cultural Studies* 21 (4–5): 570–590.

Otter, Chris. 2008. *The Victorian Eye: A Political History of Light and Vision in Britain, 1800–1910.* Chicago: University of Chicago Press.

Ouma, Stefan. 2015. "Getting in between M and M' or: How Farmland Further Debunks Financialization." *Dialogues in Human Geography* 5 (2): 225–228.

Painter, Joe. 2010. "Rethinking Territory." *Antipode* 42 (5): 1090–1118.

Palfrey, John, Bruce Etling, and Robert Faris. 2009. "Reading Twitter in Tehran? Why the Real Revolution Is on the Streets—and Offline." *Washington Post*, June 21, 2009.

Parisi, Luciana. 2013. *Contagious Architecture: Computation, Aesthetics, and Space*. Cambridge, MA: MIT Press.

Paroutis, Sotirios, Mark Bennett, and Loizos Heracleous. 2014. "A Strategic View on Smart City Technology: The Case of IBM Smarter Cities during a Recession." *Technological Forecasting and Social Change* 89:262–272.

Patel, Sheela, Carrie Baptist, and Celine d'Cruz. 2012. "Knowledge Is Power–Informal Communities Assert Their Right to the City through SDI and Community-Led Enumerations." *Environment and Urbanization* 24 (1): 13–26.

Patton, Paul. 1998. "Foucault's Subject of Power." In *The Later Foucault*, edited by J. Moss, 64–77. London: Sage.

Peck, Jamie. 2012. "Austerity Urbanism." *City* 16 (6): 626–655.

Penney, Joel, and Caroline Dadas. 2014. "(Re)tweeting in the Service of Protest: Digital Composition and Circulation in the Occupy Wall Street Movement." *New Media & Society* 16 (1): 74–90.

Perera, Charith, Arkady Zaslavsky, Peter Christen, and Dimitrios Georgakopoulos. 2014. "Sensing as a Service Model for Smart Cities Supported by Internet of Things." *Emerging Telecommunications Technologies* 25 (1): 81–93.

Perlman, Janice E. 2005. "The Myth of Marginality Revisited: The Case of Favelas in Rio de Janeiro." In *Becoming Global and the New Poverty of Cities*, edited by L. M. Hanley, B. A. Ruble, and J. S. Tulchin, 9–53. Washington, DC: Woodrow Wilson Center.

Perng, Sung-Yueh, and Rob Kitchin. 2018. "Solutions and Frictions in Civic Hacking: Collaboratively Designing and Building Wait Time Predictions for an Immigration Office." *Social & Cultural Geography* 19 (1): 1–20.

Petrolo, Riccardo, Valeria Loscrì, and Nathalie Mitton. 2017. "Towards a Smart City Based on Cloud of Things, a Survey on the Smart City Vision and Paradigms." *Emerging Telecommunications Technologies* 28 (1): e2931. https://doi.org/10.1002/ett.2931.

Pieterse, Edgar. 2014. "Filling the Void: An Agenda for Tackling African Urbanization." In *Africa's Urban Revolution*, edited by Edgar Pieterse and Susan Parnell, 200–219. London: Zed Books.

Poggiali, Lisa. 2016. "Seeing (from) Digital Peripheries: Technology and Transparency in Kenya's Silicon Savannah." *Cultural Anthropology* 31 (3): 387–411.

Pollio, Andrea. 2016. "Technologies of Austerity Urbanism: The 'Smart City' Agenda in Italy (2011–2013)." *Urban Geography* 37 (4): 514–534.

Pope-Chappell, Maya. 2014. "Hong Kong Protests: How They Unfolded on Twitter." *Wall Street Journal*, October 1, 2014. https://blogs.wsj.com/chinarealtime/2014/10/01/hong-kong-protests-how-they-unfolded-on-twitter/.

Poster, Mark. 1990. *The Mode of Information: Poststructuralism and Social Context.* Cambridge: Polity Press.

PredPol. n.d. "Overview." Accessed September 20, 2018. https://www.predpol.com/about/.

PredPol. n.d. "Predictive Policing: Guidance on Where and When to Patrol." Accessed September 20, 2018. https://www.predpol.com/how-predictive-policing-works/.

PredPol. n.d. "Proven Crime Reduction Results." Accessed September 20, 2018. https://www.predpol.com/results/.

Prefeitura de Curitiba. 2015. "Prefeitura inicia implantação do centro de gestão e controle operacional." Prefeitura Municipal de Curitiba. March 30, 2015. http://www.curitiba.pr.gov.br/noticias/prefeitura-inicia-implantacao-do-centro-de-gestao-e-controle-operacional/35989.

Prefeitura Rio de Janeiro. 2011. *Plano de Emergência para Chuvas Fortes da Cidade do Rio de Janeiro.* Rio de Janeiro: Defesa Civil Rio de Janeiro.

Prefeitura Rio de Janeiro. 2014. "Rio participa de rede global para gestão colaborativa de cidades." Prefeitura Rio de Janeiro. October 1, 2014. http://www.rio.rj.gov.br/web/guest/exibeconteudo?id=4989359.

Rabari, Chirag, and Michael Storper. 2014. "The Digital Skin of Cities: Urban Theory and Research in the Age of the Sensored and Metered City, Ubiquitous Computing and Big Data." *Cambridge Journal of Regions, Economy and Society* 8 (1): 27–42.

Rabinow, Paul. 1995. *French Modern: Norms and Forms of the Social Environment.* Chicago: University of Chicago Press.

Rashid, Mohammad A., Liaquat Hossain, and Jon David Patrick. 2002. "The Evolution of ERP Systems: A Historical Perspective." In *Enterprise Resource Planning: Global Opportunities & Challenges*, edited by Liaquat Hossain, Jon David Patrick and Mohammad A. Rashid, 1–16. London: Idea Group Publishing.

Ratto, Matt, and Megan Boler. 2014. *DIY Citizenship: Critical Making and Social Media.* Cambridge, MA: MIT Press.

Raymond, Louis, Sylvestre Uwizeyemungu, and Francois Bergeron. 2006. "Motivations to Implement ERP in e-Government: An Analysis from Success Stories." *Electronic Government, an International Journal* 3 (3): 225–240.

Redes de Desenvolvimento da Maré. 2012. *Guia de ruas Maré 2012.* Rio de Janeiro: Observatório de Favelas/Redes de Desenvolvimento da Maré. Accessed July 7, 2017. http://redesdamare.org.br/wp-content/uploads/2012/10/GuiaMare_Web.pdf.

Resch, B., M. Mittlboeck, F. Girardin, R. Britter, and C. Ratti. 2009. "Live Geography—Embedded Sensing for Standardised Urban Environmental Monitoring." *International Journal on Advances in Systems and Measurements* 2 (2–3): 156–167.

Reyes Novaes, Andre. 2014. "Favelas and the Divided City: Mapping Silences and Calculations in Rio de Janeiro's Journalistic Cartography." *Social and Cultural Geography* 15 (2): 201–225.

Rich, Thomas F. 1996. *The Chicago Police Department's Information Collection for Automated Mapping (ICAM) Program.* Washington, DC: US Department of Justice. https://www.slideshare.net/juggernautco/the-chicago-police-departments-information-collection-for-automated-mapping-icam-program.

Rockefeller Foundation. n.d. "Selected Cities: Explore the 100 Resilient Cities' Second Round of Cities." Accessed July 20, 2015. http://www.100resilientcities.org/cities#/-_/.

Rose, Gillian. 2012. *Visual Methodologies: An Introduction to Researching with Visual Materials.* London: Sage.

Rose, Gillian. 2014. "On the Relation between 'Visual Research Methods' and Contemporary Visual Culture." *Sociological Review* 62 (1): 24–46.

Rose, Gillian. 2017. "Posthuman Agency in the Digitally Mediated City: Exteriorization, Individuation, Reinvention." *Annals of the American Association of Geographers* 107 (4): 779–793.

Rose, Nikolas. 1991. "Governing by Numbers: Figuring out Democracy." *Accounting, Organizations and Society* 16 (7): 673–692.

Rossiter, Ned. 2016. *Software, Infrastructure, Labor: A Media Theory of Logistical Nightmares.* New York: Routledge.

Roubini, Sonia, and Jason R. Tashea. 2014. "After Sunflower Movement, Taiwan's g0v Uses Open Source to Open the Government." TechPresident, November 5, 2014. http://techpresident.com/news/wegov/25339/sunflower-movement-g0v-taiwan-open-government.

Rouvroy, Antoinette. 2012. "The End(s) of Critique: Data-Behaviourism vs. Due-Process." In *Privacy, Due Process and the Computational Turn*, edited by M. Hildebrandt and E. De Vries, 143–167. London: Routledge.

Roy, Ananya. 2005. "Urban Informality: Toward an Epistemology of Planning." *Journal of the American Planning Association* 71 (2): 147–158.

Rühlig, Tim. 2016. "'Do You Hear the People Sing' 'Lift Your Umbrella?' Understanding Hong Kong's Pro-democratic Umbrella Movement through YouTube Music Videos." *China Perspectives* 2016/4:59–68.

Salcedo-Sanz, S., L. Cuadra, E. Alexandre-Cortizo, S. Jiménez-Fernández, and A. Portilla-Figueras. 2014. "Soft-Computing: An Innovative Technological Solution for Urban Traffic-Related Problems in Modern Cities." *Technological Forecasting and Social Change* 89:236–244.

Saran, Cliff. 2013. "Case Study: How SAP Runs Cape Town." *Computer Weekly*, April 30, 2013. http://www.computerweekly.com/news/2240182802/Case-study-How-SAP-runs-Cape-Town.

Schrock, Andrew R. 2016. "Civic Hacking as Data Activism and Advocacy: A History from Publicity to Open Government Data." *New Media & Society* 18 (4): 581–599.

Schrock, Andrew, and Gwen Shaffer. 2017. "Data Ideologies of an Interested Public: A Study of Grassroots Open Government Data Intermediaries." *Big Data & Society*, January 1, 2017. https://doi.org/10.1177/2053951717690750.

Scott, James C. 1998. *Seeing Like a State: How Certain Schemes to Improve the Human Condition Have Failed*. New Haven, CT: Yale University Press.

Selbst, Andrew D. 2017. "Disparate Impact in Big Data Policing." *Georgia Law Review* 52 (1): 109–196.

Sentilo. n.d. "Community/FAQs." Accessed March 24, 2020. http://www.sentilo.io/wordpress/sentilo-community/faqs.

Shaw, Ian G. R. 2016. "Scorched Atmospheres: The Violent Geographies of the Vietnam War and the Rise of Drone Warfare." *Annals of the American Association of Geographers* 106 (3): 688–704.

Silvast, Antti. 2013. "Anticipating Interruptions: Security and Risk in a Liberalized Electricity Infrastructure." Ph.D. diss., Department of Social Research, University of Helsinki. http://citeseerx.ist.psu.edu/viewdoc/download?doi=10.1.1.830.1471&rep=rep1&type=pdf.

Singer, Natasha. 2012. "Mission Control, Built for Cities." *New York Times*, March 3. 2012. https://www.nytimes.com/2012/03/04/business/ibm-takes-smarter-cities-concept-to-rio-de-janeiro.html.

Skogan, Wesley G., Susan M. Hartnett, Jill DuBois, Jason Bennis, So Young Kim, Dennis Rosenbaum, Lisa Graziano, and Cody Stephens. 2003. *Policing Smarter through IT: Learning from Chicago's Citizen and Law Enforcement Analysis and Reporting (CLEAR) System*. Chicago: Institute for Policy Research, Northwestern University http://www.skogan.org/files/Policing_Smarter_Through_IT-Learning_from_Chicagos_CLEAR_System.pdf.

Smart Citizen. n.d. "Home—Smart Citizen." Accessed September 1, 2015. https://smartcitizen.me/.

Smith, Adrian. 2015. "Tooling Up: Civic Visions, Fablabs and Grassroots Activism." *Guardian*, April 4, 2015. https://www.theguardian.com/science/political-science/2015/apr/04/tooling-up-civic-visions-fablabs-and-grassroots-activism.

Smith, Adrian, Mariano Fressoli, Dinesh Abrol, Elisa Arond, and Adrian Ely. 2016. *Grassroots Innovation Movements*. London: Routledge.

Socrata. 2015. *Data-as-a-Utility: A New Era for the Public Sector*. Washington, DC: GovLoop. https://www.govloop.com/wp-content/uploads/2015/08/Socrata-Industry-Perspective_Data-as-a-Utility.pdf.

Söderström, Ola, Till Paasche, and Francisco Klauser. 2014. "Smart Cities as Corporate Storytelling." *City* 18 (3): 307–320.

Spector, Julian. 2016. "Chicago Is Predicting Food Safety Violations. Why Aren't Other Cities?" *CityLab*, January 7, 2016. https://www.citylab.com/solutions/2016/01/chicago-is-predicting-food-safety-violations-why-arent-other-cities/422511/.

Srnicek, Nick. 2017. *Platform Capitalism*. Cambridge: Polity.

Star, Susan Leigh. 1999. "The Ethnography of Infrastructure." *American Behavioral Scientist* 43 (3): 377–391.

Star, Susan Leigh, and Karen Ruhleder. 1996. "Steps toward an Ecology of Infrastructure: Design and Access for Large Information Spaces." *Information Systems Research* 7 (1): 111–134.

Straube, Till. 2016. "Stacked Spaces: Mapping Digital Infrastructures." *Big Data & Society*, September 19, 2016. https://doi.org/10.1177/2053951716642456.

Streeter, Thomas. 2014. "Panel Discussion." Presented at the International Communication Association Conference, Seattle, Washington, May 22–26.

Strengers, Yolande A. A. 2014. "Smart Energy in Everyday Life: Are You Designing for Resource Man?" *Interactions* 21 (4): 24–31.

Suchman, Lucy. 1995. "Making Work Visible." *Communications of the ACM* 38 (9): 56–64.

Swamy, Krish. 2011. "Analyzing Tesco—The Analytics behind a Top-Notch Loyalty Program." *Big Data Analytics* (blog), August 21, 2011. http://stat-exchange.blogspot.com/2011/08/analyzing-tesco-analytics-behind-top.html.

Swanson, Kate. 2013. "Zero Tolerance in Latin America: Punitive Paradox in Urban Policy Mobilities." *Urban Geography* 34 (7): 972–988.

Ta no Mapa. 2015a. *4ª Etapa do Projeto Tá no Mapa Mapeamento das favelas Pavão-Pavãozinho, Santa Marta, Tabajaras e Cabritos; Relatório I*. PDF report. November 3, 2015. Rio de Janeiro: Ta no Mapa. Accessed July 7, 2017. www.afroreggae.org/wp-content/uploads/2015/01/relatorio1-ta-no-mapa-etapa-4.pdf.

Ta no Mapa. 2015b. *Projeto Q1—Babilônia, Cantagalo e Chapéu Mangueira. Período Reportado: Entre os dias 04 e 16 de maio de 2015*. PDF report. May 4–16, 2015. Rio de Janeiro: Ta no Mapa. Accessed July 7, 2017. www.afroreggae.org/wp-content/uploads/2015/05/relatorio_ta_no_mapa-04_a_16_maio.pdf.

Taylor, James. 2011. *Decision Management Systems: A Practical Guide to Using Business Rules and Predictive Analytics*. Upper Saddle River, NJ: IBM Press.

Taylor, Peter J. 1988. "Technocratic Optimism, H. T. Odum, and the Partial Transformation of Ecological Metaphor after World War II." *Journal of the History of Biology* 21 (2): 213–244.

Taylor, Peter J., and Ann S. Blum. 1991. "Ecosystem as Circuits: Diagrams and the Limits of Physical Analogies." *Biology and Philosophy* 6 (2): 275–294.

Telesintese. 2013. "Prefeitura do Rio firma parceria com Waze." Telesintese, July 24, 2013. http://www.telesintese.com.br/prefeitura-do-rio-firma-parceria-com-waze/.

Thakuriah, Piyushimita Vonu, Nebiyou Tilahun, and Moira Zellner, eds. 2017. *Seeing Cities through Big Data: Research, Methods and Applications in Urban Informatics*. Cham: Springer.

Thomson, Amy. 2014. "Barcelona's Smart Trash Cans Pave Way for Mobile Future." Bloomberg, February 23, 2014. https://www.bloomberg.com/news/articles/2014-02-23/barcelona-s-smart-trash-cans-pave-way-for-mobile-future.

Thornton, Sean. 2013. "Chicago's WindyGrid: Taking Situational Awareness to a New Level." Data-Smart City Solutions, June 13, 2013. https://datasmart.ash.harvard.edu/news/article/chicagos-windygrid-taking-situational-awareness-to-a-new-level-259.

Thornton, Sean. 2016. "Chicago Launches OpenGrid to Democratize Open Data." Data-Smart City Solutions, January 20, 2016. https://datasmart.ash.harvard.edu/news/article/chicago-launches-opengrid-to-democratize-open-data-778.

Thrift, Nigel. 2014. "The Promise of Urban Informatics: Some Speculations." *Environment and Planning A* 46 (6): 1263–1266.

Thrift, Nigel, and Shaun French. 2002. "The Automatic Production of Space." *Transactions of the Institute of British Geographers* 27 (3): 309–335.

Tkacz, Nathaniel. 2015. *Wikipedia and the Politics of Openness*. Chicago: University of Chicago Press.

Toffler, Alvin. 1980. *The Third Wave*. New York: William Morrow.

Tomlinson, Roger. 2012. "The 50th Anniversary of GIS." ESRI, ArcNews Fall 2012. Accessed March 26, 2020. https://www.esri.com/news/arcnews/fall12articles/the-fiftieth-anniversary-of-gis.html.

Townsend, Anthony M. 2000. "Life in the Real-Time City: Mobile Telephones and Urban Metabolism." *Journal of Urban Technology* 7 (2): 85–104.

Townsend, Anthony M. 2001. "Network Cities and the Global Structure of the Internet." *American Behavioral Scientist* 44 (10): 1697–1716.

Townsend, Anthony M. 2013. *Smart Cities: Big Data, Civic Hackers, and the Quest for a New Utopia*. New York and London: W. W. Norton & Company.

Townsend, Anthony M. 2015. "Cities of Data: Examining the New Urban Science." *Public Culture* 27 (2): 201–212.

Tremayne, Mark. 2014. "Anatomy of Protest in the Digital Era: A Network Analysis of Twitter and Occupy Wall Street." *Social Movement Studies* 13 (1): 110–126.

Tufekci, Zeynep, and Christopher Wilson. 2012. "Social Media and the Decision to Participate in Political Protest: Observations from Tahrir Square." *Journal of Communication* 62 (2): 363–379.

Tyler Technologies. n.d. "Careers at Tyler Technologies." Accessed August 14, 2018. https://careers.socrata.com/.

UK Government Digital Service. n.d. "Government as a Platform." Accessed June 1, 2018. https://www.gov.uk/government/policies/government-as-a-platform.

Urbiotica. n.d. "U-Dump M2M Waste Management Sensor." Accessed February 25, 2019. http://www.urbiotica.com/en/product/u-dump-m2m-2/.

Valladares, Licia do Prado. 2005. *A Invenção Da Favela*. Rio de Janeiro: FGV.

van Dijck, José. 2013. *The Culture of Connectivity: A Critical History of Social Media*. Oxford: Oxford University Press.

Vanderbilt, Tom. 2002. *Survival City: Adventures among the Ruins of Atomic America*. Princeton, NJ: Princeton Architectural Press.

Vanolo, Alberto. 2014. "Smartmentality: The Smart City as Disciplinary Strategy." *Urban Studies* 51 (5): 883–898.

Varley, Ann. 2013. "Postcolonialising Informality?" *Environment and Planning D: Society and Space* 31 (1): 4–22.

Vlacheas, Panagiotis, Raffaelle Giaffreda, Vera Stavroulaki, Dimitris Kelaidonis, Vassilis Foteinos, George Poulios, Panagiotis Demestichas, Andrey Somov, Abdur Rahim Biswas, and Klaus Moessner. 2013. "Enabling Smart Cities through a Cognitive Management Framework for the Internet of Things." *IEEE Communications Magazine* 51 (6): 102–111.

Voutsina, Katerina, Jannis Kallinikos, and Carsten Sorensen. 2007. "Codification and Transferability of IT Knowledge." *ECIS 2007 Proceedings*, 716–726. http://aisel.aisnet.org/ecis2007/161.

Wacquant, Loïc. 2008. "The Militarization of Urban Marginality: Lessons from the Brazilian Metropolis." *International Political Sociology* 2 (1): 56–74.

Wakefield, Stephanie, and Bruce Braun. 2014. "Governing the Resilient City." *Environment and Planning D: Society and Space* 32 (1): 4–11.

Wakeford, Nina. 1999. "Gender and the Landscapes of Computing in an Internet Café." In *Virtual Geographies: Bodies, Space and Relations*, edited by Mike Crang, Phil Crang, and Jon May, 178–200. London: Routledge.

Wark, McKenzie. 2004. *A Hacker Manifesto*. Cambridge, MA: Harvard University Press.

Wark, McKenzie. 2006. "Hackers." *Theory, Culture & Society* 23 (2–3): 320–322.

Webber, Melvin. 1964. *Explorations into Urban Structure*. Philadelphia: University of Pennsylvania Press.

Weisburd, David, Elizabeth R. Groff, and Sue-Ming Yang. 2012. *The Criminology of Place: Street Segments and Our Understanding of the Crime Problem*. New York: Oxford University Press.

Whitaker, Christopher. 2012. "City of Chicago Adopts Flu Shot App Built by Civic Hackers." *Code for America* (blog), November 6, 2012. https://www.codeforamerica.org/blog/2012/11/06/city-of-chicago-adopts-flu-shot-app-built-by-civic-hackers/.

White House. 2016. "FACT SHEET: Data by the People, for the People—Eight Years of Progress Opening Government Data to Spur Innovation, Opportunity, & Economic Growth." Press release. The White House Office of the Press Secretary. September 28, 2016. https://obamawhitehouse.archives.gov/the-press-office/2016/09/28/fact-sheet-data-people-people-eight-years-progress-opening-government.

Wilson, Matthew W. 2011. "Data Matter(s): Legitimacy, Coding, and Qualifications-of-Life." *Environment Planning D: Society and Space* 29 (5): 857–872.

Worldsensing. n.d. "Fastprk Moscow—The Largest Smart Parking Project in the World." Accessed January 10, 2015. http://www.fastprk.com/media-news/newsletter.html.

Zanella, Andrea, Nicola Bui, Angelo Castellani, Lorenzo Vangelista, and Michele Zorzi. 2014. "Internet of Things for Smart Cities." *IEEE Internet of Things Journal* 1 (1): 22–32.

Zimmermann, Patricia R. 2007. "Public Domains: Engaging Iraq through Experimental Digitalities." *Framework* 4:66–83.

Zook, Matthew. 2008. *The Geography of the Internet Industry: Venture Capital, Dotcoms, and Local Knowledge*. Oxford: Blackwell.

Zwick, Charles J. 1963. "Systems Analysis and Urban Planning." Paper presented at the First Annual Conference on Urban Planning Information Systems and Programs, University of Southern California, Los Angeles, California, August 28, 1963.

Index